Woody Guthrie's Modern World Blues

Woody Guthrie's Modern World Blues

WILL KAUFMAN

University of Oklahoma Press : Norman

Library of Congress Cataloging-in-Publication Data
Names: Kaufman, Will.
Title: Woody Guthrie's modern world blues / Will Kaufman.
Description: Norman : University of Oklahoma Press, [2017] | Series:
  American popular music series ; Volume 3 | Includes bibliographical references
  and index.
Identifiers: LCCN 2016058969 | ISBN 978-0-8061-5761-0 (hardcover)
ISBN 978-0-8061-9484-4 (paper) Subjects: LCSH: Guthrie, Woody, 1912-1967—
Criticism and interpretation. |
  Technology—Social aspects—United States—History—20th century. Classification:
LCC ML410.G978 K39 2017 | DDC 782.42162/130092—dc23
LC record available at https://lccn.loc.gov/2016058969

Woody Guthrie's Modern World Blues is Volume 3 in the American Popular Music Series.

The paper in this book meets the guidelines for permanence and durability of the
Committee on Production Guidelines for Book Longevity of the Council on Library
Resources, Inc. ∞

For Judy, my safe harbor, *il mio tesoro*

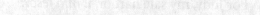

The job of salvaging
our national culture is
like today riding out
onto the pastures of
tomorrow
  To make a wild
herd of yesterdays.

Woody Guthrie, July 1942

Contents

Illustrations

Acknowledgments

Behind every solitary scholar with a laptop stands an entire community providing time, funding, source material, critical expertise, administrative effort, and moral support down to the last desperate cup of coffee. For the funding that has enabled my research, I am grateful to the BMI Foundation for the award of a Woody Guthrie Fellowship, which brought me to the Woody Guthrie Archives in Tulsa. I am likewise indebted to Robert Walsh and the Research Office at the University of Central Lancashire, as well as my deans, Isabel Donnelly and Andrew Churchill, for backing my scholarship with cold, hard cash from their research budgets.

A number of kind people have provided me with materials that have broadened my understanding of Guthrie's relation to modernity and modernism. I am grateful to Wayland Bishop at the Okfuskee County Historical Society, Kay Thompson at the *Okemah (Okla.) News Leader*, and modern dance historian Mark Franko, all of whom have given me both facts and artifacts. I wish to thank John Cohen for directing me to Thomas Crow's work on the evolution of pop art and Barry Ollman for introducing me to Norman Brosterman's compelling study of the kindergarten movement, both of which have illuminated Guthrie's artistry for me in ways that I would not otherwise have considered.

In terms of critical expertise and a willingness to wade patiently through multiple drafts of my manuscript, I must thank three esteemed scholars: Edward Comentale, whose prior research on popular music and modernity formed the bedrock of my present scholarship; Charles L. Hughes, who suggested greater attention to concepts that I had only briefly skirted; and, finally, my mentor in American folk music scholarship who remains an inspiration to me (as well as a dear friend), Ronald D. Cohen. I am grateful to Laurie Matheson of the University of Illinois Press for her trenchant comments on the earliest drafts of my manuscript and to Kent Calder, my editor at the University of Oklahoma Press, for putting his faith in this project.

Nora Guthrie and Anna Canoni at Woody Guthrie Publications have given me more than the simple permission to quote Woody's words; they have supported my research with complete trust and have always given me a free interpretive hand, for which I remain grateful. The terrific Judy Bell at TRO-Essex was tireless, thorough, and very patient in leading me through the minefield of clarifications and permissions. Kate Blalack, whom I call the Angel of the Archives, has guided me toward considerations of Guthrie's visual artistry that have vastly expanded my understanding of his output. Without Ken Levit and the George Kaiser Family Foundation, as well as Deana McCloud and all the staff at the Woody Guthrie Center, my research in Tulsa would not have been possible.

At the University of Central Lancashire, my teaching colleagues Theresa Saxon, Janice Wardle, and Alan Rice have been real troupers in their constant willingness to juggle their teaching schedules in ways that have enabled me to get away and into the archives. I owe them much.

My sons, Reuben and Theo, continue to make their old dad proud as they cross the threshold into manhood; and to my treasure, Judy Blazer, ever the Belle of Broadway, I am indebted for so much more than the title of this book's twelfth chapter.

Woody Guthrie's Modern World Blues

Introduction

Chances are that when you hear the word "modern," a picture of Woody Guthrie will not be the first thing to come to mind. The conventional images of the "Okie bard" emerging out of a dust storm, riding a boxcar, or walking along a dirt road with a battered guitar strapped to his back—the images of the rural folk myth that has been built around him—reflect an almost premodern figure. He is not widely associated with the city, although his most productive years were spent in Los Angeles and New York, or with modern technology, although machines and their physics were among his favorite subjects and metaphors. In spite of his global reputation as America's alpha hobo, bound for glory atop a "side-door Pullman" (the hobo's nickname for a boxcar), Guthrie actually spent more time on the rails as an often-disgruntled paying passenger. Moreover, if he *is* indelibly linked to the image of the long, lonesome freight train, he also wrote many songs about airplanes and even flying saucers. Fast cars were his passion, and he thought and wrote extensively about the state of America's highways. Relatively few are aware of his thoughts on the mass media, in spite of his career-long immersion in radio, recording, and—briefly—film, or with his profile in modern art, although he was a highly prolific abstract painter, illustrator, and sculptor. He thought, wrote, sang, and reflected through a myriad of artistic forms his concerns about scientific method, atomic power, and war technology. More than anything, Guthrie's primary association with folk song always threatens to obscure the other expressive areas that reveal his profoundly modern sensibilities: his fiction, essays, drawings, paintings, sculptures, letters, and

3

voluminous notebook entries. Guthrie was a fully modern figure whose immense output reflects both an individual's and a country's conflicted engagements with the phenomena of modernity. His work during a short but extraordinarily productive lifetime reflects the experience of breathtaking social and technological change.

Global historian Chris Harman observes: "There was more change to the lives of the great majority of the world's population in the twentieth century than in the whole preceding 5,000 years."[1] This was Guthrie's century, and he worked hard to make himself at home in it. As he once jotted in his notebook:

> I am a changer
> A constant changer
> I have to be or die
> Because
> Whatever stops changing
> Is dead. And I am alive.[2]

For all the exhilaration and wonder that has accompanied the maelstrom of change since the dawn of industrialization, modernity has been a source of acute human crisis. Hartmut Rosa argues that "the experience of modernity is an experience of acceleration" and, as such, is for many an experience of bewilderment, of seeming subjection to forces beyond one's control. Moreover, modernity, according to Rosa, has been guilty of a "broken promise of autonomy."[3] As Guthrie's patron, the folklorist Alan Lomax, described it, this entailed "feelings of anomie and alienation, of orphaning and restlessness—the sense of being a commodity rather than a person."[4] The mixed signals of modernity infused Guthrie with ambivalence, and his output was shot through with optimism and despair, comedy and pathos, hope and bitterness, outrage and resignation.

Edward Comentale, one of the first to examine Guthrie in the light of American modernism, argues that Guthrie's creative output "owes everything to the blustery forces of modernity that blew across the south-western plains during his youth. Its migrant spirit emerged out of the boom-and-bust cycles of the 1920s and reflects, in its own rambling way, the violently whipsawing economy that created and destroyed the little towns and cities of Arkansas, Oklahoma, Texas, and New Mexico." Comentale concludes: "Guthrie's modernity is a violent, complex affair, linked with the cyclones that bang and twist across the plains, overturning not just chicken coops and wheelbarrows, but the traditional relations and values of the past. . . . This violent energy both intrigued and frightened Guthrie; as it reorganized the structures of his life, it also ultimately served him as a model of creativity, an art that is not only engaged and motivated, but also spontaneous, fitful, and errant."[5]

Guthrie's twentieth century saw the most far-reaching mechanization of American life, labor, and culture: the broadcasting of music, speech, and pictures from faraway locations; the capturing of sound on phonographic disks; the projection of moving images on huge screens, rural and urban; the transmission of speech along telephone wires; the bulldozing of earth to construct massive dams to generate electricity. All this went by the name of progress, but the same mechanization also meant large layoffs in the industrial workforce and an army of Ford tractors and combine harvesters proliferating across the rural landscape, ravaging the land, prompting such laments as this: "The big fellows are working their farms with tractors and day labor. The peoples is walking the road looking for places. I don't know what's going to become of this here world."[6]

The juggernaut of mechanization led to a massive transformation in patterns of work—from the rural to the urban, from the agricultural to the industrial—during Guthrie's lifetime. As his singing and writing companion Millard Lampell wrote in 1941: "When the work changed, the songs changed. Boys came down from the farms to work in the mills and factories, and American songs began to lose their agrarian character and take on the clang of the stamp press and the whanging of the pressure drill."[7] Guthrie's century also saw America transformed by the rise of the automobile. As Charles McGovern observes: "For people of Guthrie's station and experience the car was central to their changing economic fortunes. The Okies and the migrants whom Guthrie chronicled largely depended upon cars for their survival. Guthrie himself rambled not only on freight trains but in Model Ts and Buicks. The social dislocation of his subjects—Okies, hoboes, farmers, and others on the road—was seen as much through the back of an old Ford as a boxcar."[8]

But Guthrie would also live long enough to witness and write about such "social dislocation" while flying in a plane or cruising aboard a modern merchant ship. He would even apply the imagery of a spaceship to comment on the possibilities of interstellar migration (as well as interstellar fascism).

McGovern also emphasizes the broader transformations brought about by large-scale migration in Guthrie's times—not only by poor white Dust Bowl migrants, Latino field workers, and African Americans from the rural South into northern cities, but also by migrants from across the seas: "American cities swelled with new immigrants, mostly peasant peoples from southern and Eastern Europe. . . . The migrants remade American cultural life as well. Both as creators and audiences, they imparted their distinct accents and experiences to American films, popular songs, Broadway and vaudeville, the comics, and professional and amateur sports. Immigrant cultures heavily shaped the attitudes and appetites of midcentury America, the place where Guthrie's work had its immediate impact."[9]

These and many other developments marked what McGovern calls "Woody Guthrie's American Century," which also saw changing perceptions and dynamics of ethnicity and race; shifting relations and expectations between genders; the crossed frontiers of atomic power; and the building of war machines such as the world had never seen. As the succeeding chapters will make clear, Guthrie took note of them all and expressed his views of them in notebooks, letters, songs, fiction, essays, play scripts, watercolors, oils, gouaches, sketches, sculptures, and ceramics, a prodigious outpouring of styles and media.

This outpouring raises the issue of an important distinction in terminology: "modernity" versus "modernism." At the risk of infuriating scholars of modernism by speaking too vaguely, as well as those general readers who do not need to be told the distinction, it is useful to attempt one while keeping in mind the lack of agreement between scholars as to what actually constitutes modernism. Is it a social condition or a mode of cultural expression—or perhaps both? It is apparently easier to define modernity than modernism. Christopher Butler, in his *Modernism: A Very Short Introduction*, refers to modernity as "the stresses and strains brought about . . . by the loss of belief in religion, the rise of our dependence on science and technology, the expansion of markets and the commodification brought about by capitalism, the growth of mass culture and its influence, the invasion of bureaucracy into private life, and changing beliefs about relationships between the sexes." Butler is less sure when it comes to modernism, arguing that it is "misleading ... to make any strict boundaries for 'modernism' or to offer a 'definition' of it. It was all sorts of things." Still, while shying away from a definition, Butler offers some useful signposts for modernism: its self-conscious "difficulty"; its foregrounding of "innovative techniques"; its indirection—its attempts to "make the world seem unfamiliar to us"; its defining associations with urbanity, not only in terms of sophistication but also "life in the city."[10] Some of these signposts can be challenged, or at least moderated, by counterexamples. Against the presumed hallmarks of "sophistication" and "difficulty" are the (sometimes hotly contested) appeals to "the primitive" and folk culture, the source material for much of modernist art. Against the presumed dominance of the city, the impact of rural modernism has long been the subject of scholarship, whether in terms of music (country and the blues), literature (William Faulkner, Carson McCullers, and Zora Neale Hurston), or the visual arts (Alexandre Hogue, Thomas Hart Benton, John Steuart Curry, and Jacob Lawrence in his *Migration Series*).

The cultural historian Michael Denning has made a bold attempt at a definition, proposing that "modernism itself might be understood as the culture of Fordism"—a reference to "the patterns of work and leisure to which Ford gave his name" (standardization, assembly-line production, depersonalization, the mass separation of workers from both the conception and the ownership of the products they produce).[11] Certainly Fordism penetrated the work culture of America's urban industrial centers as well as its factory farms. But can we really reduce modernism to this definition? How does it square with the manifestations of modernism beyond the borders of the United States? These include not only the European modernism of, say, Proust, Woolf, and Svevo but also what some are lately calling "global modernisms" (with a pointed plural)—Negritude and pan-Africanism; the Indian modernism of Rabindranath Tagore; and the Latin American modernisms of Diego Rivera, Frida Kahlo, and even Carmen Miranda.[12]

Having flagged these difficulties of definition, then, I propose exploring Guthrie's output in the following terms: his relation to *modernism*, the aesthetic and formal modes of expression that influenced him and that he used in his artistic work, and to *modernity*—the cultural, technological, and economic formations in which he lived and to which he responded. Chapter 1, "A Modern Life,' introduces Guthrie's biography, largely in the context of his engagements with the phenomena of modernity. Those already familiar with his biography might wish to skip this chapter and move on to chapter 2, "Woody Guthrie, American Modernist," which reveals a Guthrie unknown to many: the artist preoccupied with the power of the symbol; the "grapho-maniac"—the compulsive writer chafing at the limitations of language as well as triumphing over them in both song and prose; and the ceramicist, sculptor, draftsman, painter, and champion of modern dance who adopted a child's vision to create a truly modern (and modernist) body of work.

The subsequent chapters are devoted to the subjects of modernity that dominated Guthrie's thinking and his output. The first of these thematic chapters—chapter 3, "Ribbon of Highway"—targets the centrality of both the road and the automobile in Guthrie's life, just as they proved central to modern America at large. But the road and the car were only the starting points of Guthrie's passion for mobility. Chapter 4, "Long Steel Rails and Ships in the Sky," extends the discussion of modern transportation and fur-ther reveals an unfamiliar Guthrie: not the dusty hobo but the connoisseur of urban mass transit and the passenger train; not the earthbound rambler but the aficionado of the airplane and the comic visionary of the flying sau-cer. Chapter 5, "Other Wheels A-whirling," is an exploration of Guthrie's responses to the broader scientific and technological currents in American life. The wheels of science and technology in Guthrie's America appear to have run in two directions—not only forward, toward the benefits of electri-fication, mechanical production, and the saving of labor, but also backward, in view of environmental degradation, demoralization, and the enforced leisure of the de-skilled.

Chapter 6, "Hold the 'Fone—It's Radio Time!" opens the subject of media and the modern desire for mass communication, from Guthrie's love affair with the telephone to his conflicted, often testy relationship with radio, which saw his hatred of corporate control and censorship matched by his euphoria over the communicative possibilities in the age of what Comentale calls "radio-modernity."[13] The media focus is maintained in chapter 7, "Ingrid Bergman's 'Fonograft,'" which explores the connections between recording and film as they impacted Guthrie's life, not only in terms of their mutually dependent technology, but also in terms of the questions they raised in Guthrie's mind about authenticity and the legitimacy of the modern culture industries. Guthrie's ostentatious pronouncements about the corruption of Tin Pan Alley and Hollywood belie his profound dependence on recorded sources as well as his passion for the cinema and its offspring, television—a passion that, toward the end of his productive life, blossomed into the hope of securing a television career.

Chapter 8, "Dance around My Atom Fire," introduces some decidedly darker material: Guthrie's ambivalent responses to the discoveries of atomic power, its civil and military applications, and his fears of atomic conflagration. But even with the atomic genie let out of the bottle and runaway technology threatening to implode, Guthrie never lost his faith in scientific method as a route to betterment—a faith examined in chapter 9, "The Science of Struggle." Here, Guthrie is himself revealed as a would-be scientist, captivated by theories of evolution, dialectical materialism, psychiatry, and human engineering.

Guthrie's scientism dovetailed with his desire to interpret the world as a single organism, reflecting a particular modernist belief in the universality of all things and revealing his own hopes of arriving at a theory of everything. In this, he mirrored the architect Le Corbusier, who had proposed "one single building for all nations and all climates," born out of "a universal logic devoid of historical and regional references."[14] Or perhaps, closer to home, he was like Steinbeck's Preacher Casy with his "one big soul" that "ever'body's a part of."[15] In this spirit Guthrie constructed a utopian narrative of hyper-unionism, which is the subject of chapter 10, "A Unity of Disunity." Equally utopian—and equally challenged by the realities of difference and instability—was Guthrie's hope in arriving at a theory that could underpin the relations, sexual and otherwise, between genders. Hence chapter 11, "I Say to You Woman and Man," situating Guthrie on the fault line of what Denning calls American modernism's "transformation of gender relations."[16] For Guthrie this was a place that was both disorienting and enlightening.

The final two chapters, "Blacks + Jews = Blues" (chapter 12) and "Urban Centrifuge" (chapter 13), are linked in the sense that Guthrie's growing racial awareness—his conversion from casual racism to fierce antiracism—was bound up in his own progression from the rural frontier to the city. In the end, the Dust Bowl Balladeer found his home in New York by way of Los Angeles; if it was the Oklahoma plains that spawned him, it was the city that unlocked him. Just as a centrifuge keeps the densest materials at its center and disperses the others, the metropolis ultimately broadened Guthrie's outlook, globalized his senses, compounded his artistry, and enabled the distribution of his output. Sprawling, multicultural New York in particular became a great enabler, with an otherness to which Guthrie was eventually (literally and figuratively) married. His wife's Jewish culture transformed Guthrie's life, as did African American musical and political cultures. In finding his voice in the city, Guthrie gave a profound multidisciplinary and often abstract expression to the modernity into which he was born and which shaped both his outlook and his output.

I should turn briefly to the issue of that output—at least the portions of it featured in this book. Selection of sources always involves a compromise. Some readers may regret the relatively scant attention given here to Guthrie's better-known writings. "This Land Is Your Land" gets the barest mention; and *Dust Bowl Ballads*, "Deportee," and the Columbia River anthems make only the briefest appearance. References to *Bound for Glory* are fleeting, particularly in comparison to the recently discovered, posthumously published novel *House of Earth*. The majority of my sources are archival, rarely or never before seen, chosen precisely for their capacity to challenge the static imagery of the American folk icon who, up to now, has seemed imprisoned in a largely rural, pre-modernist frame. Of course, the specter of modernity has always been lurking behind even the familiar, popular imagery associated with the Okie bard. The freight trains and Ford tractors, jalopies, and power dams populating Guthrie's lyrics are in themselves flags of modernity. But in order to foreground the overwhelming significance of modernity—and modernism—in any complete assessment of Guthrie as an artist and thinker, it is necessary to privilege those sources that have lain buried in the archives, away from the mythologizing hands of his image makers (including, at the forefront, Guthrie himself). The scholarship of Edward Comentale, Mark Allan Jackson, and Martin Butler has led the discussion of Guthrie's relation to modernity. Nora Guthrie and Steven Brower, in editing *Woody Guthrie*

Artworks, have enhanced that discussion, as have Billy Bragg, Wilco, the Klezmatics, and Jonatha Brooke (among others), who have put to music Guthrie's lyrics that have served to loosen the rusty, confining frame of the Dust Bowl Balladeer. The present study is an attempt to extend the discussion even further.

One final word about the title of this book. The phrase "modern world blues" might well suggest a uniform negativity, an unbroken voicing of lament or complaint over the currents of modernity as Guthrie experienced them. But this is far from the case. In choosing the title, I take my cues from East Texas bluesman Clyde Langford, who said, "A lot of people tell you blues is just one thing, but blues can be a number of things. Blues is something in equivalence to a spirit."[17] Or, to quote Corey Harris: "There are happy blues, sad blues, lonesome blues, red-hot blues, mad blues, and loving blues. Blues is a testimony to the fullness of life."[18]

Woody Guthrie was not down on modern life; he was conflicted by it. Modernity for him was a source of exhilaration as well as depression, of immense possibility as well as confusion. It opened his eyes, provoked him, attacked his senses, and was central in making him an artist of immense power and expansiveness. He was fully equipped to sing "Modern World Blues" in all its varied registers and keys—both major and minor—across the rooftops, factories, fields, and byways of America and the wide world beyond.

1

A Modern Life

Guthrie's birth on July 14, 1912, came only five years after Oklahoma had achieved statehood and nine years after the Fort Smith and Western Railroad had reached the town. His birthplace, Okemah, was itself poised on the frontier of modernity. As early as 1909, twenty-seven years before the Rural Electrification Act, a citizen by the name of W. H. Dill had launched a rudimentary electrical service in Okemah, placing the whole town on a single breaker.[1] Still, most families, including that of Charlie and Nora Guthrie, were lighting their homes with kerosene lamps. Charlie—Woody's father—was certainly attuned to the prospects of modernity. The same year that Dill electrified Okemah, the town's newspaper reported that Charlie Guthrie had purchased Okemah's first automobile (a Chalmers) and had taken Nora on a drive over the rough dirt roads to Kansas City and back.[2] Nora herself was also a pioneer of sorts; she and her family, Woody would recall, "had one of the first phonographs in that county."[3] For a time, Charlie was prosperous, a local politician and real estate speculator. The agricultural production demands of World War I enabled him to capitalize on farm land, earning him, at one point, thirty farms that he rented out, a number of fine homes in the town, and his own hill farm breeding "prizewinning Hereford cattle, as well as hogs and pedigreed hunting dogs."[4] His currency, as his son later wrote: "Land leases. Royalties. Deeds and Titles."[5] The revenue from these sources, along with Guthrie's position as clerk of the Okfuskee County Court, allowed his family to live in relative luxury. His children—Clara, Roy, and Woody—along with their mother, especially enjoyed summer and weekend afternoons watching the movies at Okemah's Crystal Theater, sparking Woody's lifelong passion for the cinema (which would later often be camouflaged by his overbearing rhetoric condemning the pernicious influence of Hollywood).

In 1920, with the Guthrie family already shaken by the loss of fourteen-year-old Clara, fatally burned in a coal-oil fire, a major economic slump hit Oklahoma. Charlie's tenants began to default on their rents and mortgages. Within a year he was bankrupt. In desperation, he seized on the possibilities offered by the nascent automobile industry, buying a tractor with a view to securing county contracts to drag the dirt roads. As the *Okemah Ledger* reported, "Mr. Guthrie takes this work not only for the money that he secures from the work, but his pleasure at seeing good roads in the county, and expects to have the best dragged roads in Okfuskee County."[6] Thus would begin a lifetime of relying on hand-to-mouth jobs involving automobiles whenever Charlie's fortunes failed.

A potential reprieve was offered by the discovery of oil, first at Spring Hill, nine miles from Okemah, and then at nearby Cromwell and Seminole. By 1922—the year that Woody's younger sister, Mary Jo, was born—Okemah was an oil-boom town, a major supply center, thanks mostly to its railroad station. As Woody later wrote, the whirlwind of modernity hit the town with full force and with mixed results for his family: "My dad met the new comer, talked, traded, and built us a new six room house. But the speed and hurry, all of this pound and churn, roar and spin, this staggering yell and nervous scream of our little farm town turning into an Oil and Money Rush, it was too much of a load on my Mother's quieter nerves. She commenced to sing the sadder songs in a loster voice, to gaze out our window and to follow her songs out and up and over and away from it all, away over yonder in the minor keys."[7]

The population of Okemah quickly jumped from two thousand to as high as fifteen thousand, but a quiet trader like Charlie Guthrie was no match for the sharp, experienced speculators used to exploiting the rushes of the oil boom. After a brief year of success, he was bankrupt again. As Charlie struggled to provide for his family, Woody, now a young teenager, began to learn the harmonica, his first musical instrument. He would later recall, in a 1940 interview with Alan Lomax, that he had heard "the French harp" being played by "a boy that shined shoes" outside Okemah's barbershop: "That was 'The Railroad Blues' that the colored boy was playing when I walked past the barbershop door. . . . I said, 'Where in the world did you learn it?' 'Oh,' he said, 'I just lay here and listen to the railroad whistle and whatever it say, I say too.'"[8] Thus, the first sounds that Woody learned to translate into musical language were the sounds of early-twentieth-century modernity—not the pastoral song of birds or yelps of hounds but the lonesome whistle and chuff of the freight train.

The summer of 1929 saw seventeen-year-old Woody embarking on his first experience as a hobo, thumbing lifts and hopping freights from Okemah through Houston to the Gulf and back again. In spite of the hobo legend that was to grow around him, Woody's intermittent episodes in hoboing were relatively few throughout his life, but they were important in his development as an observer of American conditions. After his brief return to Okemah that summer, Woody packed up and went to Pampa, Texas, to join his father, who was now running a boomtown flophouse and brothel in the seedy section known as Little Juarez. (His mother, suffering from the barely understood Huntington's disease, had been committed to what was then called the Central State Hospital for the Insane in Norman, Oklahoma.) When Woody learned of his mother's death in the state asylum, he consoled himself, among other ways, by teaching himself the guitar, largely through copying Carter Family records.

Hungry for knowledge but indifferent to formal education (he would never finish high school), Woody ransacked the Pampa public library for books on all topics, particularly world religions, Eastern philosophy, and psychology. He ordered a raft of correspondence courses on literature, law, religion, and medicine—as his Pampa friend, musical comrade, and future brother-in-law Matt Jennings recalled, "ologies of all sorts and kinds."[9] He formed a band—the Corncob Trio—with Jennings and another friend, Cluster Baker, and together they turned to the infant country music industry for inspiration, wearing down the recordings of Jimmie Rodgers and the Carter Family. Soon they were playing at markets and barn dances across the Texas Panhandle, as well as on local radio stations.

In 1931, Woody embarked on an automobile adventure with his father and other family members, all packed into a ramshackle Model-T truck in hopes of locating a fabled silver mine supposedly staked by Charlie's father, Jerry P. Guthrie, in the Chisos Mountains along the Texas-Mexico border. Although they never found the mine, the trip wasn't wholly fruitless: it became the basis of Guthrie's second autobiographical novel, *Seeds of Man*, written in 1946–47 and published posthumously in 1977. Two years later, Woody married Matt Jennings's sister, Mary, having wooed her by a number of means, including dedicating to her a performance of the song "Take Me Out to the Ball Game" on a Panhandle radio station.[10] The following year he wrote what he maintained was his first song, "Old Gray Team of Hosses," a slapstick parlor number reflecting the coming of modernity to a rural backwater, signaled by the arrival of a Ford car that spooks a team of horses pulling a wagon with the protagonist and his belle. This song inaugurated in Woody a lifelong thread of writing about cars and driving.

Newly married, Woody struggled to make ends meet. With a preternatural talent for the graphic arts, he established himself as an itinerant sign painter for businesses around the Panhandle, but life in Pampa was turned on its head in April 1935, when the worst dust storms of the century buried much of the Midwest, including the Panhandle. This was modernity coming home with a vengeance, ironically a mere two years after the promoters of the 1933 Chicago World's Fair—the "Century of Progress" exhibition—had boasted in its visitors' programs, "Science Finds, Industry Applies, Man Conforms."[11] As the historian Donald Worster has noted, it was precisely science, industry, and humans that were responsible for the ecological disaster that first brought Woody Guthrie into the broader public sphere, namely through the "highly mechanized factory farms" that had overrun the plains: "This is how and why the Dust Bowl came about. . . . The sod had been destroyed to make farms to grow wheat to get cash."[12] Thus, in a short period of time, a mere two decades, the very machines that had served as poster icons of progress in the early twentieth century—the Ford tractors and combine harvesters—had become rampaging agents of destruction, telescoping labor hours into seconds and, in stripping the prairie of its protective grasses, undoing the patient natural work of millennia.

In November, Woody and Mary's first child, Gwendolyn, was born. Her parents had no way of knowing that she carried the gene for the Huntington's disease that would end her life at the age of forty-one, but something about her conception and birth sparked Woody's fascination with biology. He began to spend hours peering into a microscope borrowed from Mary's doctor, watching the microorganisms fighting the evolutionary struggle that would preoccupy him for the rest of his life.

The year 1936 saw Woody first hitting the highway and the rails in search of work to support his family. With the roads now flooded with newly indigent hitchhikers, Woody turned more and more to the boxcars, embarking on his most sustained period of freight-hopping. He drifted through Texas, Arkansas, Oklahoma, New Mexico, Arizona, and California, where he first saw the notorious "Bum Blockade" illegally erected at the state line by the Los Angeles Police Department, who were determined to prevent an influx of fellow-American migrants into the Golden State. With a handful of money gained by odd jobs, sign painting, and soda jerking, Woody returned to Pampa, where his interest in socialism took root in the wake of all he had seen.

In the spring of 1937, and with Mary pregnant with their second child, Sue (who would, like her older sister, succumb to Huntington's disease at the age of forty-one), Guthrie headed for California, traveling mostly by foot and by thumb. He had intended to support himself through sign painting, but once in California the music took over. Woody hooked up with a cousin—a singer and guitarist going by the name of "Oklahoma" Jack Guthrie—who was aiming to cash in on the "Singing Cowboy" craze sweeping Hollywood and further afield, thanks to the films and recordings of Gene Autry, the Sons of the Pioneers, and lesser lights. Together, in cowboy garb, the two Guthries played cowboy shows, rodeos, vaudeville houses, movie theaters, and promotional venues. Through Jack, Woody met a transplanted Missourian, Maxine "Lefty Lou" Crissman, with whom he would soon form a singing partnership. In July, Jack and Woody secured a spot on the progressive Los Angeles radio station KFVD, shortly to be joined by Crissman. Before long, the station manager, J. Frank Burke, offered them three spots a day; the fan mail rushed in. This was Woody's first taste of "big time" urban radio, for although KFVD was neither as large nor as powerful as the networks broadcasting from coast to coast, it was technologically better equipped than the small stations of Pampa and Amarillo. As Woody's later singing partner Lee Hays recalled: "The radio station was full of all kinds of sound effects. There were thunder machines, lightning machines, inner sanctum squeaky doors and electric organs, coconut shell devices. . . . Woody would wander around the studio rattling and banging and shaking on these things, just having a hell of a good time."[13]

In fact, Los Angeles offered Guthrie a new, comprehensive education in the dynamics of modernity. It was the largest city he had ever seen. Soon he was writing songs and notebook observations about the urban sprawl, the noise, the traffic, and the smog, often from the highly fabricated viewpoint of a rural rube making his first encounter with the big city. In reality, Guthrie adapted to the relative sophistication and pace of urban modernity with little trouble; if anything, he relished it. He would, for the most part, remain an urban dweller for the rest of his life. Crissman recalled him dragging her into the city's used bookstores, engaging in intense discussion on all topics with the proprietors, and introducing her to impressionism and other modern art forms at the Los Angeles museums and galleries.

Eventually the pressures of performing and broadcasting took their toll on Crissman's health, and she resigned from the station and from the duo with Guthrie in June 1938. During a brief hiatus, Burke—also the editor of a progressive newspaper, the *Light*—offered Guthrie a commission to explore the migrant camps and Hoovervilles proliferating across California and to file his reports by telephone. Guthrie would forever remember what he learned through this commission, his entry into the world of journalism: "I hated the false front decay and rot of California's fascistic oil and gas deals, the ptomaine poison and brass knucks in the jails and prisons, the dumped oranges and peaches and grapes and cherries rotting and running down into little streams of creosote poisoned juices."[14]

At this time, Guthrie was introduced to Ed Robbin, the Los Angeles correspondent for the Communist Party daily, *People's World*. Robbin had three spots a week on KFVD, and he and Guthrie became firm friends. It is likely that this was Guthrie's first personal, in-depth encounter with the world of Judaism and the politics of Zionism (both of which would inform his second marriage into a Jewish family). Robbin was instrumental in bringing Guthrie into the West Coast's progressive circles, securing his first performances for union and Communist Party events. Through Robbin, Guthrie met Al Richmond, the editor of *People's World*, who took him on as a columnist and cartoonist for the paper. Between May 1939 and early 1940, Guthrie would contribute over 170 of his "Woody Sez" columns, as well as eighty-two cartoons.[15]

Guthrie later recalled: "I went to fancy Hollywood drinking parties and rubbed my elbows with the darkling glasses that they wore over their eyes to keep down everything. I met up with an actor named Will Geer and . . . we drove my '31 Chevvery around the sad canyons to play for migrant strikers."[16] Robbin had introduced Guthrie to Geer—later the grandfather on the popular television series *The Waltons*—and Geer became Guthrie's most influential political mentor. Through Geer, Guthrie had his first experience as a film actor (albeit a nonspeaking extra), along with his pregnant wife, Mary, who had by now joined him in Los Angeles. The film was celebrated documentarian Pare Lorentz's *The Fight for Life* (1940), a dramatized tribute to the work of the Chicago Maternity Center, whose dedicated, overworked doctors and nurses ventured daily into the slums, shack towns, and tenements to bring—as someone in the film declares—"modern science to the poor women of the city."[17]

Geer brought Guthrie further into Hollywood circles, introducing him to the likes of the directors D. W. Griffith and Lewis Milestone as well as progressive actors and screenwriters with whom he would later associate as an activist—Eddie Albert, John Garfield, Waldo Salt, Melvyn Douglas, Helen Gahagan, and others. Geer also introduced Guthrie to John Steinbeck, who would go on to endorse his work and sometimes accompany him to his performances with Geer at migrant camps and at Hollywood studios and parties.

Shortly after the birth of his third child, Bill, in October 1939 (Bill would be killed at the age of twenty-three, driving his car into a train), Guthrie lost his job at KFVD after a series of confrontations with Burke over the Hitler-Stalin Pact and the Soviet invasion of Poland, both of which—in line with the increasingly uncomfortable Communist Party of the USA—Guthrie supported, to Burke's disgust. In an old Plymouth that Guthrie said he had bought "eighth-hand," the family moved back to Pampa, where Guthrie briefly took up his old job at Shorty Harris's drugstore.[18] According to the town librarian, Evelyn Todd, Guthrie boasted that he had secured a role in John Ford's film of *The Grapes of Wrath* but lost it due to his touring in the migrant camps.[19] (Guthrie would later claim to have acted as a musical consultant to Ford.)

By this time, Geer had relocated to New York to star in the Broadway production of Erskine Caldwell's *Tobacco Road*, and in a letter he enticed Guthrie with the prospect of a role in the show. This prospect was enough for Guthrie to pull up stakes and head for New York, where he arrived the following month, promising to send for Mary and the children as soon as he found work. First camping out briefly in Geer's sumptuous apartment, Guthrie soon moved to a run-down transient hotel, Hanover House, on Manhattan's Sixth Avenue, where in February he wrote a number of songs, including the first draft of "This Land Is Your Land." Although the part in *Tobacco Road* never materialized, Geer did manage to alter the course of Guthrie's life with an introduction to Alan Lomax, the assistant in charge of the Archive of American Folk Song at the Library of Congress. Together Geer and Lomax were planning a benefit concert on behalf of the John Steinbeck Committee to Aid Agricultural Organization. The Steinbeck benefit proved to be Guthrie's first significant New York appearance, if only for the reason that he was here brought together with Huddie Ledbetter—Lead Belly—and Pete Seeger. (Lomax would later date "the renaissance of American folk song" from this meeting.)[20]

Three weeks after this momentous concert, Guthrie traveled to Washington, D.C., at Lomax's invitation, to record a series of sides that were later released as *The Library of Congress Recordings*, Guthrie's first records. While Guthrie was in Washington, Lomax asked him to write an autobiography to accompany the recordings; he was presented with a typescript of twenty-five single-spaced pages, which Lomax would later compare to James Joyce's modernist masterpiece, *Ulysses*. Lomax encouraged Guthrie to keep writing—not only songs but also as much autobiographical prose as possible.

When Guthrie returned to New York, he continued to file his "Woody Sez" columns for *People's World* in San Francisco; they were soon picked up by the Communist Party's *Daily Worker* in New York. Many of these later columns fabricated the persona of an unlettered hillbilly in New York. The fabrication extended to an expressed "disdain for avant-garde art," as the art historian Ellen Landau describes it.[21] But this pose belied the fact that Guthrie had long been devoted to the experiential power of abstract, avant-garde art, as witnessed not only in his frequent visits to museums and art galleries but also in his letters, notebook entries, sculptures, and—in particular—the many modernist-inflected paintings and sketches reproduced in the remarkable 2005 volume edited by Steven Brower and Nora Guthrie, *Woody Guthrie Artworks.*[22]

Within five months of his arrival in New York, Guthrie was living with two artist friends of Seeger's, Harold and Elisabeth Ambellan. As he continued to soak up the influences of avant-garde art and bohemian life in Lower Manhattan, he perfected his half-literate Okie pose and brought it to the studios of CBS, through Lomax's patronage. His first New York City radio broadcast was on Lomax's *Columbia School of the Air* in April 1940, followed shortly by an appearance on Norman Corwin's *Pursuit of Happiness.* Ed Cray observes: "Whether singing or reading a script, the Oklahoman was the complete professional, standing out among the experienced actors and musicians with whom Corwin usually worked."[23] That same month saw Guthrie's entrance into the world of commercial recording with his *Dust Bowl Ballads* for RCA Victor. If Alan Lomax is to be believed, it was America's "second commercial folk song album," after Lead Belly's *Negro Sinful Tunes.*[24]

The cash advance from *Dust Bowl Ballads* bought Guthrie a new Plymouth coupe, and he and Seeger took their first American journey together in May 1940—first back to Washington, D.C., to begin work on their massive edited song collection with Lomax, *Hard Hitting Songs for Hard-Hit People,* then on to the Highlander Folk School in Tennessee, where they learned firsthand about the power of song in progressive educational curricula. When Seeger took off on his own to hitchhike around the West, Guthrie returned to New York, leaving his Plymouth behind, where it served as "the official car of the Oklahoma Communist Party for several years after that."[25]

Back in New York City, Guthrie joined the cast of Lomax's CBS radio program, *Back Where I Come From,* directed by future film auteur Nicholas Ray. Once again, Guthrie's public persona as the Okie rube belied his professionalism, which he demonstrated through his script editorial work, his on-air time management, and his relations with the other cast members. His radio profile mushroomed, garnering him a host of commercial contracts: *We the People* on CBS, sponsored by Sanka; *Cavalcade of America* on NBC, sponsored by Du Pont; and *Pipe Smoking Time* on CBS, sponsored by the Model Tobacco Company. Guthrie also made numerous public radio appearances, most notably on Henrietta Yurchenco's *Adventures in Music* on WNYC.

Guthrie's most lucrative contract, in terms of both salary and potential broadcast longevity, was for *Pipe Smoking Time*, for which he shamelessly bastardized his first Dust Bowl ballad, "So Long, It's Been Good to Know Yuh," into a jaunty, anodyne jingle extolling the pleasures of pipe tobacco. Soon, however, his conscience apparently got the better of him, and he appears to have engineered his own firing from CBS. He headed west in a used Pontiac purchased on the installment plan, with his long-suffering family with him. When, on a Washington stopover, Lomax asked Guthrie's three-year-old daughter Sue where she lived, she replied, "In the car."[26]

Back in Los Angeles, Guthrie had hopes of getting his old job back at KFVD, but beyond offering a brief stint for no pay, Burke was not interested in rehiring him. From February to April 1941, the Guthries lived a semi-indigent life in small rentals north of Los Angeles and in the foothills of the High Sierras, with Guthrie painting signs and cutting and hauling timber. They were rescued by an offer from the Bonneville Power Administration (BPA) to bring Guthrie to the Columbia River to write songs that were to grace a film on the building of the Grand Coulee Dam. He secured a month-long contract as "information consultant" and "narrative actor," writing a total of twenty-six songs (only three of which were eventually used in the film). The broken down Pontiac had barely made it to Portland; it was repossessed after the finance company reported Guthrie to the FBI, which opened a file on him. That same month, unbeknown to Guthrie, the paid informer Hazel Huffman was denouncing him as a Communist in testimony before the House Committee on Un-American Activities (the so-called Dies Committee).

Guthrie's month with the BPA was one of his most productive and remunerative. Equally important was its instrumentality in firing his enthusiasm for industrial projects, electrification, and mechanization. During his earliest period in Los Angeles, he had written some songs deploring how labor-saving machinery decimated the industrial workforce, but now, through the good works of the New Deal and the BPA, the Pacific Northwest would be electrified and modernized. Guthrie became evangelical about electricity and industrial production, determined henceforth to associate folk music with modernity rather than with the antique ruralism with which it was so often associated.

Guthrie's BPA contract work concluded on June 11, 1941, about two weeks before the German invasion of Russia signaled the end of the Hitler-Stalin Pact and the Communist Party's abrupt about-face from queasy noninterventionism to full-tilt antifascism. Guthrie returned to New York, minus his wife and children. Mary had reached the end of her tether and vowed she would stay put. Their marriage was basically over. Back in New York, Guthrie found that his songs still held currency in progressive circles. Martha Graham dancer and independent choreographer Sophie Maslow put together a show based on Guthrie's *Dust Bowl Ballads*, while the newly formed Almanac Singers—Seeger, Lampell, Hays, and Alan Lomax's sister, Bess—invited Guthrie to record with them. With the $250 earned for their recordings, the Almanacs bought a 1932 Buick and set out toward the West, with Guthrie naturally at the wheel, for a national tour on behalf of the Congress of Industrial Organizations (CIO). Taking in the industrial centers of Pittsburgh, Cleveland, Detroit, Chicago, Milwaukee, Denver, San Francisco, and Los Angeles, the Almanacs performed at strikers' rallies and in union halls. Lampell recalled: "Woody had a mystique about working, but he'd never really seen *industrial* workers before. I think it was the first time that Woody—or any of us—saw organized labor with this kind of strength."[27]

Back in New York, and now officially an Almanac Singer, Guthrie moved into the communal residence of the Almanacs—"Almanac House"—on Tenth Street in Greenwich Village. Very quickly the house became a bohemian salon of sorts, frequented by such visitors as Jackson Pollock, Willem de Kooning, Charles Olson, Stella Adler, and Franchot Tone. Seeger recalled that, after meeting Guthrie, Olson was "bowled over" with his autobiographical writing, encouraging him to write a full-scale work and commissioning him for an article in his progressive arts magazine, *Commentary*.[28] Guthrie began to work intensively on *Bound for Glory*, and with the Japanese attack on Pearl Harbor on December 7 he began a frenzied period of writing pro-war, antifascist, anti-Hitler songs.

In January 1942 the Almanacs were evicted from their Tenth Street residence. The new Almanac House was a flat on Sixth Avenue. The cramped conditions did not prevent Guthrie's further immersion into the world of modern art in New York. The same month, Sophie Maslow began rehearsing her new piece, *Folksay*, and invited Guthrie to perform live in the show. Through this project, Guthrie was first drawn personally into the modern dance arena, meeting Martha Graham as well as one of Graham's star dancers and method instructors, Marjorie Greenblatt Mazia, who would become his second wife and the mother of his children Cathy, Arlo, Joady, and Nora. Increasingly Guthrie's writing and his artwork would be inflected with images and metaphors from the world of modern dance, due to this encounter that transformed his life.

Meanwhile Guthrie's autobiographical work continued. In between his writing binges, he appeared with the Almanacs on a number of network radio broadcasts, riding the crest of a popularity wave as pro-war propagandists—until the right-wing press began to call them out as Communists. With the Almanacs' auditions and job offers quickly drying up, Guthrie focused even more intensively on *Bound for Glory* and secured a contract from E. P. Dutton in April 1942.

By June 1942, Marjorie was pregnant with Cathy but still determined to remain with her husband, Joseph Mazia, until after the baby's birth—not only to ensure a medically safe and comfortable delivery but also to protect her husband's security clearance (with the FBI having gotten wind of her affair with "a Communist").[29] Marjorie's decision launched a considerable period of crisis and insecurity in Guthrie, forcing his sustained reflection on new and unfamiliar patterns of domestic, gender, and parental expectations. Still, their relationship was secure enough for her to introduce Guthrie to her parents, both immigrant Jews and Zionists and one—her mother, Aliza Waitzman Greenblatt—a celebrated Yiddish poet. Guthrie would increasingly support the establishment of a Jewish state in Palestine and viciously condemned what he saw as British imperialism there. (He appears to have remained silent on the subject of the Palestinian Arabs.)

Cathy was born on February 6, 1943. She and her mother finally joined Guthrie in April. With Marjorie teaching and dancing most days, Guthrie took on an increased share of the child-care responsibilities and began keeping detailed records of Cathy's doings and, later, sayings, many of which would find their way into his most popular children's songs. But all this domestic activity was clouded by the repeated induction notices Guthrie received from the draft board, and, deciding on a more palatable (though dangerous enough) alternative to the army, Guthrie joined the merchant marine in June. The long months at sea afforded him his most extensive period of manual labor, as shipboard mess man. In between his various tasks he embarked on a massive self-guided reading course in Marxism, particularly dialectical materialism, which became a political creed for him. Increasingly seeing and writing about the world as a site of continuous evolutionary struggle, Guthrie was soon balancing his autodidactic scientism with a developing mystical and spiritual concept of union—not only in terms of labor but also in its more universalist sense, the oneness of all things. Docking in Palermo, Sicily, in July 1943, Guthrie witnessed for the first time the destructive effects of modern weaponry. In mid-September, his ship was torpedoed on the way to Tunis, sinking in Bizerte harbor. Thanks to the enforced period of liberty after this, Guthrie explored parts of North Africa, further expanding his experience with the developing world beyond American borders.

Completing his first voyage that autumn, Guthrie settled with Marjorie and Cathy in an apartment on Mermaid Avenue in New York's Coney Island, a neighborhood whose vibrant multiculturalism delighted him. But another induction notice soon arrived, so he signed up for his second voyage with the merchant marine. In January 1944 he shipped out, sailing again to the Mediterranean. Docking briefly in Oran, he explored parts of Algeria, stunned by its premodern poverty, particularly among malnourished children. In March, Guthrie sailed back to New York, and there he dove into an intensive period of recording for Moses Asch, whom he met in April. Guthrie and Cisco Houston recorded over 160 songs for Asch in a matter of days, producing what the Smithsonian's Jeff Place calls the "mother lode . . . the bulk of Guthrie's recorded legacy."[30]

The month of May brought Guthrie another draft notice and another ocean voyage, his final with the merchant marine. Passionate about the progress of what he called his "Union War," Guthrie was exhilarated by the preparations for the D-Day invasion. After docking in Liverpool and Belfast, both of which Guthrie explored, his ship sailed for Normandy, where it was crippled by an acoustic mine just off Omaha Beach. After the ship was towed to Southampton, Guthrie explored firsthand the devastation of bombed-out London before his return home.

Guthrie spent part of October 1944 touring the East Coast with the "Roosevelt Bandwagon" to support the third reelection of Franklin Roosevelt. On December 3, with Roosevelt reelected and Guthrie back in New York, the WNEW radio station took him on as the presenter of a new show, *Ballad Gazette*. The show lasted only twelve weeks, though, with Guthrie increasingly chafing at the demands of network censorship. Effectively abandoning any further hopes of a network radio career, as Ed Cray tantalizingly reports, Guthrie appeared briefly "on an experimental CBS television broadcast," the name of which has apparently been lost.[31] This was the first of a handful of Guthrie's experiences in the new medium, barely out of its embryonic stage.

When his final draft notice arrived in March 1945, Guthrie learned that he could no longer sail with the merchant marine, as the Office of Naval Intelligence had revoked his seaman's papers due to his Communist associations. Thus, on the day of Germany's surrender—May 7, 1945—Private First Class Woodrow Wilson Guthrie began his US Army service. With the US nuclear bombing of Hiroshima and Nagasaki in August and Japan's subsequent surrender, Guthrie waxed euphoric over the work of the atomic bomb. (He would about-face on this issue as the Cold War progressed.) His notebooks from this period bristle with eulogies to atomic power in general, which he would always see as a potential force for good.

In November, while on furlough in New York, Guthrie married Marjorie, inaugurating a complex and tempestuous eight-year marriage marked by many trials and separations. Upon his discharge from the army in December, Guthrie began a fitful period of child care, experiencing the sense of dislocation that was shared by many demobilized soldiers at the end of the war. But outnumbering the letters and notebook entries reflecting his frustration at this time are the many observational jottings that he would turn into some of his most renowned children's songs.

January 1946 saw Guthrie joining—at least in a nominal capacity—the board of directors of Pete Seeger's newly launched People's Songs, Inc., a musical service aimed at bolstering the postwar labor movement. But the approach of the Cold War and an increasingly paranoid anticommunism was gutting the radicalism of the movement, which seemed to disintegrate along with Guthrie's own neurological system. That spring Guthrie was back in Los Angeles, where he appeared in a short film called *Banjo Pickin' Boy*, directed by Irving Lerner. Fired with enthusiasm over a possible film career, Guthrie wrote for Lerner a treatment for a proposed film based on his own life.

The year 1947 began with Guthrie and Marjorie expecting the birth of their second child, Arlo, but devastating tragedy struck the household on February 10, when four-year-old Cathy was burned to death in a fire sparked by a faulty radio wire. Meanwhile Guthrie's graphic and plastic artwork began to shift dramatically in its appearance. As Landau notes: "The vast majority of Woody Guthrie's visual production between 1947 and 1956, the year he was permanently hospitalized, can be characterized as involuntarily childlike, its loose, suggestive, shorthand style a metaphor for the way his own mind and body were spinning out of control."[32]

The summer of 1947 marked not only the arrival of Arlo but also an acute moment of crisis in Guthrie's marriage, with his private writings replete with anguished reflections on the hopelessness of marriage as an institution and his own sense of imprisonment in a life disintegrating. Characteristically he turned to the road for respite, buying from a "mad Russian on Surf Avenue" a two-door Ford with the royalties from "Oklahoma Hills" ("the biggest chunk of free enterprise I've got so far").[33] Amid considerable marital tension and frequent periods of separation, the Guthries' third child, Joady, was born on Christmas Day 1948.

In the new year of 1949, People's Songs folded, battered by bankruptcy as well as the nation's cultural and political shift to the right. Guthrie briefly turned to a commission to write venereal disease awareness songs for a radio campaign and actively sought to land a television contract, to no avail. In September he accompanied Seeger and Hays to Paul Robeson's concert in Peekskill, New York, which was disrupted by racist and anticommunist rioting, quickly inspiring at least seventeen songs from Guthrie's pen.

Guthrie was in jail for vagrancy on January 2, 1950, the day his daughter Nora was born. Due to his increasingly erratic behavior, most of his friends and associates—as well as Guthrie himself—assumed that he was suffering from acute alcoholism. His Huntington's disease had yet to be conclusively diagnosed. His writing became episodically and increasingly surreal both in form and content, resulting in what biographer Joe Klein calls "linguistic anarchy."[34] Guthrie began spending more and more time as a drifter, usually traveling by bus but often resorting to hitchhiking and freight-hopping when he'd spent his bus fare on drink. Yet, wherever he was, he still engaged through his writing with the events of his times, whether it was the Korean War of 1950–53, atomic power, the fear of nuclear war, or the discoveries of Einstein, whose theories on relativity increasingly preoccupied him.

A much-needed respite came in late 1950, when Seeger's popular folk group, the Weavers, recorded a hit version of Guthrie's "So Long, It's Been Good to Know Yuh," earning him a $10,000 advance on royalties. The money enabled Guthrie and his family to move into a larger apartment in Fred (father of Donald) Trump's new Brooklyn development, Beach Haven, sparking a host of bitter writings from Guthrie on the development's de facto segregation policies. The money also enabled Marjorie to open the Marjorie Mazia School of Dance. Guthrie met music publisher Howie Richmond, who devised the canny strategy of making Guthrie's songs free for publication in school music books, which is how "This Land Is Your Land," among other songs, first filtered into the public consciousness.

Guthrie's penultimate recording session—for Decca, on January 7, 1952—was severely marred by his incoherence and instability. Months of hospitalization followed, and his notebooks from this period see him making significant connections between his own seeming breakdown and that of modern American society at large. Upon his discharge he headed for Los Angeles, joining Will Geer's Topanga Canyon community of progressive artists, most of them blacklisted. There he met a young married woman, Anneke Van Kirk Marshall, and they began an affair, with Anneke initially oblivious to the medical traumas that they would soon face. Running away together, they traveled to New York and then to Stetson Kennedy's place in Florida, a ranch Kennedy called Beluthahatchee. Spending just under six months there, Guthrie devoted himself to writing a surreal, science-fiction-inflected play script called *Skybally* as well as revising his manuscript of *Seeds of Man*, ever more determined to find a publisher. In July, Anneke learned that she was pregnant with Guthrie's child. Now divorced from Marjorie, Guthrie married Anneke in December, returning to New York the following month.

Guthrie's final recording session for Asch, on January 18, 1954, was a shambles, thanks in part to the combination of free-flowing drink and Guthrie's illness. Guthrie and Anneke's daughter, Lorina, was born the next month. In their cramped apartment, with Anneke working in an office and Guthrie increasingly unable to perform the child-care duties, the tension between them would sometimes explode into violence. Sensing that their marriage was hopeless, Anneke filed for divorce in October.

In mid-1956, Guthrie was committed to the Greystone Park psychiatric complex in Morris Plains, New Jersey. For the rest of his life, Marjorie took an active role in his care, devoting more and more time to projects aimed at increasing the awareness of Huntington's disease. It would largely be through Marjorie's establishment of the Committee to Combat Huntington's Disease—later the Huntington's Disease Society of America—that genetic research would enable a comprehensive designation for the disorder and, in 1994, the discovery of the responsible gene.

For the next five years, "Wardy Forty"—Ward 40—in Greystone Park would be Guthrie's home. Marjorie would bring the children to visit him and play with him on the hospital's expansive grounds, particularly around the huge, gnarled "magic tree" that spread out over the lawn.[35] In December 1956, Guthrie finally admitted in a letter to Marjorie: "I just have to really face my fact in my earthly case here all off my goody booky writing days are just all out and all over anyways."[36] Two days later, on December 14, Guthrie wrote his last letter, a plea to his children to "comey visit me in my magicy tree againe."[37]

As Guthrie's health deteriorated further, his reputation and his legend grew. In 1964, Elektra Records released the Library of Congress recordings that Guthrie had made for Lomax in 1940. The following year, the first collection of his writings, *Born to Win*, was published. By this time, Guthrie had stopped speaking altogether, simply blinking once for "yes" and twice for "no." In 1966 the US Department of the Interior recognized him with its Conservation Service Award, largely on the strength of his Columbia River anthems and "This Land Is Your Land," naturally avoiding any acknowledgment of his political radicalism. That year a resident Huntington's specialist at Creedmoor State Hospital in Queens advised that the now permanently bedridden Guthrie be transferred into his care. Creedmoor became Woody

Guthrie's final home, and he died there on the morning of October 3, 1967.

Through the combined efforts of Marjorie Guthrie and Harold Leventhal, the Woody Guthrie Archives were opened in 1996 under the direction of Nora Guthrie. This magnificent repository houses not only the bulk of Guthrie's notebooks, correspondence, manuscripts, and roughly three thousand song lyrics, but also much of his visual artwork. It is to this rich source material that we now turn.

2

Woody Guthrie, American Modernist

Guthrie once took to task the editors of a magazine—its title is now lost—that had published an essay arguing that there was no place for folk music in the modern world. As Guthrie recounted it: "The writer says that we haven't got any more folk songs, ballads, ditties, because we can't make any more about machinery and atoms and electricity and that folk music can't be made up no more because the tractor is taking the place of the horse, the gas engine is pushing out the wagon, the western frontier is all settled, the gold is all dug up, the songs are all made up, and are now only echoes of the good old past." This opinion was "dangerous," he protested; the modern world needed its folk music now more than ever—not only the traditional songs of the past but also the folk expressions of the present.[1] As he wrote to his future wife Marjorie in 1942: "The very instant that either the classics stop being changed, or folk songs, the biggest part of them is dead on the spot. There are certain big principles that stay alive in all forms of art, but unless every single day's headline news, and every day's happening and historic trends are worked into all forms of the show business, then, right then it's a dead bird."[2]

Guthrie's urge to maintain the contemporary relevance of folk expression did not set him at odds with the modern artists of his day, even if he resolutely objected to their habitual equation of the folk arts with "primitivism." As Brian Jones observes, "Modernist artists had long fostered a fascination with the work of 'primitive' peoples." Jones quotes the Museum of Modern Art's 1933 catalog *American Sources of Modern Art* in noting particularly "fundamentals of art—rhythm, design, balance, proportion, which the folk artist feels instinctively."[3] But running counter to the patronizing and anthro-pologically dubious use of the term "primitive" to account for folk expression, certain currents of American modernism had located a *contemporary* vital-ity in the folk process that had nothing to do with "primitivism"—namely "taking artefacts from everyday life and examining them as objects of artistic value."[4] It is this focus that is central to Guthrie's folk sensibilities.

Thomas Crow, in his expansive study *The Long March of Pop*, emphasizes "the preternaturally voluble and prolific Woody Guthrie" and Lead Belly, both being examples of the "anticipatory modernism" to be found elsewhere in the quotidian representations of American folk art.[5] While noting in passing Guthrie's identification with such "high-modernist intelligentsia" as Thomas Mann, Bertolt Brecht, Charles Olson, Martha Graham, Jack-son Pollock, and Nicholas Ray, Edward Comentale suggests that Guthrie "worked with the basic DNA of the folk song" to produce a new music reflective of his times.[6] In fact, Guthrie went far beyond working with "the basic DNA of the folk song." He used the whole range of his culture, both inherited *and* contemporary. It is easy to identify the "traditional" forms (the ballads, instrumentals, and vernacular styles) that were the products of Guthrie's inherited folk culture, but it is more difficult to define his contem-porary folk culture—that is, the folk culture of modernity. Asked bluntly, where—or what—is the folk culture in what Walter Benjamin called the "age of mechanical reproduction"? As Regina Bendix explains, folklore scholars, beginning in the second half of the twentieth century, saw a redefinition of what actually constituted folk expression. They began abandoning the dubi-ous and self-defeating attempts to distinguish the "folk" from the nonfolk or the "authentic" from the "spurious" in culture. Instead they began to look at the processes through which *all* people might be "recognized as active shapers of folklore," whatever their era.[7] Viewing the folk process in this light serves two functions. First, it completely eliminates the patronizing and outmoded high-modernist equation of "folk" with "primitive." Second, it allows for ever-contemporary, renewable manifestations of the folk pro-cess. Guthrie's mission to employ the imagery of industrial modernity in traditional musical settings is only one—perhaps even the crudest—example of the means by which he would choose to modernize the folk process.

Hence his habitual emphasis on the quotidian—literally, the everyday.

Not only would he take "artefacts from everyday life" and fashion them into "objects of artistic value," but he would also put everyday modes of expression and activities (labor, sex, travel, political machination, etc.) to similar artistic use. In this, Guthrie was truly modernist in his sensibilities, in fellowship with the likes of Marcel Proust and Virginia Woolf, the latter of whom, writing of Proust, observed that the "commonest object, such as the telephone, loses its simplicity, its solidity, and becomes a part of life and transparent," as do the "commonest actions, such as going up in an elevator or eating cake."[8]

In Guthrie's case, the value of the "common" everyday object is evident in his brief disquisitions on the potent ways of the symbol: "To me, everything in life is not only a symbol of my own mind and its contents; but a symbol, a living illustration of all minds and all of their contents." Here was the modernist's universalism in a nutshell. "An old wet pair of shoes on the floor, at first glance, remind me of the person that wore them, my contacts and connexions with that person. All I know about them, his good and bad habits, his cares and works and his 'low down' ways and qualities."[9]

What remains to be addressed is the sheer panoramic scope of Guthrie's artistic expression beyond the confines of the folk song. For instance, one of the most intriguing items on display at the Woody Guthrie Center in Tulsa, Oklahoma—among such other prizes as Guthrie's guitars, fiddle, mandolin, plaid flannel shirts, paintings, and sketches—is a little gem: a ceramic tile fired by Guthrie in the early 1950s, apparently meant to be used as a hotplate, and illustrated with an urban industrial scene. It depicts a red complex of apartment blocks to the left; four towering smokestacks in gray, belching smoke, in back; and in the foreground a huge, multicolored but yellow-dominated "V," reminiscent of the World War II "V for Victory" campaign (fig. 1). Whatever interpretive possibilities this tile holds, it places Guthrie at the heart of American industrial modernity and far from his rural origins.

The tile is also important for another reason: it exemplifies Guthrie's sense that each artistic medium is beset by its own limitations. As he wrote in a notebook:

> Picture albums
> Tell stories
> No singer
> Can hope to tell.[10]

Fig. 1. Ceramic tile, early 1950s. Designed by Woody Guthrie © Woody Guthrie Publications, Inc. Courtesy of Nora Guthrie.

But pictures too were insufficient: "Some things besides my brush and pen will have to fight these owners' owners."[11] And even language itself fell short. As Comentale argues, Guthrie "shared his contemporaries' frustrations with the logic of representation," particularly a "frustrated relation to language as a medium of personal and public expression."[12] Such frustration comes out in many of Guthrie's private writings. In late 1942, he confided to his notebook: "Most of the stuff I write don't sound like me."[13] Five years later, he was still struggling with what Mark Goble calls this "modernist predicament with mediation," a perceived inability, coupled with an unquenchable desire, to reflect reality accurately through whatever modes of expression were at his disposal.[14] It was a struggle that Guthrie would never give up, even as he complained, "My deep feel can't be felt by pen and ink."[15] Only the dead hand of Huntington's disease would finally still his pen.

As those who are familiar with the archival sources will testify, Guthrie's unstoppable urge to fill the page appeared close to an affliction. There are few empty spaces on the pages of his notebooks, letters, and manuscripts; spaces that he could not fill with words he filled with drawings and bright watercolor washes. Any wasted or unused creative space appeared to him a criminal act—as he wrote in his 1945 daybook: "The pages that we left blank in this book are an insult to the human race."[16] When blank pages meant for writing were not available, Guthrie would turn to other spaces yearning to be filled. Comentale observes that he "suffered from a nearly debilitating graphomania and wrestled his whole life to match up words to the people and objects around him. As he wandered back and forth across the country, he scribbled on everything he saw—papers, walls, desktops, guitars, menus, and cars. Many friends noticed his frequent bouts with binge writing, marveling at the sheer quantity and velocity of his prose, his seemingly interminable list making, and his compulsion to invent nicknames for everyone around him."[17]

Guthrie's "graphomania" may well have been, in part, a symptom of his Huntington's disease—as might his seeming compulsion to integrate such varied modes of expression into his art. Each word, he wrote, had its own "sound, tone, timber, fibre, quality, and color"—as though language itself were both plastic and musical.[18] Such sensitivity and perception may have had a neurological origin akin to synesthesia—in Daniel Tammet's

words, a "mixing of the senses . . . the ability to see alphabetical letters and/
or numbers in color."[19] Joe Klein notes that both Marjorie and Dr. John
Whittier, the Huntington's disease specialist she had engaged, wondered
aloud "if the disease hadn't worked like a drug on Woody, as a creative
spur . . . forcing the brain to continually rewire itself as cells died, forcing
new, wonderful, and unexpected synaptic pathways to open . . . forcing
the brain to become—in effect—more creative to survive."[20] Whatever the
basis, neurological or otherwise, Guthrie's astonishing multimedia output
was a reflection of his profound need and commitment to gain maximum
expressive and interpretive capital from whatever building blocks were at
his disposal.

   We might turn first to Guthrie's writing, in particular to those building
blocks at its base: the words themselves. Whether in autobiography, fiction,
poetry, essay, song lyrics, play scripts, letters, or notebook entries, words were
symbols meant to be chosen with care and nailed securely to the object or
concept that they were meant to describe. In the era before postmodernism
and post-structuralism had normalized the concept of "shifting significa-
tion" and other challenges to the presumed stability of meaning, Guthrie
fretted—in true modernist fashion—over the insufficiency of the linguistic
sign. His frustrations with semantic failure and misapplication would sometimes burst out in astonishing fits of verbal violence. While it is impossible to
identify the poor unfortunate excoriated in a notebook entry of 1947, there is
no doubting of his or her crime:

>   I hate your pronouns.
>   I hate your nouns.
>   I hate your smells in hell.
>   I hate all your adjectives
>   and hate your adverbs
>   and hate your verbs
>   and I hate your sissified
>   and piss colored sentences.
>   I hate your word forms.
>   Hate your similes.
>   Hate your shitty lip pooch.[21]

One would think, considering such an outburst, that Guthrie suffered from no expressive crises himself, that he was as omnipotent in the wielding of his pen as his boasts were meant to suggest—such boasts as: "I can make a picture with words. I can make my picture any color I want. I can make it any mood I want. I can do things that no camera can ever do, I can make pictures in peoples minds."[22] Such boasts often reflected a belligerence fully in keeping with Guthrie's conviction that words were weapons, whether to be used in the fight against fascism, against racism, or against anti-union thuggery:

> All I've got left now
> Is just these few old words
> To shoot back at you.[23]

Like his older modernist contemporary Ernest Hemingway, Guthrie compared writers to fighters, as in his unpublished review of the Folkways album *L'Honneur des Poètes: Four French Resistance Writers* (produced in 1946 but not released until 1964). Guthrie casts the four subjects—Louis Aragon, Paul Éluard, François Mauriac, and Albert Camus—as guerrilla warriors engaged in "that old run, duck, hide, and shoot" activity.[24] The written page, to Guthrie, was thus a boxing arena or battleground on which the most pugnacious threats and challenges would be flung down:

> No rich man nor no rich
> lady is going to take
> my word and my song
> and my work away from
> me.[25]

It was, of course, part of Guthrie's folksy, public pose to declare that there was nothing special to *his* writing. While others might fall at the first hurdle, it came to him just as naturally as breathing—hell, "things just happen and you just write it up and sing it out."[26] Yet Guthrie did reveal in his private writings many moments of self-doubt, of writerly insecurity, when he would admit to his failure in handling his own word-weapons adequately. "I missed too many," he would say.[27] His words were at best "crippled, but honest."[28] Time and again he confessed to an inability to say precisely what he meant, reflecting the crisis-ridden inarticulacy plaguing modernists from Woolf to Kafka to Eliot. Words, in their slipperiness or shiftiness, would either elude these writers altogether or turn around and pile in on them and threaten to bury them.

Guthrie was, like these same modernists, sometimes able to make creative capital out of the "discursive chaos" of his times, turning crisis into art. As Comentale describes it with reference to *Bound for Glory*, "all that is solid in Okemah melts into a whirlwind of voices." The streets of the boomtown are "crowded with signs and slogans. Preachers, politicians, and bosses shout each other down from opposite corners, while newsboys scream out the latest headlines and merchants loudly tout their wares. . . . In fact, in *Bound for Glory*, America at large appears as a set of bewildering commands and directives, scattering people and populations this way and that."[29] However, it is Guthrie's *House of Earth* that dwells most explicitly and extensively on the crises of inarticulacy and linguistic deluge that also mark Eliot's "Love Song of J. Alfred Prufrock" and "The Waste Land," for instance. In Guthrie's novel, Ella May Hamlin complains at one point to her husband Tike, "I don't know how to tell you how I feel. I don't think any woman can tell a man how she feels." In fact it takes a hallucination before Ella May can even begin to relate the cacophony of sound and meaning that threatens to overwhelm these dwellers in modernity—even on the abandoned plains of the Texas Panhandle. Ella May gropes for an adequate language to describe her hallucination: "But I, ah, see ten million faces inside of bells. Half like bells. Half like people singing. I see the people in the bells and the bells in the people. And they're all a-ringing together. All ringing at the same time."[30]

Here Guthrie's writing bears out the observation of Peter Nicholls, that in modernist texts, the "focus of attention travels consistently away from meaning to the texture of writing. Language begins to assume a new opacity." Words become less a medium of communication and understanding than "a medium of consciousness" itself.[31] Thus, by using them to his own ends, Guthrie—like Joyce, Woolf, and Eliot before him and Beckett alongside him—actively and creatively builds upon the gap between language and communication. Such confident applications of "discursive chaos" as in *Bound for Glory* and *House of Earth* allow for no admissions of communicative defeat, however much comprehension is challenged. Like Vladimir and Estragon in Beckett's *Waiting for Godot*, Guthrie's characters—both autobiographical and fictive—abide.

But modernist writing is shot through with contradiction, where energy is matched with paralysis and clarity with abstraction, and Guthrie was not completely immune to such contradiction. On some occasions, the failure to communicate could weigh heavily, as in Guthrie's reflection of an attempt in 1947 to decorate the window of Coney Island's Communist Party headquarters with what he had confidently assumed would be the clearest of injunctions:

> I painted, "Join the Communist
> Party" on a strip of wrapping paper
> and "Kill the Taft Hartley Slave
> Law" on some more strips. "Let's
> Have a Low Cost Housing Project
> For Coney Island" and "Read
> Your Daily Worker." . . .
> When we got it all done, I went
> in next door to a little eat shop
> and a big soda jerker told me,
> "It's just one big gigantic smudge."
> I didn't even say one single
> word. Just drunk my coffee and walked out.[32]

We have no way of knowing why, since Guthrie's signs for the party headquarters have been lost, but for whatever reason he had failed in the attempt to make himself clear, and this rankled.

Certainly there was a conflict in Guthrie between his urge toward communicative clarity and his leanings toward abstraction or, to repeat Nicholls, "a new opacity"; and it is here that we should turn primarily to Guthrie's visual artwork for instruction. It is through the graphic and plastic arts that Guthrie most powerfully revealed his passion for abstract and semi-abstract representation. One of his most remarkable letters to Marjorie, from

Fig. 2. "Conflicting Lines," 1942. Artwork by Woody Guthrie © Woody
Guthrie Publications, Inc. Courtesy of the Woody Guthrie Archives / Woody
Guthrie Center.

1942, demonstrates this; it is illustrated with a complex sketch of what he called "Conflicting Lines" (fig. 2)—a deliberate exercise in the avoidance of realistic representation. As he explained to Marjorie:

> I tried hardest to keep from
> drawing any one certain way or
> any certain object. I noticed a
> few times that I drew a box, a
> flower, a face,
> a circle, ovals,
> by mistake, and I drew a house
> and a cactus
> and a tree and
> a piece of pipe, (all from force of the copying habit)
> then I said I would
> use conflicting lines
> to decompose or to attack
> the object and every
> line I used I asked
> "does it look like a shape or a design
> of any earthly plan or object?" If it
> did I drew other splotches, blotches, and
> lines, dots, dashes, to erase the object,
> the design of the pattern.
>   Now the result of this whole page
> is all of the attacking of line against line.
> And when I looked at it I said here
> is my one, my only, real original drawing.[33]

Of all Guthrie's visual artworks, one of the richest sources of study would be what he called his "Hoodises"—so named after Cathy's perplexed queries as she pointed at them: "Who dis?" These abstract sculptures were fashioned from the concrete materials of Guthrie's times, the products and by-products of the industrial process that defined his age. Maddeningly, none of the Hoodises now exist, but Guthrie left an unpublished essay on "the philosophy of the Hoodis," in which he explains their origins in the junk piles of Okemah. They were, he said, products of his "cravery to make something out of nothing":

> I dug through our city trash piles and dump grounds when I was
> a kid in my early teens to carry pieces of brass, copper, aluminum,
> rubber, rags, bones, bottles, cow's horns, hoofs, lead, zinc, and old
> scraps of pig and castiron to weigh and to sell on the scales of our
> hometown Junkman. But I always kept back old odds and ends of
> this and that to work with around our ganghouse and at school just
> trying to make some kind of a machine, a triggerwheel, a windmill,
> or some kind of a something out of my old throwed away junk. So,
> my eye has always ran along the ground ever since feeling and seeing
> a whole big world of junkystuff that you could pick up and stick
> together into a world that's lots more fun to look at.[34]

Decades later, married to Marjorie, Guthrie had access to all the materials she had kept on hand for the upkeep of her dance outfits—"a good collection of buttons, beads, threads, spools, shiny things, bright twinklers and lots of little things she'd saved back from sewing dance costumes, hats, shoes, as well as things such as old vanity cases, mirrors, knick knacks, trinkets, jewelry, and all sorts of odds and ends which sort of give my hands a case of the gluey itches." He described making the first Hoodis for his children, emphasizing the melange of both industrial and natural objects as well as the dynamics of the composition, thus focusing as much attention on the *process* as upon the objects themselves:

> I took an old busted yoyo without no string and glued it on the flat
> top of a grey river rock. Next I squeezed some glue onto my sea shells
> and got them to stay together pretty easy. I stuck in some little straw
> red and brown flowers I bought down close to Mexico. I dropt in a
> handful of old buttons, thumb and carpet tacks, keys, marbles, banjo
> thumbpicks, and stuck a couple of red and green hat pins down
> through some button holes. I held the tube of glue up as high off the
> hoodis as I could and when I moved it back and forth the glue dried
> real fast and looked like some kind of a spidery web that caught
> everything and held it there. It wouldn't stand up because it was too

heavy on the lefthand side, so I dipped our little flat slate rock from Lake Ontario and stuck it into the right hand side.[35]

The process was not complete until the Hoodis was brought to light by the effect of a candle moved in front of it, casting bizarre, surreal shadows on the wall behind it. In terms of the imaginative work it enabled, the Hoodis was a grassroots challenge both to old media like the shadow-puppet shows of Indonesia and to newer media like the motion pictures:

I walked back away from them, then I walked to the right side and back to the left side, and we watched the shadows jump, stretch, twist and climb our walls and turn the hoodisses into everything that you could possibly imagine. Boats, ships, gunfights, scrapes, forests, animal fights, storms, floods. . . . Marjorie said it made her think of odd and curious kinds of stages set up for a thousand shadows and reflections to match the moods and moves of actors and the wild actions of a dancer. . . . I wanted to show everybody in every room on earth how our one little two-cent candle and our hoodiss made out of old junk could give us just as much of a new kind of fun as thirty dollars spent going to fancy places and seeing other kinds of lights fixed up to catch your eye and your memory.[36]

The Hoodises—and his writings on them—are important as examples of Guthrie's oppositional responses to high-modernist aesthetics and practice, particularly with regard to deliberate elitism and self-conscious difficulty. Joyce, who would keep the world guessing, said, "I've put in so many enigmas and puzzles that it will keep the professors busy for centuries arguing over what I meant."[37] But Guthrie happily explained what the Hoodis meant to him: "To me, a hoodis goes to show you that you can take all of your ugliest things, your brokest and your worn outtest things, and stick them together the way mama nature does her leaves and her stems and her weeds and her grassblades, and make out of your trashiest things your very nicest and prettiest of flowers." He proclaimed the Hoodis a product of a *democratic* modernism—"no matter if nobody in this world ever called you a big artist with a high name. . . . It goes to prove that your lowest, dirtiest, and your ugliest people . . . can slip out of their old raggety clothes and grow up to be the best people and the prettiest people to look at in your whole world here." Finally, and in spite of their proud and deliberate lowliness, Guthrie's Hoodises were products of the modernist mission to *make it new:* "Your hoodis is like a brand new song and when you get it made, it is way yonder different from any other picture, song, statue, dance, painting, drawing, sketch, book, poem, or loveletter made by any living human hand out of ten thousand centuries and ten million years of hands making things."[38]

The Hoodis is representative of one further—and crucial—aspect of modernism's engagement with reality: the urge to represent the un-representable. Modernism is filled with the voices of artists and think-ers who have been stymied in their efforts to make artistic sense of their times, whether it was Theodor Adorno arguing that to "write poetry after Auschwitz is barbaric" or Philip Roth complaining that "the American writer in the middle of the twentieth century has his hands full in try-ing to understand, and then describe, and make *credible* much of the American reality."[39] In Guthrie's case, one of the most conspicuous events that threatened to still his voice, forcing him into a fitful series of artistic modes, was the 1927 double execution of Sacco and Vanzetti. First he attempted a song cycle, having been commissioned by Moses Asch in 1946 to develop a concept album for Folkways. (After many false starts, the album would not be released until 1960.) As Guthrie wrote to Asch from Boston, the site of the executions, the writing task seemed beyond his abilities, dumbfounded as he was by the injustice and absurdity of the case: "I refuse to write these songs while I'm drunk and it looks like I'll be drunk for a long time."[40] Next, while he was able to complete a number of drawings to accompany the album, he was stopped cold in his attempt to give a realistic reflection of his incredulity at the phrase "consciousness of guilt" as it had been used by the hostile judge and prosecutors (fig. 3). He then veered toward the abstract, executing in November 1947 an obscure black and red watercolor wash with the legend "Conscious of Your Guilt" scrawled across it (fig. 4).

In the end, though, it was a Hoodis that enabled him to complete the work of representation. While the Hoodis has disappeared, Guthrie's expla-nation remains:

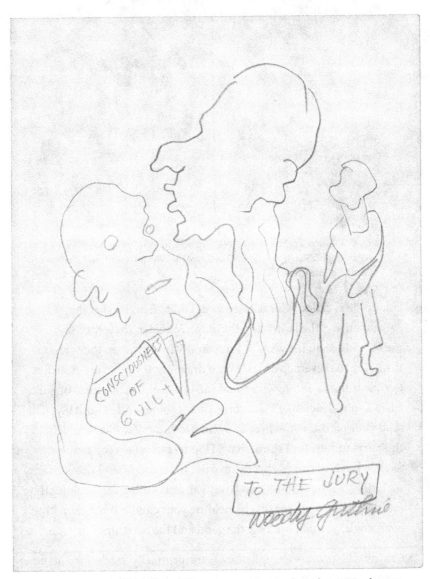

Fig. 3. "Consciousness of Guilt," 1946. Artwork by Woody Guthrie © Woody Guthrie Publications, Inc. Courtesy of the Woody Guthrie Archives / Woody Guthrie Center.

Fig. 4. "Conscious of Your Guilt," 1947. Artwork by Woody Guthrie ©
Woody Guthrie Publications, Inc. Courtesy of the Woody Guthrie Archives /
Woody Guthrie Center.

Hoodis #8 is called "Consciousness of Guilt." This is what the
patrolmen and the jailers and the judge, Webster Thayer, all said
they could see on the faces of Sacco and Vanzetti when they arrested
them. I made several pen and brush drawings trying to get at such a
terrible thing as a thing you could call just the consciousness of guilt,
when I would look like I was conscious of some kind of guilt if you'd
send your patrolmen in here to my house and my workroom right
this very minute. . . . I think that a Hoodis can reflect the sad and
terrible kinds of things that fly up from my mind when I think of any
such thing as the whole Sacco [and] Vanzetti killing and their legal
murder. So, you can see that by holding your candle at the right kind
of an angle, you can even see the good and the bad things men do.[41]

Clearly, then, even though they were primarily made for the entertainment of his children, Guthrie's Hoodises were capable, through their
abstract elasticity, of generating profound, complex associations. In this
sense, there was nothing all that childish about child's play. Other modernists knew this as well—indeed, as the art historian and architect Norman

Brosterman argues in his inspiring study, *Inventing Kindergarten*, child's play may well have been the very basis of the modernist movement in the first place—the "seed pearl of the modern era."[42] Brosterman's study (like Guthrie's candle) throws valuable light on the philosophy of the Hoodis as well as Guthrie's other artworks and writings inspired by the play of children. Focusing on such pioneering modernist painters as Georges Braque, Piet Mondrian, Paul Klee, and Wassily Kandinsky, as well as the architects Walter Gropius, Frank Lloyd Wright, and Le Corbusier, Brosterman argues that their common history as the first generation of kindergarteners set the stage for their adult forays into abstraction. During these figures' late-Victorian childhoods, the kindergarten—the dream child of German educationalist Friedrich Froebel, with its emphasis on play as education—was still in its relative infancy. Brosterman notes that while the kindergarteners' "play objects—balls, blocks, sticks, paper, pencils and clay—were not in themselves new, the integrated educational method in which they were used was, and radically so." Froebel's pedagogic aim had been for children to engage with the abstract forms of "nature," "knowledge," and "beauty" through "short sessions of directed play."[43] Frank Lloyd Wright, for one, recalled:

> For several years I sat at the little kindergarten table top [and played] with the square [cube], the circle [sphere] and the triangle [tetrahedron]—these were smooth maple-wood blocks. . . . Eventually I was to construct designs in other mediums. But the smooth cardboard triangles and maple-wood blocks were most important. All are in my fingers to this day. . . . I soon became susceptible to constructive pattern *evolving in everything I saw.* I learned to "see" this way and when I did, I did not care to draw casual incidentals of Nature. I wanted to *design.*[44]

A similar compulsion to turn child's play into art overtook Guthrie vicariously, through watching his own children at play. He described in an unpublished article, "Child Sitting," aimed at the parents' magazine *Two to Six,* the ways in which three-year-old Cathy had both adopted and inspired a surreal vision through her childish, abstract drawings:

Each page, she made me stop what I was doing and write down with pen and ink what the picture was all about. One was, "All About Peter And The Wolf an' here's granpapa with th' trees all around him." Another one was, "A Zoo with every kind of an Animal you are looking for." Another was, "A Ferry Boat With a Pumpkin driver On Top." . . . One said, "This Is The Alligator biting the Mother Turtle an' the' Mother Turtle bites the Alligator On His tail." . . . I don't know why I wrote her words down on all of these drawings. It's just a little thing I started doing a year or so ago and now it's a wild thing, a thing of no control, a spreading fire, a blaze, a smoke, some kind of a thing like the blackmarket, like gambling, like using dope, it's something that has got so big that I can't stop it by myself."[45]

Eventually Guthrie wrote a much-loved and still thriving body of children's songs, most of them based on his daughter's utterances and many of them bearing the abstract visions of the kindergarten—literally, the "children's garden"—as Guthrie himself makes clear: "She sang songs while she drew her pictures . . . and forced me to take down the words as she sang them. . . . I've sold two albums of fonograph records of kids songs just by putting little tunes and guitar notes to her songs she sings . . . and still I've not scratched the first crust of top dirt in her garden of the soul."[46] Thus were Cathy's abstract voicings turned into abstract songs, with, for example, her own "CHUCKIE CHOOKIE CHOOKIER / CHICKEE CHIEKEE CHEEKEEBOO" feeding into Guthrie's "Hoodoo Voodoo" as recorded by Billy Bragg and Wilco:

> Hoodoo voodoo
> Chooka chooky choochoo
> True blue, how true;
> Kissle me now.[47]

There is one further connection to be made between the kindergarten vision and Guthrie's art—a connection made concrete by the cover of his popular Folkways album *Songs to Grow On for Mother and Child*.[48] In the line drawing adorning the cover, Guthrie offers a rendering of a dance, a woman in motion holding a child, alongside the legend "Dance Around and Around and Around" (fig. 5). Dance, arguably the most abstract of modern

Fig. 5. "Dance Around and Around and Around," 1946 (cover, *Songs to Grow On for Mother and Child*, Smithsonian Folkways, 1991). Photo courtesy of Kate Blalack, Woody Guthrie Archives.

arts alongside atonal music, was central to Froebel's kindergarten curriculum, not only in the literal terms of children dancing but also figuratively, in terms of the various abstract forms that children would make with their building blocks, patterns that Froebel called "dance forms" in reference to their seeming incorporation of movement.[49] Guthrie's perceptions and output as a graphic artist were highly influenced by the movement and kinetic energy of Marjorie and her colleagues in the Martha Graham and Sophie Maslow companies (figs. 6 and 7).

Guthrie thought and wrote about dance extensively, in published articles, notebooks, and letters, and countless of his drawings and paintings are

Fig. 6. "Atom Dance," 1949. Artwork by Woody Guthrie © Woody Guthrie Publications, Inc. Courtesy of the Woody Guthrie Archives/Woody Guthrie Center.

Fig. 7. "Lost John," 1949. Artwork by Woody Guthrie © Woody Guthrie Publications, Inc. Courtesy of the Woody Guthrie Archives/Woody Guthrie Center.

reflections of dance movements. He clearly viewed dance, like his Hoodises, in the light of modernism's prime dictum to make it new. As he argued, "It is the job of the dancer to move in a way that no other human has ever moved and make it look like everybody moved that way. And to find some original move as a dancer is like a farmer hunting for some new way to plow or to plant and raise a seed. Like a singer trying to find some new mixture of notes. Like a miner hunting for some new mineral."[50] It is hardly surprising, then, that Jim Longhi, in his recollections of his time spent with Guthrie and Cisco Houston in the merchant marine, should recall a significant moment just prior to their ship hitting an acoustic mine. Guthrie, Houston, and Longhi were sitting on their bunks below deck and talking. Among the things that Guthrie said were "worth dying for" was "Jane Dudley dancing the Harmonica Breakdown":

> "What's 'Jane Dudley dancing the Harmonica Breakdown'?"
> Woody raised his eyebrows. "You mean you've never seen Jane Dudley dance the Harmonica Breakdown?"
> "No, Woody." I imitated his amazed voice. "I've never seen Jane Dudley dance the Harmonica Breakdown."
> "Well—before—you—die—" Woody's lips were now moving in slow motion and he was slowly rising through the air, strangely floating upward toward the overhead. "Before—you—die—you've—got—to see—Jane—Dud—ley—dance—the—Har—mon—i—ca—Break—down." And he kept rising until his head touched the overhead. I watched in awe as he hung there, and then BOOOOM! I heard the mind-shattering explosion! *We were hit!* An enormous underwater force![51]

Harmonica Breakdown was one of the signature pieces of Popular Front modern dance, choreographed by Dudley between 1938 and 1941 and set to a harmonica-based score recorded by Guthrie's colleague, Sonny Terry. As Mark Franko explains, *Harmonica Breakdown* relied on a "resolutely modern" dance vocabulary combining "the double sense of breakdown as dance with psychological and physical breakdown in words."[52] Thus, there may have been something particularly intimate and personal in Guthrie's reaction to this piece. While it would be impossible to conclusively assign artistic influence directly from Dudley's choreography to Guthrie's drawing, there is clearly a parallel between the stylized contortions of Dudley's dance (fig. 8) and those of some of the figures in Guthrie's drawings for *Bound for Glory*, notably his mother succumbing to the "physical breakdown" of Huntington's disease (fig. 9). Guthrie had begun working on his *Bound for Glory* drawings not long after his initial immersion into the modern dance milieu of New York.

In his notebooks, Guthrie left a fictionalized account of his introduction to this milieu (as well his first meeting with Marjorie), an engagement that had him yearning for greater inclusion in the dance arena. Casting himself as an aspiring actor named Tom Harris, hired as a narrator by a radical dance troupe, Guthrie creates a scenario that reflects his perceptions of industrial modernity and the way these perceptions could be played out in the motions

Fig. 8. Jane Dudley dancing the *Harmonica Breakdown*. Photo by Barbara Morgan, courtesy of Mark Franko.

Fig. 9. Illustration from *Bound for Glory*, 1943. Artwork by Woody Guthrie
© Woody Guthrie Publications, Inc. Courtesy of the Woody Guthrie
Archives/Woody Guthrie Center.

of the dance: "The dancers moved like a thousand people working in a factory. . . . He could hear them puffing for wind and breathing like steam engines. Tired from a week or two of hard and heavy rehearsing, stumbling, banging and bruising their feet and toes, their muscles and skin, jumping, leaping, whirling and even rolling over and over across the floor, the whole group was working smoother and better and lots harder tonight." For Tom, the apparently seamless blending of music, singing, and dance becomes a metaphor for proletarian progress itself: "He felt for the first time in his life like here he was a part, a part of something. . . . Here he felt his mind was more close-connected with fifteen or twenty other people working, thinking, and moving, not 'every man for his own self,' but sort of all for one and one with all of the others."[53]

Guthrie's re-creation of himself as an actor speaks volumes, just one more indication of his desire to break free from the confines of a given artistic medium and to find connections and correspondences between all modes of artistic expression. In his notebooks he argued that "being a good writer means also being a good actor and acting means that art and science of stretching your mind around quick, to cover and to enter and reflect any given situation and then to let your face and eyes and mouth and body, hands and legs, to move accordingly."[54] In the end, the actor, the writer, the singer, the dancer, and the visual artist were all engaged in the same task: the expression of both individual and universal experience and—fully in line with modernism's elevation of the artist into a holy status—the redemption of the human race. The artistic mode did not matter: "The very moment when you stop creating for us, why, then you become a leech, a dead weight, a useless burden to the world."[55] Redemption was redemption, in whatever form.

Indeed, in the immediate wake of Cathy's death, Guthrie, in the midst of his profound grief, turned to the art that had been produced and inspired by her play for all its redeeming power. In a heartfelt letter to Pete and Toshi Seeger written within weeks of the tragedy, he wrote: "She decorated and ran this house here. Her decorations are still here to let us look at them every day and night and get brighter. She did not leave us as a robbery or a loss, but as a complete gain." He urged the Seegers to ensure that their own son, Daniel—not yet six months old—would have the ground prepared for him so that he too, through *his* art-as-play, would eventually offer the same redemption to his world:

> Give him your problems and give him your knots and puzzles.
> Give him your crazy feelings, your ups and your downs, give him
> everything. He will give you back lightness for dark, brightness for
> sorrow, calm rest for quivering guts, laughs for grunts and groans,
> and jokes and tall tales to tell to the other little Dannys you will be
> snatching off from that sweet and bitter root tree. He will give you
> wild and dancy limbs and leaves, the closest and truest contact and
> closeness, your own mental rights to operate and to live and to work
> in your highest shapes and forms. Give him your old nervous work
> and he will give you back sheaves and piles of pages that will ring
> every telefone around the world.[56]

"Decorations"; "knots and puzzles"; "wild and dancy limbs"; "shapes and forms"; "sheaves and piles of pages"—these were both the raw materials and the finished products of an art that would transform and uplift all who might come into contact with it, in an age before the glib theories and surface practices of postmodernism would call into question any such transformative powers of art. In Guthrie's modern world, it was still possible for art to be a holy pursuit.

3

Ribbon of Highway

On February 16, 1940, Guthrie set foot in New York City for the first time. He had started out on a car journey from Pampa, Texas, with his father, in a beat-up Chevrolet that had broken down and died on a hill approaching Konowa, Oklahoma. There Woody's brother George had lent him enough money for a bus ticket to Pittsburgh. From Pittsburgh, in the midst of the worst snowstorm that the Northeast had seen in decades, Guthrie managed to hitchhike as far as the Susquehanna River bridge at Harrisburg before nearly succumbing to the cold in a snowbank along US Route 22. Rescued by a forest ranger whose wife fed him clam chowder and whose parents gave him three dollars for the bus fare from Philadelphia to New York, Guthrie arrived in the metropolis with his head full of the sights he had seen on the "ribbon of highway" that he would memorialize one week later in the first draft of "This Land Is Your Land."[1]

As Guthrie thawed out from his journey, first in Will and Herta Geer's sumptuous uptown apartment on Fifty-Ninth Street, and then in the shabby Hanover House hotel on Sixth Avenue, other citizens in nearby Flushing Meadows, Queens, were seeking warmth and enlightenment inside the pavilions of the New York World's Fair, which for a year had been trumpeting "The World of Tomorrow" as its theme.[2] By far the most popular exhibit at the fair had been Norman Bel Geddes's *Futurama*, which offered a dazzling vision of a 1960s America transformed by the modernization of the highway system. Bel Geddes later recalled that between five thousand and fifteen thousand people a day had queued for the automotive ride through

Fig. 10. General Motors *Futurama* Exhibition, New York World's Fair, 1939.
Photographer unknown. Courtesy of the General Motors Media Archives.

the landscape of America's future, enjoying what amounted to an aerial view over a detailed model of imagined townscape, cityscape, and countryside (fig. 10), all connected and enriched by a unified, planned motorway system that in many ways prefigured the interstate highway system inaugurated by federal law in 1956.[3]

As Edward Dimendberg observes, "Bel Geddes occupied a unique position in 1940s American highway development, gliding effortlessly between the roles of professional visionary, corporate image maker, motorway lobbyist, and popularizer of European modernist trends in architecture, design, and city planning."[4] Bel Geddes's argument was passionate: the American highway system was a "planless, suicidal mess" that for the most part had "originated as animal tracks" and haphazard byways "laid out for the different needs of gold-seekers in California, of missionaries in the South-west, fur traders and explorers in the Northwest, covered-wagon pioneers in the Great Plains, buffaloes in the Middle West and Indians in New England."[5] His vision was futuristic even by today's standards: "We have come out with transcontinental roads built for a maximum of one hundred and a minimum of fifty miles an hour. We have come out with cars that are automatically controlled, which can be driven safely even with the driver's hands off the wheel. We have discovered that people could be driving from San Francisco to New York in twenty-four hours if roads were properly designed."[6]

No record of Guthrie's having visited the World's Fair has yet been unearthed in the archives, but he certainly had the opportunity, since the fair ran until October 1940. In any event, he was strikingly attuned to the Bel Geddes vision, as indicated in a notebook entry of 1941:

> Cars are built for higher speed; but it is the roads that will not stand it. The curves are too sharp and the roadbed slants wrong; the roads are too thin and too weak and big holes wear out on the sides and in the center; 4 and 6 lane roads suddenly quit off and you've got to crowd onto a small, narrow 2 lane road. You have been traveling at a fast gait and all of a sudden you find yourself packed and jammed onto a rough, worn out, low speed road. This causes the driver to get all mixed up. There's a lot of accidents but I'm surprised that there aint a lot more.[7]

It is hardly surprising that the automobile should be a central figure in Guthrie's writings on the modern experience. As Michael Denning points out, at mid-century the entire American economy was anchored to its fortunes—an economy "built on the technologies of oil, rubber, and steel fabricated into the automobile."[8] The end product of this economy, for all its potentially dehumanizing impact on the workforce, was the cultural icon that Guthrie perhaps loved the most. If, as Roland Barthes suggested, the car has been "the Gothic cathedral of modern times," then Guthrie was one of its most devout worshippers.[9] Indeed, what he recalled as "the first song I ever wrote"—"Old Gray Team of Hosses," written in 1934, five years after his arrival in Pampa—re-creates the intrusion of the automobile into a hitherto premodern setting, proving itself the agent of good fortune:

Fig. 11. "The Oldest Ford in Okfuskee County," ca. 1920. Woody
Guthrie sits in back seat, fourth from left. Photographer unknown.
Courtesy of Okfuskee County Historical Society.

> I was in a buckboard wagon going down the old plank road,
> When I spied a Ford a-coming down my way.
> I will tell you just what happened, how I lost my wagon load
> When that old gray team of hosses run away.

Spooked by "the rattle and the clatter of the car," the team of horses bolts
down the road; the narrator's terrified companion throws herself upon him,
and he heroically regains control of the runaway team:

> At a standstill there I kissed her when at last the hosses fell,
> Quite exhausted from the run that they had made,
> And I married sweet Melindy, so I'm happy in my soul
> That the old gray team of hosses ran away.[10]

Guthrie was entranced with cars and fast driving. He was highly attuned
to the caste system of automobile brands, enough to use their names repeatedly in his attempts to distinguish between various categories of modern
American experience. For him, the top of the line was the Cadillac, which he

eulogized in two songs written on the same day in October 1946, "Cadillac Cadillac" and "Cadillac Eight." In the former, he boasts:

> If your Chevvy
> Touches me
> I will run you
> Up a tree.
> > If your Dodge
> > With me gets wise
> > I will pass you
> > In the skies.[11]

In "Cadillac Eight," the lowly Buick, Oldsmobile, and Pontiac endure the same abuse.[12] The Cadillac (or "Gitalong Eight" or "Skiddalack Eight") was his automotive benchmark of quality.[13] Guthrie wryly admitted of his own meager fortunes, "Best I ever done was some pontiaccing."[14] Indeed, it was thanks to his "pontiaccing" that J. Edgar Hoover knew of Woody Guthrie as a potential car thief as much as a Communist—or so one FBI memo from June 1941 would imply:

> A confidential informant advises that subject person is a
> Communist. Subject is from some place in New York State and is
> driving a 1941 Model Pontiac Sedan bearing 1940 New York license
> plates XX32. . . . The General Motors Acceptance Corp. in New
> York City is said to be looking for subject because of his failure
> to make car payments. Was stopped by Oregon State Police upon
> entering Oregon from California on or about May 15, 1941, because
> of having 1940 license plates on auto. Disposition of case in Oregon
> unknown.[15]

Regardless of the brand name, the automobile provided Guthrie with some of his most potent imagery and subject matter. Ensconced in Los Angeles shortly after fleeing the Dust Bowl in 1937, he turned his attention to urban sprawl, still a bewildering and sometimes frightening novelty to him. The subject enabled him to develop the slapstick approach that he would go on to perfect in one of his greatest Dust Bowl ballads, "Talking Dust Bowl Blues" (1940), in which the Okie family's "Ford machine" suffers "a breakdown, sort of a nervous bustdown of some kind," and, overturning on a hairpin curve, scatters "wives and childrens all over the side of that mountain."[16] In Los Angeles, it is a series of close encounters on the over-crowded streets that drives the slapstick of "Downtown Traffic Blues" as sung on KFVD in 1938:

> Lost a radiator at Fifth and Main,
> And a carburator at Sixth and Spring,
> On Figueroa I lost my door,
> They left me settin' on top of the frame.

In the end, the narrator ruefully concludes, "When you get to Heaven there'll be no drivin,' / There'll be no downtown traffic blues."[17] Below the set of lyrics in his KFVD notebook, Guthrie pours on the hillbilly caricature to emphasize the disjuncture between the urban and rural experience, particularly regarding the unwanted by-products of the burgeoning automotive industry, urban congestion, noise pollution, and smog:

> The hardest thang in the world to git chused to, is car smoke so
> thick you could cut it up and sell it fer coal. I reckon you've been
> Downtown. Anyhow, you no doubt noticed they wuz some other
> folks down there. They all seem to take a notion to go down there at
> th' saime time. They mought have some silent runnin' cars at home,
> but it shore aint the ones they taike to town. Then when they all git
> there, they all taike the same notion at the saime time. Theyll pick
> out some parkin' place and all run fer it, and then when one gits
> it, the rest jest sirkel the bloc a waitin fer thet one to buy a cream
> comb.[18]

Indeed, the novelty and absurdity of the urban driving experience captivated Guthrie, as evident in a number of songs, written not only in Los Angeles but also later in New York. For the next two decades he continued to use cars and driving as metaphors for all kinds of human predicaments. On KFVD he chastised the "reckless drivers," "drunken drivers," "sweethearts and lovers" with their "one handed driving," "road hog drivers," "speed demon drivers" and all-around "lousy drivers" who, if they didn't wise up, were "bound to get lousy in Lincoln Heights Jail."[19] In New York he updated the old folk equation "for want of a nail, the shoe was lost; for want of a shoe, the horse was lost" in the unrecorded "No Parking Place Down Here":

> I am driving to my work with a letter in my hand
> Looking for a mail box on the way.
> Well, I lost my job and letter, and I lost my car and house,
> 'Cause I couldn't find a place to park that day.[20]

As he demonstrated in one of his most popular children's songs, "Riding in My Car" (or "Car Song"), the automobile could be the instrument of the kind of boundless, childlike joy that Guthrie captured from his own children ("Climb, climb, rattle on the front seat; / Spree I spraddle on the back seat; / Turn my key, step on my starter, / Take you riding in my car").[21] More soberly, the car could provide the onomatopoeic soundtrack to loss and separation of the kind that Guthrie and Marjorie increasingly experienced after Cathy's death in 1947:

> Swish swasshh
> Swushity swissh
> My windshield wiper moans. . . .
> You're not here
> To hum with me
> Our windshield wiper song.[22]

Taking a leaf from the blues tradition that had used the car as a means of describing sexual activity, triumph, and frustration (as in Robert Johnson's "Terraplane Blues"), Guthrie employed surreal automotive imagery to express even his raunchiest desires:

> I'd like to get you to
> flush my radioator [sic] out
> and to drain my cranker
> case a time or two every
> few hours.[23]

Guthrie's private writings are replete with references to the automobile as an index of time passing, generational change, and personal or historical progress. One of his most noteworthy rhetorical strategies is to reverse the

time-honored anthropomorphic approach and to "automorphize" humanity, its functions, and its constituent parts. In a notebook passage addressed
to his newborn daughter, he writes:

> You're our newest model, Cathy. You are what you call a streamliner.
> None finer. None sassier. None can bubble more and bubble quieter,
> or none can flip a nipple any fancier than you.
>
> When I was new I knew that I was tougher than all the old horses
> and wagons I seen all around me and I felt like I was so fast they was
> only in my way. . . .
>
> But you've got more than old slow horses and buggies to outrun
> and outwork. You've got cars that can still do 70 per all day long—
> and you call them the old ones nowadays. You've got to live and work
> and love about 80 or 90 per at least, to be a new model.[24]

The human mind, he argued, was like an automotive transmission system,
working at differing speeds for differing temporal and emotional land-
scapes:

> Your mind is a lot like a gear shift on a car—it has three that move—
> one past—one present—one that shifts toward the future and there
> is a fourth shift but it dont move in either direction—it seems like
> sort of a neutral shift when your mind stops to look its own business
> over—to look at its past, present, and future, to more or less turn
> the mind's eye on the mind itself and this 3 way action is what takes
> place in love—that is—love sees the past and present and the future
> in this very sensitive way.[25]

Or the mind was like a motor that, when "crank[ed] up," enabled one to
"travel around and look and think" and "find out it's a really big race."[26] And
for all those who would clog the routes of knowledge and communication
with obscurity and obfuscation, Guthrie offered some terse automotive
advice—"Put It Light":

> Whatever you got to say at the breakfast table, say it plain. Same
> thing about talking about your work or what's on your mind, Keep it
> on the road.

> Your talk is kind of like your car lights, it's a good idea to be
> bright when you're out on a fast open road; but when you see another
> feller coming, dont turn on so bright that you blind his eyes.[27]

Guthrie even viewed the capitalist system, which he so hated, as an automobile:

> This private profit machine
> has got eight cylinders.
> Greed. Fear. Lies. Hate.
> Jail. Court. Asylum. Tomb.[28]

Guthrie's preoccupation with the car as a means of perception and
description, as well as mobility, is linked to his embrace of the road itself.
He indeed perceived that the American highway, as Bel Geddes had argued,
was the route to a national transformation. But while Bel Geddes waxed
lyrical about the engineers who designed the roads, he was quiet about the
labor that built them. His *Futurama* pavilion was bankrolled by General
Motors, itself hostile to the New Deal labor programs that Guthrie eventually championed.[29] It is no surprise then, as Dimendberg notes, that Bel
Geddes should have been silent: "Within the domain of the Futurama, labor
conflicts, unemployment, poverty, urban blight ceased to exist. Pulled along
its trajectory, like workers on an assembly line (production never *really* disappeared from these exhibits), spectators were addressed as consumers and
drivers."[30] For his part, Guthrie was adamant about the missing variable in
the equation. As he wrote in *Hard Hitting Songs for Hard-Hit People:* "You
built that Highway and they can put you in jail for thumbing a ride on it."[31]

The relation between labor and the road is as central to Guthrie's biography and output as it is to the history of the United States in the twentieth
century. Denning writes of the "midcentury earthquake," with one of its
greatest tectonic shifts being "the largest internal migration in US history, a
migration of black and white southerners to the North, remaking the industrial working class."[32] While Guthrie could never be considered a member
of the "industrial working class," he was inextricably linked to its migration
along the highways of America. His ambivalence about the road is a defining aspect of his response to modernity—as we shall see, an ambivalence

that only disappears when he is able to yoke the road and all its hard-rock imagery to the progress of the American proletariat. Otherwise, for all of his glorification of the hobo's life, many of Guthrie's private and public writings betray his unease, guilt, and longing for the stable domestic space that often undercut his wanderings.

Hence the sentimental melancholy of "Stepstone," a parlor song adapted by Guthrie, which became one of his earliest and most popular KFVD hits:

> Goodbye to my stepstone, goodbye to my home,
> God bless the ones that I leave with a sigh;
> Fields will be whitening and I will be gone
> To ramble this wide world alone.[33]

A note below the manuscript lyrics to this song—perhaps, but by no means certainly, patter meant for a broadcast or songbook—challenges the listener to deny the lure of the road that threatens to overpower the pull of the domestic heartstrings (as well as the deadening security of a place in the modern industrial or bureaucratic workforce): "You might kid most folks, but you caint kid me: They is a Hobo feelin' rises up in yer bosom. Picture yoreself a strollin' slowly along a dusty little road, about the middle of th' mornin' when the Day is at its best—warm, cool, lazy-like. Dont tell me you dont feel it."[34] Likewise the notes he writes to accompany the text of Goebel Reeves's "Hobo's Lullaby," a song so powerfully associated with Guthrie that many continue to mistake him as its composer.[35] Below the lyrics, in the manuscript of the *Woody and Lefty Lou* songbook offered to his KFVD audience, Guthrie paints a picture calculated to defamiliarize the confining urban patterns of work and living: "Yes, pardnah, it is another world—another Life, drawn apart from the one you know. . . . A hobo's Life moves swiftly, broadly, talking and moving in terms of states, countries, seasons instead of the narrow, suffocating, life of City Living so hemmed in on every side."[36]

It might be relevant to point out that these notations were written in the midst of Guthrie's first marriage, which was already being tested by the strains of parenthood, financial insecurity, and a growing incompatibility of outlook between Guthrie and his wife, Mary. Yet in the early years of Guthrie's relationship with his second wife, Marjorie, particularly during their unwanted periods of separation, his yearning for a stable home was passionate. In 1943, with Marjorie still living with her husband and pregnant with Cathy, Guthrie's envy shone through in a notebook address to her: "You know how I respect your planned living and your organized home. Your little band box is a world in a world. All so clean and pretty and neat. Every single article hung in its place. Every speck of dirt and dust gone. Clean corner and sweet beds."[37] By November 1943, with Cathy already nine months old and Marjorie having definitively left her husband for Guthrie, the prospect of a home was like the sweetest dream: "I think of our little house and this clean little bed and in the next little room there our good little baby—and mama—oh mama—this is where I can do my best to fight for a freer world."[38]

Nearly two years later, with a year of seafaring behind him and four months of the army left in front of him, Guthrie—stationed at Scott Field in Illinois—wrote in a notebook-length letter to Marjorie: "No man dreams up any more dreams about the road and the sea than I do. No man has travelled circles around me under his own power. But I don't think there is any man that craves a house and ground [to] work any more than I do." He described to Marjorie how far he had come—at least in his own mind—from his rambling days:

> Ed and Clara [Robbin] told me, "The only real cure for your
> footloose restlessness is to build you a house and get into it and feel
> the sense of pride in yourself which comes no other way and is never
> even guessed at by the cagiest and cleverest of renters."
>
> I might have argued against him. I have forgot. But since I have
> put so much ground and ocean under my feet I have thought it
> through to a conclusion that is the hottest of all my cravings outside
> of you. That craving is to own a house and a lot yard, trees, garden,
> water pool, and all.

Guthrie even went so far as to describe and illustrate the construction of their modern dream home using some decidedly Bauhaus-influenced imagery (fig. 12). He wrote, "We will arrange our windows big and sunny and fit their frames (steel) into place as we raise the walls. The raising of rock or concrete wall is no scarey job with a Ten Cent Government pamphlet telling you step by step just what to do. Pipes, plumbing is put in place and sealed

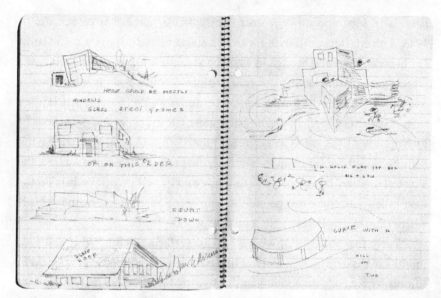

Fig. 12. Architectural jottings, 1942. Artwork by Woody Guthrie © Woody Guthrie Publications, Inc. Courtesy of the Woody Guthrie Archives/ Woody Guthrie Center.

over, around, and all drains and sewer connections are set into place."[39]

Still, the siren call of the road was always there. After only three months of home life, following his army discharge, the cramped conditions of Guthrie's new domestic setting prompted him to spin a slightly embellished tale of a return to his rambling ways: "Our apartment is too small for me to get much done around the house, but I write on trains, busses, in box cars, hotels, jungles, Hooversvilles, wherever I am."[40] There is some credibility to Wayne Hampton's observation that "Guthrie's hoboism" was "essentially apolitical and escapist," glorifying a selfish individualism at the expense of not only his family but also "the community and the communal ideal."[41] Yet, if Guthrie is to be believed, the road was *precisely* the site of a "communal ideal," however transient and mobile, as befitted a nation of people increasingly on the move. As he wrote to Marjorie, he was no freeloading escapist, but rather a dedicated public servant:

> They said, "I just picked you up for company" "To talk to" "To sing
> me a piece" or to "keep me awake so I'll not run off of the road." I
> earned my ride.

I helped to clean a spark plug, chip carbon, fill a radiator, fix a tube, pump up a tire. I rolled wheels down to the garage to get them fixed. I drove. I told stories. We sang. As I got out I asked if I had paid my way. I said I had been called a vag and a bum by too many already. I wanted to earn the mile we covered.[42]

It was on "that big open road called the People's Highway," Guthrie wrote, that the most valuable communal stories were to be found.[43] He wrote to Marjorie, "Travel is the only way to get material to write about."[44] In this sense, the road was indeed Guthrie's natural habitat. Yet, as he also reminded Marjorie, "the road is your love and your hate."[45] Throughout his work, the references to "hard travelin'" along the road that made him are too many to enumerate. Many of his eulogies to the road are compromised: for all the reasons to celebrate it, the road was "long and tired and lonesome. . . . It's been pleasure, it's been pain."[46]

For one thing, the road proved a microcosm of the social and economic divisions of the land that it traversed. As a result, Guthrie heaped scorn, often laced with perceptible envy, on those a negligent economy had enabled to secure a more comfortable and convenient relationship with the road. Time after time, his narrator is obliged to breathe the exhaust of the wealthy, the beneficiaries of modernity's uneven bounty. What can "an asphalt highway / Teach you?" he asks in an unpublished poem:

> How long a mile is
> When you've got to walk it.
> What a blistered foot feels like
> When you stop to cool it.
> What a big rich car sounds like
> easing up behind you
> And what a limousine looks like
> Throwing
> Smoke and dust and dirt
> In your face.[47]

Thus, for Guthrie, the road could be as much a site of retrogression as progress, especially for the pedestrian doomed to a premodern mode of transport—*walking*—as he recalled in 1943 in a letter meant to be read later in life by Cathy. Recounting one of his westward rambles, he describes "lots of cars passing me, lots of folks laffing and kidding, joking at me out their car and truck windows, and I yelled and raved, threw rocks at them, cussed them and called them bad kinds of names." Attacked by a swarm of ravenous desert ants as he rests by the roadside, Guthrie can only look yearningly at a seeming mirage of modern salvation off in the distance: "that place out acrost yonder where the red and green neon lights burned on and off to look pretty to make you hungry, thirsty, and to make you stop and spend your money in their slot machines, pin ball games, and for things you eat and drink." Yet the point of salvation seems always to recede into the distance before him, like Jay Gatsby's dream (and there are indeed apt correspondences with *The Great Gatsby*, in which the automobile too proves an instrument of fate): "I'd swore to my own self that I would walk to that eating place, but, well, the air out here on this desert is so clear and so funny that it fools you, it makes things look closer to you, or makes them look farther from you, but things never do get to where they look just like they are, I mean, to look just right."[48]

The neon lights (in an ironic comparison to the green light beckoning to Gatsby from Daisy Buchanan's dock) are as viscerally seductive to the famished Guthrie as any siren light to a love-struck millionaire. Condemned to his own personal valley of ashes—literally "in amongst these old rotten stumps, limbs, and little dry fire sticks, here on the desert, here where every bug has got a stinger, every crawler has got a poison tooth, every four foot animal has got a hungry mouth, and every bird has got a set of pinching claws"—Guthrie's green and red lights mark his own decidedly downscale "orgastic future" (as Fitzgerald put it in *Gatsby*): a meal, a drink, and four walls and a roof to protect him from the merciless elements and night creatures. He extrapolates from the "little old green and pinklike neon sign" that he recognizes as "the flash of a filling station, a coffee shop, and an eating joint, all nice and warm, all nice and friendly, all full of boys and girls eating, . . . busloads of men and women half asleep dropping [in] to eat a little bit of a snack under the very flicker of that neon sign, that red, that greenish funny looking flash that I could see so far out over the tops of my brushy patch." It is Guthrie alone, in extremis, who can appreciate the magnitude of what these lights represent: "Did any of these folks see the flicker and flash of these neon light colors, and did they think anything about it? . . . Did it mean life or death to anybody waiting for the bus driver to come back and holler, Cheyenne, Las Vegas, Denver, Omaha?"[49]

The blacktop highway, the signal site of American modernity amid the landscape of Fordism, along which progress rolls and fortunes are made and lost, becomes, in Guthrie's writings, "marked with blood where a million feet have trod."[50] Hence his repeated renderings of the downtrodden outcasts on the byways of America—on the Will Rogers Highway, Route 66, "lined with jalopies as far as you can see," where "all day you're hot, all night you freeze," where

> Ten thousand people you see every day
> Camped under the bridges and under the trees,
> With rattle-trap cars that have come apart
> From old Oklahoma to Los Angeles.[51]

And hence the desperation of young Guthrie and the other protagonists of his novel *Seeds of Man*, a story of modern hopes and failures, where fortunes are based on the ability of a rattletrap Model T truck to make the journey to the brow of a hill—powered by much more than the "drip gas" illegally siphoned off a pipeline in the Texas-Mexico borderlands: "The wind's not pushing our truck. Our truck is pushing the winds along. Our dreams are pushing the wheels along. Our hopes are shoving the bearings and the spark plugs along."[52]

Given his own experience of—and witnessing on—the road, it is understandable that Guthrie should conclude that indeed the "road to heaven is rough to ride."[53] Thus was born one of his most persistent and pervasive metaphors for progress, social improvement, and proletarian effort: building a *new* road. The old road he had walked, thumbed, and driven down had been his teacher, for it was there, he implies in the unrecorded "Setting by the Highway," that the battles dearest to his heart had been thus far played out: there were "rich and poor folks riding this highway," with the "poor folks" fighting for "union" and the "rich folks" fighting against it "like hell."[54] The "old road" had merely "led to the back door, there for to beg."[55] But the new road would be "a big smooth road so everbody could travel easier on it, and it would be a government road."[56] Guthrie wrote his ode of that name—"The

Government Road"—the day after completing his first draft of "This Land Is Your Land," celebrating both the "ribbon of highway" and the New Deal that had proved such anathema to General Motors (and which, in any case, was about to be terminated in the transition to a war economy). As Guthrie argued, American poor people had been condemned to travel along a primitive "buffalo trail" where the only road markers were hardship and obstacles, but the New Deal programs and the roads they built represented change for the better:

> Buffalo trail is sticks and stone;
>> build a government road,
> It'll all be paved when I get done;
>> build a government road.[57]

Thus, through the triumph of labor and public ownership, Guthrie's utopian vision could be achieved, a utopia to match any envisioned by Bel Geddes and the designers of *Futurama*. Guthrie waxed euphoric: "The mountains can be tunnelled and scraped down as level as a floor, and the deserts can be watered and raised full of pretty farms with thick orchards and gardens; wide, safe roads and speedways can go winding and rolling over the biggest mountain humps and shooting straight across whole deserts and mountain backs and gliding from coast to coast, wide, strong, and good and smooth."[58] In thus completing the equation left uncomfortably blank by the technocratic and corporate visionaries of mid-century America, Guthrie found his voice and his place on the road, becoming one of the most lyrical proponents it has ever had. In this sense he was as true a bard of American modernity as any highway planner or engineer.

4

Long Steel Rails
and Ships in the Sky

For many people, the name Woody Guthrie will immediately connote the long, lonesome freight trains of "Hard Travelin'" and *Bound for Glory*: the "highballs," "rough riders," "dead enders," and "flat wheelers" transporting the semi-mythicized Guthrie out of the Dust Bowl and westward toward California's promised land. Guthrie's boxcars transport a veritable microcosm of the nation through lightning storms, fistfights, arguments, and sing-alongs. Some will recall Guthrie's description of the fear instilled in him by the freight train, its "hundred tons of heavy machinery" that made him feel "so soft and little" as he clung to a ladder between two cars in the freezing cold, nearly slipping onto the rails as he replayed in his mind "the tales of the railroaders, people found along the tracks, no way of telling who they were." They might recall his near-epiphany: "That was the closest to the 6x3 that I've ever been. My mind ran back to millions of things. . . . And, no doubt, my line of politics took on quite a change right then and there, even though I didn't know I was getting educated at the time."[1] Readers of *Bound for Glory* would thus have perceived the freight-hopping experience as a signal moment of Guthrie's political radicalization, with the brutality of the railroad bulls, detectives, and vigilantes sparking the antifascism that marked his life.

In historical fact, Guthrie spent much less time on the freights than the mythology would suggest. Joe Klein notes that as a teenager Guthrie had seen a friend lose a leg falling from a boxcar, and "for the rest of his life, Woody only used the trains as a last resort: they were too dangerous and uncomfortable."[2] Klein is referring to freight trains specifically, for Guthrie had much experience with, and much to say about, railroad travel as a paying passenger, not only in the wide open spaces of the transcontinental journey, but also in the cramped conditions of the urban transit system. Examining Guthrie's relationship to the train, both aboveground and underground (subways), not only extends our understanding of his engagement with American modernity at large, it also—perhaps surprisingly—throws light on his overpowering fascination with another mode of travel with which he is not widely associated: aviation. Guthrie yearned to escape "the surly bonds of Earth," as poet-aviator John Gillespie Magee Jr. phrased it.[3] This is reflected, for example, in a brief but highly telling simile in the "Off to California" chapter of *Bound for Glory*, where the freezing train on which Guthrie rides gains altitude "almost like an airplane."[4]

The perceptible shift of interest from trains to planes in Guthrie's writing is in keeping with a larger American cultural expression that has often tried to release the train from its earthbound rails and send it flying (for example, Roy Acuff's country hit, "Streamlined Cannonball," written in the mid-1930s in response to the transition from steam to streamlined, with its train hurtling along "like a star in its heavenly flight").[5] But moving beyond the simple celebration of speed, there is a rich body of folk and literary expression using the train as a metaphor for a spiritual journey. Long before Charles Davis Tillman and M. E. Abbey published the gospel song "Life's Railway to Heaven" (1890)—which itself drew on a murky plethora of existing folk and broadside sources—Nathaniel Hawthorne chose to fashion his parody of John Bunyan's *The Pilgrim's Progress* as "The Celestial Railroad" (1843). As Norm Cohen notes, it was almost inevitable that the railroad should have superseded the "Sweet Chariot" and the "Old Gospel Ship" as the preferred carrier to heaven in the nineteenth and early twentieth centuries. Among the many songs that Cohen has examined, from both the black and white traditions, are such indicative numbers as "If I Have My Tickit, Lawd," "The Gospel Train," "The White Flyer to Heaven," and "The Glory Bound Train." On the dark side, leading to the opposite destination, would be the likes of "The Devil's Train" and "The Hell-Bound Train."[6] Guthrie's adoption of the lyrics to "This Train (Is Bound for Glory)" for his autobiography and his recording of the admonitory "Little Black Train" are just two indications of his familiarity with the uses of the railroad as a spiritual folk metaphor.[7] A third indication would be his unpublished song "The White Ghost Train," which not only promises a ride "into Heaven" but also into "Hell at midnight" as well as a number of earthly stops along the way: Reno (for "when the honeymoon, it's over"), Lovelost, and finally, Death Valley.[8] Given Guthrie's sensitivity to the forces of countermodernity within modernity—entropy, neglect, decay, and systemic breakdown in the midst of supposed "progress"—it is unsurprising that he should turn to the railroad for some of his bleakest (if also most comedic) scenarios. Conversely, given his optimism for the "better world a-comin'" through the proletarian revolution, the trains served him well as the symbolic carriers toward a "Union world."[9] In the end, however, with the train being, at best, *almost* like an airplane, Guthrie would turn his eyes skyward for new metaphors for progress.

While he indeed had some firsthand experience with the "flat wheelers" and the "rough riders," the juddering, bone-rattling boxcars that all hoboes were prepared to take in their stride, Guthrie was distinctly unimpressed with the state of many passenger train services. His notebooks are filled with grumbles about the discomfort that fare-paying passengers had to endure on their journeys: "I put my feet on the seat + floor + ceiling + window, + rail + cushion + rack + wall + door + knob + behind my back as well as in my pocket and I still just cant seem to make my feet feel at home on this train. It's cleaner than this on the freights."[10] Some of his manuscript song lyrics— those that were clearly written on passenger train journeys—are practically illegible. One unfinished song, "Railroad Guys," written in 1947 on the "PRR NY Tx" (the Pennsylvania Railroad's "Texas Special," running between New York and San Antonio), abruptly breaks off.[11] The peevish notation: "FINISH LATER. TRAIN TOO ROUGH."[12]

The relationship between the train and the market was naturally a subject of Guthrie's considerable scorn. Just as he had been attuned to the resentment and envy of those without the resources to enjoy the conveniences of the modern highway, so too was he sensitive to the plight of those for whom the luxury of rail travel was also out of reach. This sensitivity was certainly informed by the brutal experiences he shared with the many hoboes harassed and ejected from rolling stock by thuggish railroad bulls:

> There's a train on the track
> That I'd sure like to ride
> But I cain't ride that train
> So I aint satisfied.[13]

On the back of the manuscript lyrics to this song, "I Aint Satisfied," Guthrie explained how it had been inspired during a train journey taken with Will and Herta Geer: "The most important thing that I saw on this trip was a man walking down the railroad track and there I was a setting up there . . . and as the train whistled past him I just set there and tried to think what he could be thinking, what was the first thing that struck his mind and it come to me like you see here in this song."[14]

Guthrie likewise sought to extend such empathy to those unseen, unsung, and often sacrificed laborers who had made the rail journey possible in the first place—just like their fellow road workers facing arrest for thumbing a lift on the highways that they had themselves built:

> And while you ride my railroad rails
> And sip your ice cold cocky tails,
> Some good soul died for each cross tie
> To ride you on my railroad.[15]

Guthrie would also turn to trains as the agents of separation, loss, and disappointment. His unpublished "Gyro Locomotive"—picking up on the new engine technologies trumpeted throughout the Soviet Union in the 1950s (and which he most likely read about in the *Daily Worker*)—plays with a newfangled idea to comment on a very old blues problem:

> Gyro locomotive when my
> heart backs up to leave
> You may [have a] gyro compass but
> your heart aint never free
> Born to be a hustler on this
> old steam pressure line
> You may be somebody's baby
> but baby you aint mine.[16]

Indeed, during his early separations from Marjorie, Guthrie would dream of "a world where we're always together, out where the trains don't keep nobody apart."[17]

There is, as ever, a flip side. If Guthrie sometimes saw the trains as the agents of separation, he also appealed to them in his dearest project of spreading the union gospel. While trains could tear people asunder, they could also bring them together, and this provided Guthrie with some of his most rousing and hopeful imagery. Using the templates laid down for him by generations of evangelical songsters, he secularized both the heavenly journey and the blessed destination:

> There's a Union Train a coming;
> A coming down the Line;
> It's full of Union Comrades
> And it got here just in time;
> . . . That Union Tra—in! That Union Train![18]

In Guthrie's railroad vision, heaven thus gets translated back into an earthly realm, where fortunes are determined not by pie in the sky but by politics, negotiations, production, and activism. "Our country here is called the Union," he wrote. "Union of our whole big forty eight states over which in various boxcars I've rolled and been rolled. The word 'union' means 'all hooked together' like a big high rolling train. The people is the fast locomotive and the cars behind it are our forty eight states full of our work and our goods."[19] Guthrie was thus well aware of the symbolic power of the railroad journey; he worked with its rhetorical capacity to evoke not only the crossing of continents but also the crossing of political and spiritual frontiers, and he is perhaps best known for such expansive evocations.

But an equally important, if lesser known, side to Guthrie is his relationship with the urban mass transit system, which began to preoccupy him immediately upon his arrival in New York in 1940. One of his earliest responses to the phenomena of New York mass transit was occasioned by the arrival of his first wife, Mary, and their children at Grand Central Station. As Mary recalled, "We didn't know you had to have a meeting-up point. We figured it was a small depot with a lightbulb, like we had in Pampa."[20] Guthrie exaggerated the resultant confusion, making up "a little song to tell you about it."[21] "The New York Trains" is a slapstick account of a rural south-ern family's first encounter with inflated urban prices ("You better bring a wagonload of greenback dollar bills") and an overstretched, underfunded subway system:

> The subway trains are crowded and when they make a stop
> You're at the wrong dern station and you're pushed off by a cop
> They heave and push and squeeze and squirm. They slip and
>   slide and crowd.
> And when your station comes along, it's then you caint get out.[22]

Guthrie expanded his discourse on the overcrowded subways in his "Woody Sez" column for the *People's World*: "They could have more people in these subway trains if they'd lay 'em down. When you got to your station they could shoot you home like a torpedo."[23] Guthrie's milking of his new urban perceptions extended to his "Talkin' Subway Blues," which uses sim-ilar slapstick imagery to enhance the bizarre unreality of a transit hell that New Yorkers had long been conditioned into accepting as normal:

> I run down 38 flights of stairs,
> Boy, howdy, I declare,
> Rode the elevator twenty two,
> Spent my last lone nickel, too,
>   Feller in a little cage got it,
>   Herded me through a shoot-the-shoot,
>   Run me through 3 clothes wringers,
> So many people down in there you couldn't even fall down.[24]

Whatever the impressions of discomfiture given in these writings, an important fact of Guthrie's life is his easy adaptation to the New York subways. Indeed, one moment stands out in the surviving tape of his final recording session, January 18, 1954, when Guthrie, firmly in the grip of Huntington's disease, descends into musical anarchy while playing with Sonny Terry, Brownie McGhee, and Jack Elliott.[25] A telephone is heard to ring, and the music-making stops. Guthrie answers the phone and, after a brief pause, launches into a confident, detailed set of instructions for the caller to negotiate the myriad routes and changes on the subway lines in order to get to a party that night. Guthrie is clearly as facile with the system as any native New Yorker.[26] Indeed, when it came to the city's subways, he knew a "perty good train" when he saw one:

> The Brighton Line, folks,
> It's a fast free wheeler, folks;
> Justa thirty six minute bounce
> Down to old Times Square.[27]

From the moment of his arrival in New York, Guthrie had perceived the subways as fertile sites of community engagement, especially for purposes of morale boosting on the eve of, and during, World War II. Among the most widely circulated images of him are the publicity stills taken for the promotion of *Bound for Glory*—the balladeer in his merchant marine cap and peacoat, singing for the subway passengers, one of them in uniform, with his guitar boasting the handwritten sign, "This Machine Kills Fascists" (fig. 13). There are also a number of extant accounts describing the impact of Guthrie's musical agitation on the subways, including Mike Quin's article for the *Daily*

Fig. 13. Woody Guthrie performing in subway car, 1943. Photo by Eric Schall. LIFE Picture Collection/Getty Images.

Worker on an entire carload singing "The Sinking of the Reuben James" and E. P. Dutton editor Joy Doerflinger's recollection of the passengers reveling to "All You Fascists Bound to Lose." As Quin wrote: "If anyone should ask me: What's the most effective way of distributing a leaflet? Or if anyone should ask me: what's the best possible way to have a good time? I'd give them both the same answer: Go singing in the subways with Woody Guthrie."[28]

Ultimately, however, the train—whether underground or above-ground—appears to have eventually exhausted its rhetorical and symbolic potential for Guthrie, as he moved on to demonstrate precisely the imaginative process described by Norm Cohen: "As technology advances, more modern imagery replaces the once-familiar notions of railroads to heaven or hell." Enter the airplane, another mode of modern transportation not readily associated with the Dust Bowl Balladeer but one with which he was enthralled. In this, Guthrie was certainly not alone among musicians operating in the folk tradition. As an example of the tradition's regeneration through the adoption of new technological imagery, Cohen cites Mother McCollum's "Jesus Is My Air-O-Plane" (1930):

> Full salvation is the engine's name,
> Oil in the vessel to run just the same;
> So goodbye, Fords, and also the trains,
> We are going on to glory in the airoplane.[29]

Guthrie was writing in a similar vein as early as February 1939, when he introduced "Airline to Heaven" into his KFVD repertoire. Generally apolitical, the song would have played well to the overwhelmingly conservative, religious majority of Dust Bowl migrants that made up his audience:

> Your ticket you obtain on this heavenly airline plane
> You leave your sins behind
> You have got to take this flight, might be daytime, might be nite
> But you caint see the way if youre blind.
>> Those got ears let them hear—those got eyes let them see
>> Turn your eyes to the Lord of the Skies
>> Take that airline plane it will take you home again
>> To your home beyond the skies.[30]

Initially the airplane proved an easy source of comedic inspiration for Guthrie, as he entertained his radio audience with scenarios about America's encounters with aerial modernity. In 1939, when Guthrie had yet to experience his first airplane ride, he imagined for his audience a comic scenario in which a car purchased on "the easy payment plan" launches into flight. Guthrie's aim was to comment on the "High Priced Cars" after which his song is named:

> Well, I just drove it down the street,
> To see what she would do.
> I was a jumpin' gulleys,
> And a skippin' through the dew.
>> I throwed out the unusual joint,
>> And then I throwed a wheel.
>> I passed up a couple of aeroplanes
>> In my automobile.[31]

Guthrie appears to have taken his first airplane ride on March 22, 1946, when he flew with Pete Seeger and Lee Hays from New York to Pittsburgh and back on a two-day trip for a rally in support of Westinghouse strikers. After that he experienced only a handful of flights before his final documented flight in April 1950. He has left a comprehensive record of the defamiliarization of his entire world through the experience of flight, very much in keeping with the "sensorial reorientation" described by Lauren Rabinovitz in relation to the introduction of railway travel—"new ways of seeing and relationships to the world at large."[32] Railroad historian Wolfgang Schivelbusch borrows a phrase from Karl Marx to examine likewise the "annihilation of space and time" enabled by new modes of transport.[33] On the day Guthrie returned from Pittsburgh, he recorded his impressions of how both time and space had indeed been annihilated for him, courtesy of the airplane. Crucially, his most detailed point of focus was the industrial landscape, his most fervent wish a means of applying the benefits of flight to the good of the labor movement:[34]

> I flew from Pittsburgh to New York this morning. Left at 2:15 am, got here at 4:30 or 5:00 am.

Flying after dark was as good as the trip yesterday, and yesterday was a very clear sunny day for this early in March.

The lights from towns and farms were a sight I had never seen before. I've walked up mountains and pulled over humps in cars and trucks, but never just drifted over a whole range of them like a big bird.

I looked down into the red hot stacks and furnaces of steel mills all across Pennsylvania. I saw fiery vats of moulds full of white hot iron and steel. Saw car loads of hot slag pound down the dumps. I had almost as much fun seeing the world from up here as I had singing for Ten thousand Westinghouse Strikers. . . .

I only wish I could have seen this Westinghouse Strikers rally from up in a plane. I wished we could fly a jet down and spray everybody with phonograph records and Peoples Songs.[35]

Years later, Seeger sent Guthrie a copy of the first song he ever wrote on an airplane, with an undated accompanying note: "Dear Woody—On my desk the other day I was sorting out papers and came across all the verses you wrote on the plane to Pittsburgh. I don't know if you realized how god damn envious Lee and I were that while we snored or fretted over one thing or another, you were creating poetry."[36] Guthrie's song, titled simply "Airplane," captures a remarkable moment in his life: the moment of his "sensorial reorientation" marked by the adoption of airborne imagery and his immediate determination to draw politically progressive conclusions from his new way of seeing. First, he uses the flight to comment on the legacy of the Almanac Singers, disbanded during the war but—in the persons of Seeger, Hays, and himself—still fighting the good fight: "Almanac Singers fly over town / You can't keep a good man down." The visual reorientation from five miles high reaffirms his all-inclusive humanism:

I see people like the head of a pin
I can't make out the color of your skin

Everybody in the world could stand in place
Still have plenty of room and space.

Quite naturally, Guthrie also reveals the apprehension of a passenger on his first airplane ride, keenly uncomfortable with being hurtled through the air in a metal cylinder held together with rivets, locks, and latches: "Emergency knob here by my hand / No guarantee just where I land." And, finally, he gives himself over to the sheer delight of having defied the laws of gravity:

> You bring whisky, I bring beer
> Have a little time in the stratosphere. . . .
>
> The higher I fly, the better I sing
> Silver wings are the latest thing.[37]

Seven months later, on October 20, 1946, Guthrie was on a plane again, this time from Cleveland to New York. The song he wrote during that flight, "Lady in the Plane," builds upon the experience of being asked by a flight attendant "if there was something she could do." Guthrie takes the opportunity for some labor agitation five miles above a country wracked by industrial turmoil, waves of postwar strikes, and an unbridled, runaway economy:

> What can you do to raise the workers wages
> Or to keep high prices down?
> Oh what can you do to kill the black market
> That is running so wild all around?
>
> Say, what can you do to make Mister Truman
> Give us back our price controls?
> Is it true your boss of the airplane company
> Really loves me as much as you are told?

Finally, in Guthrie's wishful scenario, his questions have provoked in the flight attendant the shared understanding of an ally:

> She went to her seat and looked out her window
> All down across our land
> By the look in her eye she's a good union lady
> In love with some good union man.[38]

In March 1947, not yet six weeks after Cathy's death, Guthrie was on a flight to Montreal for an unrecorded event, most likely a labor rally or performance. He was apparently in the combative, stoic mood that characterized much of his response to tragedy. In this case, the aerial vision seems to have emboldened him: "The pretty country down below me here with a light sprinkle of blown snow is Canada in the middle of March. The fields, hills, trees, and rivers are froze up and snowed over with lots of pretty patterns, shapes, designs, and look to me to be maps of victory."[39] But with the Cold War launched just nine days before, through the Truman Doctrine of March 12, and the anticommunist, anti-union Taft-Hartley Act soon to come into force, the American political landscape was undergoing a dramatic, disorienting upheaval. On that same flight, Guthrie drafted an unfinished song, "Looking Down on You," which takes advantage of the aerial perspective; but the distance afforded by the airplane seems to result in a lack of clarity, an imprecision as to what is actually occurring in the struggles on the ground:

> You might be some big shot
> On your highest seat
> You might be the lowest one
> Walking down the street
> Everybody looks so little
> I caint tell who is who
> I ride my silver winger
> Looking down on you.
> (Finish later)[40]

The year 1948 saw Guthrie pen "Plane Wreck at Los Gatos" ("Deportee") in response to the California plane crash that had wiped out twenty-eight unnamed Mexican migrant workers along with three crew members and a US immigration officer. The media's unconcern over the identities of the dead migrants (as opposed to the crew and the officer, who were all named) prompted Guthrie's outrage and the song that emerged from it.[41] Much of the world is familiar with the harrowing images of the aircraft's explosion—the "fireball of lightning" that "shook all our hills"—and the scattered passengers, falling "like dry leaves to rot on my topsoil."[42] It is clear, through reading Guthrie's correspondence, that he had been preoccupied with the relationship between mechanical failure and capitalist greed since the death of his daughter, set afire by a spark from a faulty radio wire. As he had written to the folk song collector John Lomax, corner-cutting and cheap production in the interests of "the greedy profits of a manufacturer" had not only killed his daughter, but also those "in the airplanes that fall down from their upper places to fill our papers and our radio speakers with only some dim echo of the living eyes and faces that got marked out in their fall."[43] Here again were the vaunted promises of progress and modernity falling fatally short.

By 1949, the novelty of flight for Guthrie had clearly begun to wear off as he grew more accustomed to the vertical distance it enabled. He still appreciated "the pretty sights of seenery"—"the world from ten thousand feet up above the clouds" that looked "like a scrabbled up patchwork quilt by daytime, and like a jewelry thief's dream after night."[44] He also remained curious as to "how many songs & song ideas [he] could pick up at that height," as he wrote to his Oklahoma relatives shortly after a flight in April 1949: "One song I knocked out right up there above your head was a tune called OKLAHOMA CLOUDS. If it gets famous you might hear it. Listen for it, anyhow."[45] While the lyrics to "Oklahoma Clouds" appear to have been lost, a tantalizing snippet of it has been left in the recollection of folklorist John Greenway, who—through "a coincidence which would pale the most egregious of Thomas Hardy's into insignificance"—found himself sitting next to Guthrie on that same flight:

> While we were flying across Oklahoma next day, I prodded Guthrie awake and pointed below to Oklahoma, covered by an unbroken bank of clouds. "There's your old home," I said. He looked soberly at the clouds for a moment and then asked me if I had a pen. I handed him a particularly fluid ball-pointer and in a matter of seconds he had written a song beginning "I want to lay my head tonight on a bed of Oklahoma clouds." Amazed, I asked, "Do you always write a song that fast?" "No," he drawled in his expansive, impersonal way, "only when I got a good pen."[46]

But in spite of Guthrie's readiness to make creative capital out of the picture beyond the frame of the airplane's windows, his airborne writings increasingly betray an evident regret over the lost clarity of the closer view that the aerial viewpoint had prevented:

> The lady tells me friendly we're up over
>   my home state, Oklahoma, but I can't
>   see anything down there that looks like
>   my Oklahoma to me.

Apparently, the airplane had become an instrument of dehumanization to Guthrie. The same distance that enabled bomber pilots to drop their bombs and fire their rockets with little perception of the humanity of their targets also obscured the tangible realities that had enhanced his life on the ground:

> Two Fifty every hour that's how fast
>   our shadow flies from the sun
>   down cross the creek there. Did
>   you hear us way up here? Did my
>   shadow taste the ragweed and the
>   gypsum in your yard?
> Couldn't see no red nor grey clay which
>   I beat on School House Hill.[47]

If indeed the airplane had been used up as a fertile source of inspiration for Guthrie, that too would be in keeping with the revitalizing process suggested by Norm Cohen in his study of railroad imagery: "It can be only a matter of time before some modern-day songwriter recounts an astronaut's heavenward voyage. And what will be left after that? Sci-fi enthusiasts already know about teleportation; somehow, this seems a much more appropriate way to get to heaven."[48] In a rambling, undated, unfinished verse tentatively titled "Woke Up This Morning with a Foggy Brain," Guthrie briefly signals his own yearning for yet a new aerial perspective, beyond the frontiers already crossed by the airplane: "Wish I had a plane without no wing / Wish I had a girl without no ring."[49] The "plane without no wing" is a mildly surreal image, perhaps suggesting the smooth, streamlined rocket ships that pervaded the science-fiction culture of the American 1950s.

In fact, Guthrie had already been applying a fairly surreal catalog of images to his reflections on the possibilities of space travel. As early as World

War II, in an undated version of "Talking Hitler's Head Off Blues," he envisioned the Nazis attempting to "hijack the earth, and the Planets Next":

> But I cain't picture my kids a packing their grip
> And going off to school in a rocket ship
> Skipping through the orbs and orbits . . . studying up on
> how to conquer the planets with a paint brush.[50]

Bizarre as this scenario is, it at least manages to generate an accessible political commentary at the expense of the failed Austrian painter who had plunged the world into terror. But in terms of its surrealism, this version of "Talking Hitler's Head Off Blues" pales in comparison to the Dalíesque poem, "Jet Plane," written in December 1952:

> Jet Plane, steam train,
> I'll stop your jet plane,
> I'll stop your steam train
> And let my pomegranite go through
> Go through
> To let my pomegranite go through.[51]

The poem defies rational interpretation. Even if the Soviets' *Sputnik* did somewhat resemble a flying pomegranate, that was still five years into the future.

Guthrie's wholly inexplicable pomegranate imagery makes tepid and innocuous his "My Flying Saucer," a song frequently trumpeted as evidence of the Dust Bowl Balladeer's surprising engagement with the space age:

> My flying saucer where can you be
> Since that sad night that you sailed away from me?
> My flying saucer I pray this night
> You will sail back before the day gets bright.[52]

As Billy Bragg recalled soon after releasing the song on the second *Mermaid Avenue* album, "I came across a song about a flying saucer, which is not what you expect from Woody Guthrie, and there was a note in the top left-hand corner with two very un-Woody Guthrie words: 'Supersonic boogie.' Those words opened up the whole [*Mermaid Avenue*] project. When you realize Woody Guthrie was writing about flying saucers in 1950, and he wanted the song to be a supersonic boogie, you realize the Woody Guthrie we think we know is not the real Woody Guthrie."[53] If "My Flying Saucer" could prompt such a stunning awakening, what must his "Jet Plane" be capable of?

In fact, with American culture in the grip of a Cold War–inspired UFO craze in the late forties and early fifties—think of the "Roswell incident" (1947) and such alien-invasion films as *The Day the Earth Stood Still* and *The Thing* (both 1950), with the aliens doing a fine job as stand-ins for the invading Reds—Guthrie could hardly have been immune to the wonderful possibilities of surreal expression born from the disorienting condition of American paranoia.[54] Flying saucer imagery increasingly appeared in his writings of the 1950s. After being stopped—bearded, disheveled, and otherworldly looking—for hitchhiking in Pennsylvania in June 1950, he wrote: "Reports about me flooded the entire state of Pennsylvania. Bushy headed spy nabs convoy seecrits. Is he from a flying saucer?"[55] It was surely the nervous energies of Cold War paranoia that at least in part drove Guthrie's incomprehensible play script, *Skybally*, written in 1953 with the help of Jack Elliott, Guthrie's wife, Anneke, and the expressive idiosyncrasies of Huntington's disease. In this mad scenario, flying saucer invasions dovetail with folksinging, labor agitation, the Ku Klux Klan, protohippie communalism, and out-of-control campfires.[56]

Given the experience of defamiliarization that has often accompanied the introduction of new technology, not least with regard to modes of transport, a degree of surrealism has perhaps always been attached to the experience—how otherworldly the horseless carriage must have once looked! Indeed, how strange must have been the first wheel fashioned by human hands. The long path from chariots to space stations has often been marked by surreal responses in narrative, song, and visual imagery. Where Guthrie's pomegranate fits into this chain of development is anybody's guess; but surrealistic transport goes at least as far back as the Old Testament, with the prophet Ezekiel's vision of the Merkabah, or Heavenly Chariot (Ezekiel I: 1–28). Guthrie sang of this too, along with Cisco Houston and Sonny Terry, in an adapted version of the African American spiritual, "Ezekiel Saw the Wheel," recorded for Moses Asch in 1944. Like the biblical verses on which it is based, the old spiritual is surreal enough without the benefit of modernist intervention:

> Ezekiel saw that wheel
> Way up in the middle of the air
> Ezekiel saw a wheel a-whirling
> Way in the middle of the air.[57]

Ezekiel's vision, both in the Bible and in Guthrie's version of the spiritual, can certainly give Dalí a run for his money in terms of its surrealism. (Indeed, a 2010 *YouTube* posting of Guthrie's version has prompted a number of users' comments confirming the song's surreal impact: "I realized that way back in 1972 on acid"; "The Merkabah is a heavenly chariot . . . Which is a ufo driven by the Sumerians"; "LOL he's talking about seeing a ufo people!")[58] Thus, it would seem that, well before the arrival of twentieth-century modernism, the wheels of technology had been inspiring responses to defamiliarization that can only be described as surreal.

The point of this observation is not to undercut Guthrie's claim as an American modernist. Rather, it is to suggest that modernism is as much a sensibility as a historical marker. In this respect, perhaps the invention of the wheel was itself the first step toward modernity, and the long-lost human response to it—maybe a cave painting somewhere—the first step toward modernism. In Guthrie's case, the wheel's turning has not been limited to the physical gears, sprockets, drive wheels, tires, and turbines that have driven the process of modernization and, it must be said, the degradation that has always been a part of it. As the next chapter shows, Guthrie himself saw many other technological wheels a-whirling, beyond the realm of transport. He marked their revolutions and counterrevolutions with all the conflicted sensibilities that have defined the modernist predicament of simultaneous progress and retrogression.

5

Other Wheels A-whirling

In his "new theory of modernity," Hartmut Rosa writes of a "circle of acceleration" in which advancements in technology drive the "acceleration of
social change," which in turn drives the "acceleration of the pace of life,"
which in turn drives further advancements in technology . . . and so it goes
in a seemingly endless circle.[1] As we have seen, Guthrie was not immune
to the exhilaration of the dizzying ride enabled by the revolutions of the
wheels of progress. At the same time, he was compelled to register those
countermodern forces—the brakes on modernity—that ever threatened to
slow the wheel's turning or even reverse its direction altogether. Guthrie's
engagement with scientific and technological advancement is a complex
story of wayward encounters, shifts of position, reversals of opinion, celebration, and condemnation. Partially, it was the result of his being made
sadder but wiser with the accumulation of knowledge and experience.
As Tom Gunning points out, one of modernity's symptoms is a need for
constant adjustment: amazement at the possibilities of new technology—a
"heightened astonishment"—eventually "fades into understanding as
the dazzle of the first encounter yields to knowledge."[2] Beyond this store
of diminishing returns is what Zygmunt Bauman calls "the horror of
ambiguity"—the "ambivalence" spawned from the perceptions of disjuncture, of countermodernity challenging the smooth narrative of modern
progress.[3] In Guthrie's case, the accumulation of social and technological
knowledge—both positive and negative—was compounded by considerable
personal trauma.

Perhaps the most public and well-known body of work attesting to Guthrie's initial euphoria over the liberating possibilities of applied science and technology are the songs and other writings celebrating the introduction of electricity to previously benighted areas of the United States. His many odes to the Grand Coulee Dam are only part of this work; his letters and fiction are another. Guthrie's awareness of a seeming premodern existence in the midst of the twentieth century explains, at least in part, his declaration in "Talking Columbia" that "the whole country ought to be run by electricity," as well as the futuristic vision only half-jokingly offered: "Atomic bedrooms! Plastic! / Ever'thing's gonna be made out of plastic!"[4] Other writings make the appeal for the blessings of electricity far more soberly, such as the unpublished "I Can't Be Happy This a Way," which begs for this and other promises of modernity to touch the poorest and most neglected corners of the land:

> I might of read the bible better
> If I'd of had 'lectricity
> But I didn't have 'lectricity
> So I cant be happy this a way.
>
> I'd do my warshing better
> If I had a gasoline motor
> But a bendin down a rub board
> I cant be happy this a way.[5]

When Guthrie was in Oregon in 1941, in the midst of writing his Columbia River anthems, his giddiness over the blessings of publicly funded power was palpable in letters to friends back east. Thanks to the New Deal, there was surely hope for all the unhappy families still yearning for the magic currents of the age to touch their lives. As Guthrie wrote to Millard Lampell: "Electricity means pumps. Pumps mean water from river or wells. Also good lights for study, kids get educated. El. stoves, heaters, cook stoves, fans, ice boxes, barns lit up like a sainted church, the el. milkers, grinders, cream separators, churns, . . . savings to pay higher wages, improve homes + business joints."[6] In light of such boosterism, it is unsurprising that even Guthrie's own proletarian odes should have been powered by electricity, at least metaphorically. As Guthrie told Alan Lomax in September 1940:

"Tonight I'm a writing this by a light, a floor lamp with three shifts forwards and a radio with 3 backwards and I've got the light and the other folks can have the music. Music is some kind of electricity that makes a radio out of a man and his dial is in his head and he just sings according to how he's a feeling."[7]

Wayne Hampton accounts clearly for Guthrie's euphoria, particularly in 1940–41, at the tail end of the New Deal that for a brief but powerful interlude seemed to put the democratic—even protosocialist—seal on America's technological progress: "What excited Guthrie about the Bonneville Power Administration, the Tennessee Valley Authority, and other New Deal public works projects was that the government (meaning the people) was building these massive dams and highways. This was a revolutionary slap at the private enterprise system and to Guthrie and many others on both sides of the issue it was an important step toward socialism. His political dreams seemed to be coming true."[8]

But with Guthrie poised at such a fever-pitch of excitement over the possibilities of socialized public utilities, it was inevitable that his dreams should come crashing down with the change of political climate at the end of the war. Cut to 1946–47, with the New Deal dead and buried along with Franklin Roosevelt, with Harry Truman at the helm on the eve of the Cold War, and with his administration (as well as the pliant trade unions) presiding over the legislative gutting of radicalism in the labor movement and sweeping the decks for the elevation of private enterprise amid vengeful and vicious anticommunist purges.[9] Writing *House of Earth*, Guthrie injected into Tike Hamlin—fretting in the mid-1930s—a bitter cynicism that could only have come from the postwar depths: "You think them 'lectricity fellers is gonna spend eight thousan' smackeroos to put a power line two 'er three miles all th' way over ta our place even if it was built with three barns an' two houses an' all made outta Portlan' seement? Hell no."[10]

The most harrowing event of 1947 ended Guthrie's love affair with electricity altogether. "Yes," he wrote—with all the bitterness of a man personally betrayed by the failures of the New Deal vision at the hands of triumphant, venal capitalism. "That wire that shorted out and burnt Cathy to death was a cheap wartime wire with too much profit in it."[11] Six months after Cathy's death, her grieving father composed "Wires That Won't Burn":

By the spark and the

flash of a wartime radio wire,

Tell every little kid and

tell every big kid

Don't run your high factory

to bring home crazy old wires.

Give your hands a lot more

money so's your heart will sing

and dance while your wheels run

out pretty wires that won't burn

your new pink dress.[12]

If electricity in the hands of private profiteers could prove the arch betrayer for Guthrie, so too could the machinery born of it—just as machinery put to the greater benefit of "the people" could take on the status of holy instruments for him. At times Guthrie revealed his wonder and unbridled admiration for the pure physics of machinery, as distinct from the uses to which it was put or in whose hands it lay. For this reason he turned to machinery time and again for its descriptive imagery and for its potential as analogy—most famously for his own guitar, the "factory machine" that killed fascists (not a phrase of his own, but rather one that was borrowed from the home-front factories during the war).[13] In fact, he applied such mechanical imagery to all forms of labor, whether manual or artistic—"just like you get to working over an old machine and maybe you invent a new gadget of some kind for it or maybe once in a while you invent a whole new machine that works faster and lots better. Music and acting and sawing timber is the same way. And so is writing."[14] For Marjorie, he fashioned one of his most optimistic and endearing mechanical images, that of the "hoping machine": "I can turn it on something like a radio, and go around listening to all kinds of hopes. Hopes from the Okies. Hopes from the sharecroppers. Hopes from the refugees in Europe."[15]

Still, it was the *applied* uses of the machine, both in the literal and the figurative sense, that would repeatedly undercut Guthrie's admiration for it. One the one hand, he could celebrate (for instance) the jackhammer in a number of his Columbia River songs, not only in the published and recorded versions of "Jackhammer John" and "Jackhammer Blues" but also in an unpublished version of the latter:

> Jack Hammer, Jack Hammer,
> Eatin' that rock away—
> Jack Hammer, Jack Hammer,
> Eatin' that rock away—
> Takes 14 shovelers, to
> Follow me around all day.[16]

On the other hand, the same agent celebrated here—the single machine that can do the work of many hardworking men—is the agent of disaster elsewhere, from "Dust Can't Kill Me" ("That old tractor run my house down") to "Poor, Hard-Working Man Blues."[17] In the latter, the desolate laborer may be an agricultural one ("One man run the combine, / Ninety-nine went a-begging") or an industrial one:

> I went to work in a big steel mill,
> And I guess I'd have been there still;
> But they invented a big machine,
> And a million men went over the hill
>> To the poor house—unwanted,
>> Unneeded, unwelcomed guests.

In either case, a machine could only be as beneficent as its master, and it made all the difference whether that master was a public or a private owner:

> I always thought of a big machine
> As the way the Lord His people blessed;
> But in the hands of a selfish man,
> The more you're blessed, the worse it gets.[18]

Indeed, for all his boosting of machines in his moments of political optimism, Guthrie could assign to them almost ghoulish qualities in settings of social and economic destitution—such as in *House of Earth*, as Ella May shudders in the dark, with no electricity, facing the unseen monster of a prairie nightmare, not merely the indifferent instrument that bulldozes farmhouses, scatters families, and spawns refugees, but something even more personally malign:

> "This awful dark is pushing down on top of me like a tractor running over me. It makes me see old Dan Platzburgh like I saw him when he cranked his tractor and it was in gear and pushed him over backward and climbed on top of him and the blades on the front wheels cut his two arms right off at the elbows, and the big back wheels stabbed him all through and through with long muddy cleats, and the harrow plow and the back end came along and tore him into a thousand different pieces and scattered him all over our field. And you can't hardly set your foot on an inch of these wheat lands that somebody's meat and bones hasn't been scattered over with."[19]

Guthrie assigned a similar malignancy to the political machinery surrounding him. In January 1946, reflecting the Cold War paranoia of the immediate postwar era (and with no likely knowledge that he had actually been the subject of FBI surveillance since 1941, when he was first written down as a Communist deadbeat), he declared: "The big machine sends men or things called men around to poke through all my thoughts to see if any of my visions are set against the wheels of the big machine."[20] This was a far cry from the lightheartedness with which he had earlier commented on the "wheels" of political machinery, in a note beneath the lyrics of "Ezekiel Saw the Wheel" in the manuscript of the *Woody and Lefty Lou* songbook for KFVD:

> Never will forget the Cyclone that come 'way in the Middle of the Air. Ole Ezekiel must uv done come frum somewhere down South. That's where you can shore nuff see all kinds of wheels in the air. Cultivator wheels, buggy wheels, and wagon wheels, and Ford wheels, and tracter wheels, skate wheels, kiddy car wheels, wheelbarrow wheels, spinning wheels, winning wheels, skinning wheels, dealing wheels, all kinds uv wheels. Sometimes some of the Wheels out of the Crooked Political machine—most often found in "windy" places— like a courthouse, or congress hall, or specially during Election. In Politicks, the Little wheel runs on "gas" and the middle size wheels on "hot air" and the Big Wheels on pure dee "wind."[21]

As the sprockets on the political, industrial, and economic wheels enmeshed with one another and drove American society further into the twentieth century, a new monster raised its malevolent head: the threatened destruction of the biosphere, savaged by the ruthless juggernaut of mechanical production. By 1962, as Guthrie lay languishing in Brooklyn State Hospital, Americans were waking up to the warnings of Rachel Carson's *Silent Spring* and other writings that were injecting new urgency into ecological debates that had been opened by such earlier conservationists as Henry David Thoreau, John Wesley Powell, John Muir, Theodore Roosevelt, and Aldo Leopold. Of these activists, only Leopold and Carson had witnessed such a dramatic and terrifying environmental disaster as the Dust Bowl—only they had been allowed to see firsthand the "circles of acceleration" spinning to such devastating effect. But if indeed Guthrie the artist was, in a sense, born out of the Dust Bowl, that environmental trauma was itself born out of a much larger cycle of technological and economic activity dominating the first three decades of the twentieth century. As Donald Worster argues, "The attitude of capitalism—industrial and pre-industrial—toward the earth was imperial and commercial; none of its ruling values taught environmental humility, reverence, or restraint. This was the cultural impetus that drove Americans into the grassland and determined the way they would use it."[22]

Guthrie's own environmental awareness has been the subject of some discussion, which began, perhaps, with his receipt of the US Department of the Interior's Conservation Service Award in 1966, the year before his death. As Secretary of the Interior Stuart Udall wrote to him in conferring the award: "Yours was not a passing comment on the beauties of nature, but a living, breathing, singing force in our struggle to use our land and save it too. . . . You have summarized the struggles and the deeply held convictions of all those who love our land and fight to protect it."[23] Such sentiments have provoked more than the dismissive comments from Guthrie's friends, such as Irwin Silber ("They're taking a revolutionary and turning him into a conservationist").[24] They have also provoked concerns about the environmental consequences of projects that Guthrie himself cherished, notably the Grand Coulee and the other Bonneville Power Administration (BPA) dams. Hence a parody of "Roll On, Columbia" written by the environmental activist

Daniel B. Botkin, who—as the son of the eminent folklorist, Benjamin A. Botkin—knew Guthrie as a child:

> Now sixty years later the salmon have fled
> The dams in the river have busted their heads
> We need to do something before they're all dead
> But the BPA rolls right along.[25]

As another environmentalist, Thomas DeGregori, writes: "If Guthrie were alive today and sang 'Roll On Columbia,' he would probably be booed by the ideological descendants of those who earlier cheered him." Still, DeGregori has a kind word: "Guthrie's vision of irrigation and cheap power running factories, filling 'shiploads of plenty,' and curing the economic problems of the depression may seem naive in retrospect. But at least he had a vision."[26]

To be fair, Guthrie had more than a "vision" about the benefits of industrialization; he also had at least a vague environmental concern that was marked out even in his earliest writings. While he never appears to have arrived at the point of recognizing the concept of a biosphere, he certainly identified pockets of environmental degradation that—like any other human-made ills—could presumably be sorted out by concerted public effort. His awareness shows itself in one of his earliest songs, lodged in the "Alonzo Zilch" songbook that he produced in Pampa in 1935—an awareness prompted by the devastating pollution left in the wake of the oil booms in both Pampa and Okemah:

> If I was President Roosevelt,
> I'd make the groceries free—
> I'd give away new Stetson hats,
> And let the whiskey be.
> I'd pass out suits of clothing
> At least three times a week—
> And shoot the first big oil man
> That killed the fishing creek.[27]

Within a decade, Guthrie would elaborate on this verse in his reflections on the Okemah oil boom in *Bound for Glory*, as he chronicled the poisoning of what had previously been a prairie idyll. In retrospect, he implied, he had been too young to appreciate fully the implications of the "pretty" oil slicks floating on the surface of the Canadian River: "It reflected every color when the sun hit just right on it, and in the hot dry weather that is called Dog Days the fumes rose up and you could smell them for miles and miles in every direction. It was something big and it sort of give you a good feeling. You felt like it was bringing some work, and some trade, and some money to every-body, and that people everywhere, even way back up in the Eastern States was using that oil and that gas." Soon, however, the "rainbow-colored gold drifting hot along the waters" revealed its true colors for the young Guthrie and all the inhabitants of his boomtown:

> Oil laid tight and close on the top of the water, and the fish couldn't get the air they needed. They died by the wagon loads along the river banks. The weeds turned gray and tan, and never growed there any more. The tender weeds and grass went away and all that you could see for several feet around the edge of the oily water hole was the red dirt. The tough iron weeds and the hard woodbrush stayed longer. They were there for several years, dead, just standing there like they was trying to hold their breath and tough it out till the river would get pure again, and the oil would go, and things could breathe again. But the oil didn't go. It stayed. The grass and the trees and the tanglewood died. The wild grape vine shriveled up and its tree died, and the farmers pulled it down.

Thus, in the end, a bleak mathematics had played itself out in Okemah: "The oil had come, and it looked like the fish had gone. It had been an even swap."[28]

And as it had been for Okemah, so it was for Pampa, the second important oil-boom town in Guthrie's biography. *Bound for Glory* paints a hellish pic-ture of Guthrie's last glimpse of the town, descended into a Gothic industrial nightmare, as he hitchhiked away westward toward California: "I looked out my window and seen it go by. It was just shacks all along this side of town, tired and lonesome-looking, and lots of us wasn't needed here no more. Oil derricks running up to the city limits on three sides; silvery refineries that first smelled good, then bad; and off along the rim of the horizon, the big carbon-black plants throwing smoke worse than ten volcanoes, the fine black powder covering the iron grass and the early green wheat that pushes up just in time to kiss the March wind. Oil cars and stock cars lined up like herds of cattle."[29] Only such witnessing could have inspired the mildly epiphanic passage in *Seeds of Man*, in which the clear air of the mountainous borderland all too briefly serves as an antidote to the industrial poisons that had choked the life out of both Okemah and Pampa. As Guthrie recalled it: "The feel and the breath of the air was all different, new, high, clear, clean, and light. None of the smokes and carbons, none of the charcoal smells of the oil fields. None of the sooty oil-field fires, none of the blackening slush-pond blazes, none of those big sheet-iron petroleum refineries, none of those big smoky carbon-black plants. No smells of the wild oil gusher on the breeze. No smells from that wild gas well blowing off twenty million feet into the good air every day."[30]

It was during Guthrie's month-long tenure with the BPA in 1941 that environmental depletion became an increasing preoccupation of his. In an epic song written in May that year—"Lumber Is King," which he never recorded—Guthrie envisioned the dethroning of the lumber trade that for so long had been king in the Pacific Northwest. On the one hand, he was clearly aware of the need for a managed tree-felling program if the trade were to continue at all, even in a diminished state:

> King Lumber might live for 100 years, too,
> If when you cut one tree, you stop to plant 2;
> But, boys, if you don't, he's on his way down;
> 'Cause Lumber's just King in a Lumbering town.[31]

On the other hand, Guthrie could not remotely foresee the environmental fate that would come with the triumph of the dam-building project. On a brief return visit to Portland with Pete Seeger in September 1941—roughly three months after he had finished his odes to the Grand Coulee and the other Columbia River dams—he painted a grim picture in a letter to Lampell in New York: "Some factories are dumping refuse + chemical garbage into the nations greatest salmon, power, stream, the Columbia river. Millions of fish are destroyed and the Indians are plenty sore. The dried salmon means grub for the hard winter. A disposal plant was offered the company for a few thousand dollars, but the company refused. All running water is public property under Federal law—why this poisoning of the river?"[32] Guthrie was convinced that the BPA dams would be a corrective to this dire state, unaware that in the succeeding decades the dams themselves would be implicated for their part in making the Columbia "one of Oregon's most polluted rivers" (as stated by the Oregon Environmental Council), thanks largely to the runoff of toxins from the "farms, roads, construction sites and stormwater systems" enabled by the dams.[33] As for the "pretty sore" Indians lamenting the loss of their salmon fisheries, Guthrie envisioned the return of a bountiful store with the completion of the BPA dams:

> When old King Lumber's asleep in his grave,
> The Royal Chinook leap the white ocean wave
> To the Great King Columbia's spawning ground;
> 'Cause Lumber's just King in a Lumbering town.[34]

In fact, the sacred deep-net fishing grounds that for centuries had supported the Wasco, Wishram, and other Chinook tribes—sites such as the Celilo Falls and Kettle Falls—were lost forever with the creation of Lakes Celilo and Roosevelt, resulting in massive cultural dislocation and bitter litigation.[35] All of these developments were beyond Guthrie's vision.

And as it was on the West Coast, so it was in the East, where another bout of "poisoning" was taking place (in addition to that which was already killing the Hudson River, not to be revived until the 1970s, largely through the efforts of Pete Seeger's Clearwater project). One day in 1947, as Guthrie took a sad walk along the Coney Island beachfront, he was reminded of his childhood days in Okemah. He thought not only of the oil that had suffocated the fish in the Canadian River, but also the detritus of industrial production that had briefly been his only source of income at the age of fifteen. As he had described it in the "Junking Sack" chapter of *Bound for Glory*: "Every day I combed the alleys and the dump grounds with my gunny sack blistering my shoulders, digging like a mole into everybody's trash heaps to see if I couldn't make a little something out of nothing. Ten or fifteen miles walking a day, with my sack weighing up to fifty pounds, to weigh in and sell my load to the city junk man along about sundown."[36] Now, in New York, the "garbage waves" filled him with a disgust that had made his "junking" seem like a pastoral activity:

I stand here
in Coney by the garbage
waves and I swim with
the condoms and oil and
crap flushed down your
toilet and sink and drain
and I feel like my old
junking sack was clean.

Still, Guthrie's solution to the problem suggests that he had yet to think of the long-term implications of the current waste disposal practices. He simply asks

you city health
guys why you don't flush
this crap out in the
Atlantic a few more miles.[37]

Beyond water and land pollution, Guthrie clearly had worries about air pollution as well. To some extent, these worries were reflections of his concern for the conditions in which industrial laborers were making billions for the mine, mill, and factory owners across America. One of Guthrie's relatively microcosmic points of focus was silicosis, a particular miner's affliction. As he wrote in the introductory notes to "Silicosis Is Killin' Me," one of the songs collected by Alan Lomax for *Hard Hitting Songs for Hard-Hit People*:

You get the silicosis a working in hard rock tunnels.

Dust is deadly poison. . . . It killed an average of a man a week on rock drilling jobs in New York City. Sixteen Union men died in 4 months from it. No masks to keep it out of your lungs. They'd set off the dynamite and make you go right in; the law says you got to wait thirty minutes for the dust to settle. To hell with the law, the big shots figured, and they hired spies to stand in the mouth of the tunnel and holler when a inspector was a coming, so's they could hide their illegal tools, the ones that makes so much dust.

Wanted: More and bigger and better Cuss Words to tell what I think of a man that would do a thing like this just to squeeze a extry dollar out of a working man's dead body.[38]

Out of this concern came Guthrie's "Dead from the Dust," of which he noted on the manuscript, "I wrote up this song to try to tell you how I feel about this silicosis dust that blows from the mines"—implying his fear that it was not only the miners who would be affected but also those living and working in the vicinity of the mines:

> You can build a machine for a few silver dollars
> That would clean all this dust that poisons the skies;
> I'd rather dig coal than to stand digging grave holes
> For my people cut down by the dust from the mines.[39]

A visit to Los Angeles in 1952 reintroduced Guthrie to a situation that had apparently not seemed as acute during his residence there in 1937–39—not acute enough to have prompted any songs specifically devoted to it. However, during the 1952 visit, the Los Angeles smog caught his full attention, giving rise first to his "Smoggy Old Smog," an updating of "Dusty Old Dust" ("So Long, It's Been Good to Know Yuh"), which had inaugurated his Dust Bowl commentary seventeen years previously:

> I'm not smoggin' here 'cause I just want to be;
> I've come in like a cloud or a fog from the sea;
> I've got to burn all of these noses and eyes
> That spill'd these wild chemicals up in my skies.

As had been the case with "Dead from the Dust," Guthrie readily pointed his finger:

> I come partly to warn 'bout the fact'ry boss greed;
> Partly to warn everybody I see
> About all kinds of wrong thoughts and fears you let rise
> Up here to foul up our skies.[40]

Guthrie wrote two more parodies during that same visit: "Smoggy Mountain Top" (based on the Carter Family's "Foggy Mountain Top") and "On Top of Old Smoggy." In the latter song, it is clearly not enough simply to blame the factory boss. Rather, Guthrie explicitly calls for concerted collective agitation and resistance:

> Come all you smoggy weepers
> Red eyes and hot nose,
> We'll trail that dern fact'ry lord
> Wherever he goes.

> If this smog gets much worser
> It'll kill us like frogs;
> The only way we c'n best it
> Is to fight it like dogs.[41]

In "Smoggy Mountain Top," Guthrie draws in another vital element in the fight—the legislation that must follow the agitation:

> I will build a big machine to wash y'r dam smoke clean;
> I'll put it in by hand if th' law allows;
> But if we dont pass my law to clean y'r fact'ry smoke,
> We're gonna die fr'm y'r smog, anyhow.[42]

It is clear that by 1952 Guthrie had begun to sense the acuteness of the air pollution problem in America. The urgency of his L.A. smog songs is a far cry from the blitheness of only eight years previously, when, toward the close of the war, he had been looking to the postwar era with shimmering optimism for the "better world a-comin'." He appears to have had no problem with the ecological implications of what he hoped would follow on the heels of an Allied victory in his "Union War," as he jotted into his notebook late in 1944:

> Gonna take more smoke
> from more factories
> to build the world up
> than it took to blow it down.
> I'll work with everybody.[43]

Thus, like many observers of American modernity, Guthrie had conflicting responses to the industrial technology that had so transformed the domestic landscape, as well as waterscape and airspace, during his lifetime. As the following chapter shows, he was equally conflicted over the transformation of a more abstract dimension: the nation's (and the world's) *soundscape* through the wonders of sonic technology. Guthrie's insatiable desire for communication, matched by that of modernity itself, brought him a host of mixed blessings.

6

Hold the 'Fone—
It's Radio Time!

In *Beautiful Circuits: Modernism and the Mediated Life*, Mark Goble observes that "modernism itself desired communication and the many forms it took." The connection between communication and desire may at first seem curious, but then consider Guthrie's lifelong fixation on a communicative device that had been quite a novelty during his formative years in Okemah (1912–29) and not yet all that common during his Pampa years (1929–37). This was the humble telephone, which in the early twentieth century was, as Goble notes, "an essential emblem of class status and modernity."[1] But the attractions of the phone had to do with much more than status. The phone was also about consciousness and effect, phenomena intensely preoccupying many modernists—including Guthrie, who often closed his letters with the salutation, "Hold the 'fone!"

Of those modernists who paid particular attention to the telephone as an instrument of desire, the most significant, perhaps, would be Marcel Proust. Sam Halliday's study *Sonic Modernity* explores, among other subjects, Proust's disquisitions on the telephone in his *Remembrance of Things Past* (1913–27). The major attraction of telephony for Proust was its capacity to separate and heighten the aural sense in the same way that (as Virginia Woolf had noticed) other supposedly mundane activities could heighten the experience of consciousness and ignite the process of involuntary memory. For Proust it might be riding in an elevator, tasting a madeleine, or talking with his grandmother on the telephone. In the latter case, as Halliday argues, "the device not only separates vision from audition, but in doing so, makes each of these senses somehow more themselves."[2] As such, the desire for heightened consciousness becomes, among other things, a desire for communication as an experience rather than as a mere function.

Guthrie's own telephonic desire permeates a remarkable extended discourse he wrote for Will and Herta Geer in February 1945, when he and Marjorie were scouting for a nursery school for Cathy. Here the school's telephone crowds out every other aspect of the letter, including its nominally main subject, the school itself. Not the least striking aspect of this communication is the sensuality—even the sexuality—with which the telephone is rendered. It is, Guthrie says, "one of the prettiest telephones that I believe I ever did see and I could just set down there . . . and pet that telephone and talk to it and drink with it. . . . I've seen Poland China hogs that same color and almost that slick when they was well oiled and greased, seen horses run in the sun and get all sweaty and shine like that fone did." Soon the school's telephone prompts a recollection of another phone, one that Guthrie had had in a rented room. That phone had managed to surpass even a wife in its satisfying potential: "You never get to knowing a wife as good as you do a fone. A wife won't set and listen to you talk like a fone does. I never found a wife yet that I could put as much of my confidence in as I did that there fone of mine." Finally, as Guthrie himself admits, the telephone had indeed become—in his life as well as in this particular letter—a full-blown, overpowering obsession: "I seen a picture show the other night with a telephone in it and I completely forgot the names of the folks that was in the show. I think this was what got me so nervous and heated up about fones. . . . And, well, you know when you see a phone, somehow you feel your hand reaching out for it almost before you know what in the devil you're going to say to it."[3]

The telephone became a central instrument of both hope and frustration in Guthrie's relationship with Marjorie, not only during the difficult early period when Marjorie was still living with her husband, but also during the later periods when Guthrie's behavioral changes led to one separation after another. In the former case, a single phone call from Marjorie, late in 1942, apparently had the power to alter the very shape of existence for Guthrie. In the midst of a mildly despairing letter to Marjorie, he writes:

BUT YOUR PHONE CALL JUST CAME, and so that changes not only all of this, but me, and the world, and everything, even my part in the war.

THAT CRAZY PHONE CALL I MADE TO YOU, the best thing is to just forget it. Or maybe not.[4]

But how fickle the telephone could prove to be when, after a series of bitter observations about Marjorie having gone back to her "band box" to live with her "long-term man" and three-week-old Cathy early in 1943, Guthrie scrawled:

> I called long distance on
> my telephone
> and said
> "Please let me speak to the
> only one
> In this whole world that knows
> my
> Deeper self."

But the telephone offers no consolation, no connection, only the mockery of a jeering electronic pulse:

> The line was busy.
> All I got was
> Buzz * *
> Buzz * *
> Buzz * *
> Buzz * *
> Buzz * *
> Buzz * *
> Buzz * *
> Buzz * *
> Buzz * *[5]

Later, in 1949, when Guthrie's erratic behavior led to a particularly dramatic separation from Marjorie, the telephone—so often an instrument of torment and mockery—was now the very vessel of salvation:

> But when I called
> you on our fone wire, and you let me
> know that I could still come back to you,
> . . . well—you led me back to you
> through the mansion of the dead.[6]

October 1950 saw Guthrie tapping into the popular music currents that had begun to seize on the telephone as a means of bringing sexual partners together (Glenn Miller's dance number, "PEnnsylvania 6-5000," from 1940) or keeping them apart (Rose Murphy's "Busy Line," from 1949). Guthrie's "DRexell 23883" anticipates by sixteen years Wilson Pickett's "634-5789," turning his telephone into any woman's sure and certain conduit to pleasure:

> Well, if you feel sad and lonesome, too,
> Gonna tell you just what ta do;
> Step right in to your old fone booth;
> Call DRexel Two Three Eight Eight Three.
> DRexel Two Three Eight Eight Three.[7]

Clearly, then, like modernism itself, Guthrie desired "communication and the many forms it took." Telephony was only one of those forms, and it cannot helpfully be considered in isolation from the other modes of communication that also sparked modernist desire. Goble goes so far as to declare that "the phonographic era . . . *is* modernity" (my emphasis).[8] This belief is shared by Edward Comentale, who argues that "the mediation affected via sonic form . . . becomes nothing less than the mediation of modernity itself."[9] Such claims as these do not quite appear exaggerations when one considers the advancements made in sonic technology during Guthrie's lifetime, advancements made on the back of the telephone. Not for nothing did Lee de Forest, the inventor of the Audion, the triode vacuum tube that made possible the amplification and broadcasting of electrical signals, first call his developing medium the "wireless telephone," which he later called the "radio telephone" (to distance himself from his archrival Marconi's preferred term, "wireless"). "Radio telephone" would soon be shortened simply to "radio."[10]

We know relatively little about Guthrie's early consciousness of radio—or the condition of "radio-modernity," a phrase coined by Comentale to describe

"radio and the modernity it represented"—during his formative years in Okemah.[11] Guthrie makes no mention of radio in the early chapters of *Bound for
Glory* or other recollections of his Okemah years. Given that, for all intents and
purposes, radio broadcasting did not develop before 1922, it is unlikely that
a radio would have been a household fixture, even if the up-and-down fortunes of the Guthrie family would have enabled the purchase of an expensive
battery-operated set.[12] (AC-powered "plug in" radios were not developed until
1927.)[13] Ed Cray surmises that "if he came upon a radio" in Okemah, Guthrie
might well have listened to "KVOO, 'The Voice of Oklahoma,' broadcasting
from Bristow. . . . The station thirty miles north of Okemah boasted live broadcasts by local performers, including Jimmie Wilson and the Catfish String
Band, and Otto Gray and his Oklahoma Cowboy Band."[14] However, KVOO
did not begin broadcasting until 1925 (under the call letters KFRU).[15] Joe
Klein notes that the *National Barn Dance* from Chicago's WLS and the *Grand
Ole Opry* from Nashville's WSM—along with increasingly powerful stations
broadcasting what had yet to be called "country music" from Fort Worth and
other Texas cities—would have brought folk musical influences into a soundscape otherwise dominated by religious, popular, and "semi-classical" music.[16]
But the *Barn Dance* and the *Opry* only began their broadcasts in 1924 and
1925 respectively, so this leaves a precious four or five years in which a young
Woody Guthrie *might* have been directly influenced by the radio in Okemah.

A clearer picture emerges with Guthrie's arrival in Pampa in 1929.
There he not only learned a range of traditional, topical, and popular
songs broadcast on the Pampa and Amarillo stations, but he also learned
through imitation "the outlandish 'hillbilly' posturing of the comedians on
such popular radio shows as *Grand Ole Opry*."[17] He developed a local radio
presence, playing in barn dance and comedic country bands on Amarillo's
WDAG and Pampa's KPDN stations. As the rustic, cracker-barrel philoso-
pher "Alonzo M. Zilch," drawing on templates laid down by his hero, Will
Rogers, Guthrie honed his between-song patter as well as his facility with
what he would come to call the "microbephone."[18] By the time he decided
to migrate to California in 1937, Guthrie had in mind a career as a singer
of cowboy songs on the radio, with his cousin, "Oklahoma" Jack Guthrie.

Given the relative lack of autobiographical commentary, it is useful to
turn to *House of Earth* for an indication of Guthrie's perception of the radio

experience for a poor family on the Texas plains in the early 1930s. It is, in the first place, tied to the restrictions of the Hamlins' disposable income, which is virtually nonexistent. While the radio was lauded as a relatively cheap source of entertainment and connectivity to the wider world, the state-of-the-art technology is not within the Hamlins' grasp. Ella May, writhing under the weight of her unborn child, pleads with Tike for some "perty music" to sweeten her ordeal:

> Ella May lifted the weight of the baby in her stomach and went over across the room to connect the naked ends of two wires that would make the radio play. . . .
>
> As she sat back down on the edge of the bed, she worked the knobs of the radio. It was an old one, in a green metal box, and the loudspeaker stood up on top of the box like an air ventilator on a ship. . . .
>
> "I don't see what ever did possess you to go and give that much for such an old junk heap as this, anyway," she scolded him. . . .
>
> "Goshamighty whizzers, lady, that ain't too much to pay for a good radio. An' that's a good one. I seen an ad in a big magazine that said so. Company speaks might well of it."
>
> "Yes. I should suppose the company would. I would too if it made me a millionaire."[19]

In spite of the advertisers' spin, the radio—like every other mode of communication at the mercy of unevenly distributed infrastructure—proves such a source of frustration in *House of Earth* that it almost drives Tike and Ella May mad in their attempt to get a clear signal. Tike resorts to a frantic rain dance of sorts to get the radio to play, before collapsing at Ella's feet:

> He was so out of wind that he could hardly talk, but finally did manage to say, "Playyy!"
>
> Ella May's voice sounded thin and a long ways off. "Play."
>
> A hum, a scratchy rasping blur of noise, a rattle, a whine, a clicking, clacking, several high and low zooms, far-off rumbles, sobs, sighs, and then a terrible clatter came from the mouth of the loudspeaker. This was the only answer that it made to all of Tike's sweating and working and dancing. (112–14)

Eventually, in a tantalizing moment, a man's faint voice is heard just beyond the wall of sonic interference—but "there were parts of his words that the weather whipped to pieces." When finally the interference subsides, what comes from the speaker makes a mockery of the Hamlins' dirt-poor reality. A smug "big Government man" is heard to declare:

> "It is a very plain and simple problem with a very plain and simple answer. Our modern machines and our modern factories and our modern systems of labor have simply given us more of everything than we can use. There is no demand for this oversupply. Prices are falling because all of the storage rooms are full and overflowing and nobody will buy the excess. There is too much. Too much of everything."
>
> And a look that was half hate and half silly, a grin that was more of a sneer [appeared] on Tike's face. Outside he heard the rattle of the cold wind against the dry house. He thought of the years that he had raised growing things and said, "Oh yeah? Too much." (124)

The "oily" voice of the "Government man" thus impresses upon the Hamlins that they share little in common with the well-fed pontificators in the state or federal capitol buildings. For them, the promised radio connectivity just reinforces their sense of deprivation and alienation in a land of abundance in the midst of the "Century of Progress." There is, in fact, only one moment in which the radio works its magic to the extent that it can bring Tike and Ella into some sort of communion with the wider world, and this is through music:

> For some unknown reason the speaker had gotten quiet, and it was for some few minutes that they listened to the sounds of an orchestra. It was so soft that they strained their ears to hear, because of the dead batteries, but the notes of the music were easy to hear. It was the horns and the saxes, hot trombones of a Saint Louis dance band playing some dreamy, bluesy Louisiana ragtime. The shuffle of the trombone and the blare of the little wet trumpet sounded jazzy, wiggly, fiery, and Tike saw people all around the world move their hips and rub their bellies. (120)

Tike's brief moment of transportation, enabled by what Comentale calls "the snaky wires and alien tubes of a radio set," is a powerful reflection of a contradictory desire, as well as its satisfaction, that was still very new in the mid-1930s—the experience of total immersion from a distance. Comentale writes: "With the simple flick of the dial, the mind of the rural listener was freed from habit to travel the airwaves, sampling cultures and voices from abroad in a *detached* way. According to Bob Coltman, 'Radio's gift to Depression listeners of distant visions of culture and confidence proved especially fascinating to country people, changing their lives, their understanding of the world, their tastes, among other things in music.'"[20]

Indeed, as a "rural listener," Tike represents precisely the figure that remained at the heart of the earliest discussions about the value of developing a radio broadcast system in the first place. As Steve Wurtzler notes in his study, *Electric Sounds*, "The farmer became a crucial rhetorical figure in the initial debates about radio that claimed the medium's identity resided in its capacity to conquer distance." Champions of the new technology "highlighted broadcasting's ability to end rural isolation. Long nights on the farm—particularly in the winter—might soon be accompanied by the uplifting sounds of urban symphonies and operas, or by edifying talks featuring the nation's great speakers."[21] Wurtzler points out that lobbyists for broadcasting investment not only claimed future successes in "the conquest of distance" but also in the medium's ability to "redress the uneven development characteristic of modernity."[22] However, in true countermodernist fashion, Guthrie's rendering of the Hamlins' "radio-modernity" depicts both these benefits and their opposites. Yes, there is the brief moment of musical communion; but the radio also reinforces Tike and Ella May's sense of "rural isolation," of alienation from the policy makers and bureaucrats of an out-of-touch government. In terms of "uneven development," the ramshackle condition of the Hamlins' radio set—puffed up as it was by the lies of an advertising pitch—places them at odds with the type of promotional material that was used to reel in the early consumers of "country radio." As Comentale notes: "Souvenir programs took listeners into the studio, providing pictures of stars, directors, technicians, and sound engineers. Spreads and pictorials featured the 'completely modern studio' and provided illustrations of control panels, amplification tubes, and high-voltage rectifiers."[23]

Wurtzler's study of radio also focuses on a process that became a major concern for Guthrie as his broadcasting career developed. As early as the 1930s, within only ten years of the industry's birth, mass media ownership and control in the United States was "in the hands of progressively fewer, larger horizontally and vertically integrated firms. . . . The establishment of radio networks, the institutionalization of network-affiliate relations, and the increasing role played by national advertisers in programming content centralized the economic control of U.S. broadcasting."[24] Denning elaborates on "the mixture of advertising and programming" that characterized commercial broadcasting during Guthrie's tenure as a radio artist: "The programs . . . were a way of attracting an audience to the advertisements: they were, in a way, advertisements for the advertisements. The radio programs of the 1930s and 1940s were not only sponsored by advertisers, but were produced by advertising agencies."[25] Yet, for Denning and some other cultural historians, Guthrie's radio career may well have represented at least a small chink in the armor of capitalist control, with the radio and other centers of "the cultural apparatus" becoming "a contested terrain between the Popular Front and the Advertising Front, as working-class styles, stars, and characters emerged alongside the sales plug."[26]

When Guthrie joined the KFVD stable in July 1937, he indeed stepped for the first time onto that "contested terrain" between Popular Front activism and "the Advertising Front." As was the case with most of Guthrie's battles, the lines of conflict were not so neatly drawn, for Guthrie was compelled at times, and for various reasons, to join that very "front" that he so often professed to despise. Although the owner and manager of KFVD, Frank Burke, was a politically engaged progressive behind the campaigns of local and national New Deal figures, his radio station was a solidly commercial concern. Consequently, Guthrie and his KFVD singing partner, Maxine "Lefty Lou" Crissman, were indebted to the largesse (and subject to the editorial pressure) of such local businesses as the Perfume Man, the Victor Clothing Company, and Sal-Ro-Cin Headache Pills.[27] In a note scrawled into his copy of the published program songbook *Woody and Lefty Lou's Favorite Collection, Old Time Hill Country Songs*, Guthrie actually pays a grudging compliment (if somewhat backhanded and a touch sarcastic) to the phenomenon of radio sponsorship:

A sponsor is a highly refined member of the animal species, possessed of a peculiar ability to get what they can and can what they get. They have a strange tendency to hide away in business places where no Hillbilly can find them. When approached by a Musician, they scamper away and seldom come out except during very good business seasons. However, we strive to understand them, for they use their natural gift of accumulation sometimes in favor of Hillbillies who have none. And often are found doing the thinking for Hillbillies that are unable to. So let us lend an ear to the worn-out messages given you daily by sponsors of all sizes, over all radio stations.[28]

Clearly irritated by the patronizing superiority of his sponsors, who always seemed to know best, Guthrie nonetheless welcomed their sponsorship as he began to develop his own promotional techniques. He would plug his radio show in the four local newspapers to which he contributed his cartoons and columns—the *People's World*, the *Light*, the *California Progressive Leader*, and the *Hollywood Tribune*—and he would plug these newspapers on his radio show.[29] As Guthrie admitted, if advertising could be used in the service of a progressive cause—such as raising funds for the migrant workers or offering an alternative to the dominance of Tin Pan Alley—it was worth it: "We used every trick and device of the trades of salesmen, show men, P. T. Barnum's, Flo Zeigfelds [*sic*], Jimmie Rogers, and every twist of the nipple that filled California's dry and native soil with a fighting kind, a more personal, human, kind of folk song, folk dance, folk yell."[30]

In January of 1938, Guthrie and Crissman were invited by the Consolidated Drug Company to cross the border and broadcast from the Tijuana, Mexico, station, XELO. As Klein notes, the various "X" stations would fill the airwaves with "commercials hawking products of a less than savory sort, especially quack cures too raunchy to make it past American censors and Better Business Bureaus." In this case Guthrie and Crissman were obliged to sing between "loud, pushy, obnoxious ads for Peruna Tonic, which was Consolidated's cure-all, plus Colorback hair dye and other questionable items."[31] In spite of the corrupt nature of the enterprise, what galled Guthrie most were "the blue pencil lines drawn across the several censored verses of each song," with the sponsor's agents mercilessly policing their output.[32] Never having been subjected before to such a degree of censorship (not even on KFVD), Guthrie recalled the experience with considerable bitterness—a bitterness that would only grow with each encounter with the "blue pencil lines," whether drawn by commercial agents, network standards-and-practices officials, or even collaborators such as the Almanac Singers.

Following his brief sojourn in Mexico, Guthrie spent another year at KFVD before his terminal confrontation with Burke over the Hitler-Stalin Pact and his relocation to New York in 1940. March of that year proved a very opportune time for Guthrie to meet his most influential patron, Alan Lomax, and the following month he met a friend of Lomax, radio producer Norman Corwin. Lomax himself was only a recent convert to the radio and its potential, or so he suggested when asked in 1939 to devise a twenty-six-week-long series on folk music for the long-running CBS program *American School of the Air.* "I thought this was a joke. . . . I didn't know that anybody could be seriously interested in working on the radio, a pile of crap. Then I heard Corwin's broadcasts and I did a flip. I realized that radio was a great art of the time."[33]

Thus, on April 2, 1940, Guthrie made his first New York radio appearance, singing "Do Re Mi," "Talking Dust Bowl Blues," "Blowing Down the Road," and a few other songs on *American School of the Air.*[34] Three weeks later, with Lomax's help, he was on Corwin's Sunday afternoon show, *The Pursuit of Happiness,* also on CBS. When Lomax was invited by CBS to produce a folk program, *Back Where I Come From,* in August 1940, with Nicholas Ray as the director, Guthrie was signed on as a regular. Other frequent guests included Josh White, the Golden Gate Quartet, and, after persistent lobbying from Guthrie, Lead Belly. Guthrie was hot radio property immediately after his first appearance on *Back Where I Come From.* Radio stations (and their sponsors) courted him with invitations—CBS's *We the People* (Sanka), NBC's *Cavalcade of America* (Du Pont), and CBS's *Pipe Smoking Time* (Model Tobacco Company). Guthrie gushed to Lomax: "They are giving me money so fast, I use it to sleep under. Handed me fifty bucks the other day just to see how far it would knock me."[35] And, for the briefest moment in his career, Guthrie seemed like he was willing to do anything to make money, including rewriting his first Dust Bowl Ballad into the smarmy jingle that he would regret for the rest of his life:

> Howdy friend, well it's sure good to know you
> Howdy friend, well it's sure good to know you
> Load up your pipe and take your life easy,
> With Model Tobacco to light up your way
> We're glad to be with you today.[36]

After six weeks of *Pipe Smoking Time*, Guthrie could take his self-betrayal no longer. It is unclear whether he consciously engineered his own firing, but he soon turned his back (for the time being) on network radio as well as New York City itself, fleeing to California. He jotted into his notebook some opaque speculation: "Well I guess the main reason Pipe Smoking Time fired me was on account of I done just what they told me to do and it was no good. It didn't make me feel none too good because it sounded like too much war—so what I done wasnt good—so I'm broke again. I feel natural but just aint satisfied."[37] The reference to "too much war" is confusing: was there "too much war" between Guthrie and his sponsors, or—given his strident noninterventionism, which would last until June 1941, with the end of the Hitler-Stalin Pact—was there too much pro-war talk at the station? In any event, he was clearly pinning his hopes on a return to KFVD, but Burke would have none of it.

Next Guthrie sent a begging telegram to Nicholas Ray, asking for his old job back on *Back Where I Come From*—only to be told that the program had been axed by the network. Upon reflection, Guthrie surmised that the program—which, to him, had seemed so riddled with artistic compromises—had turned out to be "so honest nobody would pay money for it."[38] The cancellation was yet another symptom of a potentially liberating industry falling into the hands of the advertisers and the hegemonic class. As Guthrie wrote to Lomax in disgust: "Oh well, this country's a getting to where it caint hear its own voice. . . . The rich folks likes to lull their self off to sleep and sort of float 1/2 way between a drink of scotch liquor and a tile shit house—and listen to a raft of songs that's about as close to the real as I am to foreclosing on a farm."[39]

Guthrie's West Coast options seemed all but completely shut down. He was rescued by his productive month of songwriting for the Bonneville Power Administration, but his thoughts were still on radio when he returned to New York in June 1941, prompted by an invitation from Pete Seeger to join the Almanac Singers. Having about-faced from strict noninterventionists into fervent pro-war activists in the wake of Pearl Harbor, the Almanacs were invited onto Corwin's CBS radio program, *This Is War*, broadcast under the auspices of the Office of War Information (OWI). On February 14, 1942, to a nationwide audience on all four major American radio networks, the Almanacs sang "Round and Round Hitler's Grave," with a dazzling career as wartime propagandists apparently ahead of them—until the New York *World-Telegram* outed them three days later as "the favorite balladeers of the Communists."[40] The Almanacs were dropped from the network as well from as the OWI, and they were pilloried in the press. Nicholas Ray and other Popular Front radio figures such as John Houseman would follow them into the cold within another two years, as the remnants of the New Deal vision were purged from the federal broadcast agencies. As Denning phrases it, "The Popular Front vision of the anti-fascist war was defeated by the corporate vision of an American Century in the OWI."[41]

Guthrie still managed to secure a few more independent broadcast appearances for the OWI, such as Corwin's *Labor for Victory* in July 1942. It would not be long before all but the barest traces of such Popular Front activism would be erased from government-sponsored broadcasts like this, but for now Guthrie could eulogize "Union Radio" as a metaphor to compete with the "Union Train," the "Union Rock," or any other of his symbolic "Union" fashionings:

> There's a union radio that's built in every workers heart, and it
>   never falls to pieces
> and it never breaks apart
>   Our union's got a sending set and also receiver, too, and every
>   member's got both in
> his heart out yonder, and back here, too
>   So just remember, comrade, no matter where you may go, we can
>   talk to one another
> on our union radio.[42]

During the early war period, Guthrie kept his faith in the radio as a potent educational resource for America's young antifascists, making some return appearances on *American School of the Air*. After a session in November 1943, he wrote to Marjorie: "This is quite a big program and I always like to be on it, because it has got an enrolled listening audience of ten million school kids who bring their radios into the school rooms and listen and of course, is picked up by many homes, cars, ships, and so forth. I'd like to put on some real tough anti fascist shows for the school children."[43] Radio's potential for progressive education was a subject to which Guthrie persistently returned. He argued that folk song programs would present, from the ground up, a vibrant alternative to the hegemonic history handed down in schools and through the culture industries: "It wouldn't be unfair for the U.S. to have an hour a day on a coast-to-coast, nationwide radio station, just putting on this one particular brand of American history."[44] *American School of the Air* and *Labor for Victory* were perhaps the closest that Guthrie came to seeing such a broadcast curriculum realized.

His enthusiasm for OWI radio notwithstanding, Guthrie grew scathing in his commentaries on the state of American radio broadcasting as the war progressed. In 1942—at about the time he was appearing on *Labor for Victory*—he pointed his finger at the industry with the charge of deliberately sapping the fighting spirit of the nation:

> Morale is just simply "knowing" what you're fighting against, and
> fighting for and knowing that a few hundred million of us are
> thinking, working, and living and dying to back you up. Songs ought
> to, they've just naturally *got* to tell you this. Got to tell you over and
> over and over ten thousand times a day, so that when you feel like you
> need a couple of buckets of fresh, brand-new morale, all you got to do
> is to just walk over and turn on your radio, and out it comes, as free
> as the breeze, and as fresh as the air, and as tough as the nickel plated
> center of the earth, and as sure and certain as the ocean rolling in.

That was the ideal; but the reality was otherwise: "You can tune in your radio and listen twenty four hours a day, and about twenty two of it will [be] for the business of selling you something instead of making you want to fight and win this war against fascism."[45]

During his long days at sea in 1944, radio proved a mixed blessing for Guthrie. It was not *all* unbearable, and occasionally he would admit to a grudging satisfaction with at least some of the programming. As he wrote to Marjorie: "We hear some good radio programs and some good old folk songs over here. The old things are good, but where they try to go modern and commercial I writhe in my skin."[46] While he accepted and valued the medium's capacity for maintaining communion even across the ocean waves, he still sensed a lost opportunity, perhaps even a betrayal of radio's original potential: "The songs are slushy and dont speak for you nor for us, yet it is a noise and it comes from the place you live in and this reminds me of you. Someday maybe the radio will sing songs that speak for both of us, we away, you at home, and then the dreams of the inventor will come a bit closer to coming true."[47] It was during a period of shore leave in London, in July 1944, that Guthrie was invited to sing on BBC program *The Children's Hour*, which introduced a segment of the British population to his anticapitalist ballad "Pretty Boy Floyd."[48] He had a soft spot for the BBC. Not only had the state-owned, noncommercial corporation broadcast Lomax's antifascist ballad opera *The Martins and the Coys* (with Guthrie in a lead role), while no US network would touch it, but also, as Guthrie told Marjorie, the BBC didn't "try to sell you a wild axe handle every few minutes."[49]

In December 1944, Guthrie managed to secure what would become one of his last contracts with a commercial radio station—a weekly fifteen-minute spot on New York's WNEW, *Ballad Gazette*, which he introduced with "This Land Is Your Land." On the show's first broadcast Guthrie declared defiantly: "I could hire out to the other side, the big-money side, and get several dollars every week just to quit singing my own kind of songs and to sing the kind that knock you down. . . . But I decided a long time ago that I'd starve to death before I'd sing any such songs as that. The radio waves and your jukeboxes and your movies and your song books are already loaded down and running over with such no-good songs as that anyhow."[50] The spot lasted only twelve weeks before conflicts over censorship led to Guthrie's departure: the management refused to allow him to broadcast his proletarian anthem "When I Get Home," which he had written especially for the show. Mistaken in his belief that WNEW was "owned by Patterson McCormick," the anticommunist proprietors of the *New York Daily News*, he fumed that "their whole way of thinking is a fascist one."[51] Guthrie asserted that "their system of censorship protects Franco, Churchill and Hitler, and puts the chains of slavery on the microphones and the legs of the people."[52] Although he was wrong about the station's ownership and perhaps a bit hyperbolic about the reach of the network's editorial policy, he was gathering enough evidence to substantiate his claims, given the relentless turn toward post–Popular Front purging and reaction in the broadcast industry.

Within a year, Guthrie was in the army, writing to Marjorie wistfully from his base at Scott Field, Illinois, about what may have been a literal or a metaphorical encounter:

> A little brown cricket
> Sings in the corner here
> In back of a broke down
> Old wrecked radio
> He sings these words
> To all his world and soul,
> "I'm singing my loudest
> To fill your radio!"[53]

This fragment harkened back to an allegory that Guthrie had written in January 1941, about a "certain old cricket back where I come from that used to sing me off to sleep of a night and wake me right up early next morning"—a cricket that would sing no song but the one he wanted to sing.[54] Whether or not the singing cricket was a representation of Guthrie himself (as Ed Cray believes), or Lead Belly (as both Joe Klein and Robert Shelton suggested), it was clear that he did the job that so many radio singers appeared to be avoiding—getting into the "rot" and singing to make it better: "Crickets sing in under chunks of old rotten wood. . . . Anywhere there's anything rotten. This is because, you might not believe, but this is a warm place. This is good fertilizer for this kind of singing. Erosion, mold, rot, decay, damp, crooked work, lies, broke promises, profit snatching, you will hear him singing around all of this."[55]

Implicitly, you would not hear such a cricket "singing around all of this" on a commercial station at the end of World War II and at the dawn of the Cold War. By the early 1950s, Guthrie appears to have lost his faith in radio as an instrument of progressive change (his valedictory project having been his venereal disease awareness songs for a Columbia University broadcast in the summer of 1949). It had all seemed so different in 1940, the year of his arrival in New York. Back then, to repeat his hopeful analogy, music could have made "a radio out of a man"—the dial would be "his head" and he could just sing "according to how he's a feeling." The intervening years had proved that singing one's feelings was a much more difficult enterprise than he had imagined—at least on the radio, in the midst of the Cold War, and with the remnants of the Popular Front lying in tatters before the victorious "Advertising Front" in those ascendant years of the American Century.

7

Ingrid Bergman's "Fonograft"

In an undated notebook entry sometime in the late 1940s, Guthrie made an observation that is highly revealing for what it demonstrates about the impact of media technology upon him as a modern artist and thinker. Since "all art is nothing more than being able to enter into and in some way portray all of the different states of mind, emotions, moods, feelings, and all," he writes, "then it is like a radio set." Then again, for the artist, the same "care and attention should be given to looking after bodily health as [to] keeping a delicate movie camera or television outfit up in good repair or else the recording nor the projecting would be true."[1] The ease with which Guthrie taps into these various communicative arenas—radio, cinema, and even at such a technological dawn, television—indicates his awareness that media technology could offer the most fertile imagery for making a point in contemporary terms.

Guthrie's similes raise another important issue. His integration of all three of these media reflects a perhaps more troubling process of integration that had been playing itself out since the early decades of the twentieth century and that still has enormous repercussions for us all. As Douglas Gomery observes, Hollywood studios had been quick to seize control of the music publishing business as the film industry developed, so that by 1929 "over 90 percent of the popular music in America was being generated by music publishers owned by Warners, Paramount, RCA, or Loew's."[2] The corporate control went well beyond publishing, with media conglomerates reaching further and deeper into the cultural landscape. Steve Wurtzler pays attention to the "process through which individual corporations gained interest in multiple media forms," systems, properties, research and development, and human resources. By 1930, for instance, "RCA held substantial interests in consumer sound equipment sales, but it also controlled several important radio stations, NBC's two radio networks, the film studio RKO and its chain of movie theaters, and Victor's phonograph recording and manufacturing facilities as well as its exclusive contracts with performers." By the late 1920s, most of the studios had "forged institutional relationships with various entertainment interests across media lines, extending their financial interests and control well beyond the nation's movie studios and theaters."[3] Edward Comentale adds another element to the equation: Madison Avenue, by which the "new forces of technology (cinema, phonograph, radio, etc.)" were "bound to new forces of . . . commercial marketing (advertising, publishing, synergy, etc.)," Michael Denning's ultimately triumphant "Advertising Front."[4]

There was thus some good reason for Guthrie, in his repeated diatribes, to tie together "fake magazines, fake moving pictures that talk at the same time, and fake phonograft records, fake Hollywood, fake Broadway, [and] fake Tin Pan Alley junk," at least insofar as it showed his awareness of these interconnections within the culture industries.[5] It would logically follow that he should also tie them together as he outlined his solution to the problem of capitalist control of those same industries. As he wrote in an article for the *Sunday Worker* entitled "Me . . . and Ingrid": "When the workers own and control their own movie sets and studios, own their theaters and radios, then we can have real facts of life played and acted for us by artists even more capable, more social conscious than the ones we got now."[6]

In spite of Guthrie's concerns about the conglomerate control of the culture industries, as well as his obvious debt to the "folk process"—the handing down of songs from generation to generation that was part of his home background—it is a fact that commercially produced records were the primary source of his musical education. As Comentale observes, the advent of cheap, commercially reproduced records took the mimetic process "to a whole new level. . . . Musicians honed their craft through records, and the average farmhouse was crammed full of spinning black discs, giving listeners a chance to try out the new attitudes and styles engraved upon them."[7]

Ed Cray recounts how, in Pampa, Guthrie fell in musically with his future brother-in-law, Matt Jennings: "Woody was practicing guitar, Jennings said, trying to master 'the Carter Family lick' shaped by Maybelle Carter on a series of RCA Victor shellac records. Because 'he wanted to do all the runs,' Jennings explained, Guthrie listened to the records repeatedly in Shorty Harris's drugstore, imitating exactly what he heard."[8] In so doing, Guthrie was extending a long-established chain of reliance on commercially recorded sources, since the Carter Family themselves had acquired much of *their* repertoire from recordings by the likes of Vernon Dalhart, Riley Puckett, and numerous popular performers.[9]

When Guthrie and Maxine Crissman began to assemble their repertoire for the *Woody and Lefty Lou* program on KFVD, they were no less indebted to records and other commercial sources. Peter La Chapelle has analyzed the bulk of their program material and has arrived at some telling statistics. Out of their KFVD repertoire of some 272 separate songs, the origins of 155 have been "firmly verified." Out of these, "more than three-fifths, or 62 percent, were songs whose tunes or lyrics, or both, had been previously recorded commercially or printed as commercial sheet music." Of the remaining verifiable songs, "only 14 percent" were unrecorded folk ballads "that Guthrie or Crissman likely heard from old-timers, relatives, or other folk performers." La Chapelle concludes that "Guthrie and Crissman's KFVD repertoire demonstrates just how tenuous the distinctions were by the 1930s between 'folklore,' that vestige of a supposedly pristine preindustrial culture, and 'poplore,' a term Archie Green has applied to folklife material and traditions 'spawned by mass media.'"[10]

The extent of Guthrie's indebtedness to the recordings from which he learned certainly problematizes his frequent lashing out against the pernicious influence of the recording industry. Rather than admitting a recording's potential to spawn new musicians and heighten the performatory benchmark (as had been his own case), he tended instead to fixate upon the detrimental impact of records on live music and musicians' livelihoods. He wrote in his "Woody Sez" column for the *People's World*:

> Use to be when a musician walked in a saloon he was cinched to
> make a good stake, 'cause he was welcome.

Now days the bartender says "no music wanted—we got Bang Crosby right over there on the electric fonograft—" an the crowd roars. An the musician sleeps under a bridge.[11]

Later, when Alan Lomax, Guthrie, and Pete Seeger were editing their *Hard Hitting Songs for Hard-Hit People*, Guthrie crowed about the organic, noncommercial purity of the book's contents—it would "reap the nation's harvest of the songs of the working people . . . and it'll bring new life back to the soil."[12] What Guthrie failed to acknowledge was the extent to which even this volume of songs relied on Lomax's patient examination of commercially released sources. As the book's eventual publisher, Irwin Silber, explained, while many of the songs were drawn from Lomax's Archive of American Folk Song, others "came from commercial recordings issued by the major record companies, RCA, Columbia, Decca. . . . This, too, was a huge undertaking for Lomax, because it involved going through the files of these companies, listening, culling, copying, from out-of-print, highly breakable 78 rpm discs."[13] In the compiler's postscript, Lomax himself proclaimed his debt to those songs that would have been lost altogether had they not been preserved by the commercial labels: "When, in the Spring of 1937, I ransacked the files of Columbia, Victor and Decca record companies for anything that had a folk flavor, I found not only the early Blue Grass, not only urban blues tradition, I found scores of songs of protest and social comment by urban and country folk singers."[14]

Guthrie claimed in the book's introduction that "you don't ever hear these songs played and sung on the nickel boxes in the saloons and pimp joints."[15] By "nickel boxes" he was referring to what Denning calls "the public phonograph, the juke box (which took 60 percent of record sales in 1939)."[16] And while it would take an enormous survey to determine the truth or falsehood of Guthrie's claim, his strident objections to the influence of the "fonograft" put him at odds with his own musical origins, his modes of musical acquisition, and his professional desires as a recording artist (which included more than once the hopes of securing lucrative commercial contracts). Moreover, they belie his own status as a fairly studious record collector, which can be seen through a perusal of the remains of his personal collection housed in the Woody Guthrie Archives: "Guthrie himself annotated many of the record jackets, noting how he acquired the record, the date he received the album, and his thoughts on either the artist or the lyrics."[17]

When it came to the prospect of developing his own recording career, Guthrie could be positively giddy in reporting even most the tenuous hint of a possible contract, not least—and quite understandably—for the financial rewards that it might bring. Hence his boast to his Oklahoma family about the remuneration that would be sure to flow in from the Weavers' recording of his first Dust Bowl ballad, "So Long, It's Been Good to Know Yuh": "So if & when another dustybound hobo squeezes his way into your backdoore with a fistful of Hundred dollar bills and tosses them all around over your floor and furniture, the traveler and the dust both will be me."[18]

As a result of such potential windfalls, Guthrie could be highly jealous over the issue of copyright, not only resisting the Almanac Singers' decision to credit the group collectively as the authors of their songs but also making sure to redress copyright infringements of his other songs, such as "Oklahoma Hills." Guthrie wrote to Marjorie of his surprise upon hearing the song played on a diner's juke box, recorded by his cousin Jack Guthrie, who had brazenly claimed authorship: "'Oklahoma Hills' is there in the Library of Congress (typed black) book. You can look it up and see that the words are identical. This typing and filing by the Library constitutes a patent and a Copyright and I performed it [in] public hundreds of times under my own name. So just where Mr. Jack gets this idea that he can just sort of take it is beyond my reach."[19]

Despite his own attempts—and sometime successes—at securing commercial recording contracts (as well as his euphoria when the royalty checks came in), for Guthrie, the worst symptom of commercialism in music was the inauthenticity that was supposedly its hallmark. Nothing commercially produced could be "authentic," by definition. Hence the repeated epithets—"the fake and the phoney"—that Guthrie flung at the output of Broadway and Tin Pan Alley, as opposed to the integrity of what he called "people's music"— folk music.[20] In his configuration, the "truth" of folk expression, its inherent authenticity, was in a bitter contest with the deceptions of Tin Pan Alley and the cabal supposedly behind it—the "big shots" who wanted "'illusions,' 'fronts,' 'glamour' and 'oommmph,'" as opposed to "the working people" who wanted "'facts,' 'truth,' and credit for their talents, their fights, and the

work they've done." The commercial culture industries had been highly negligent in their educational duties, Guthrie charged, keeping the truth from
the hungry masses: "Strikers have been blowed to the ground with machine
guns all over the country, and union organizers have been murdered in big
numbers; but where is it on the stage, screen, radio or the records?"[21] The
conspiracy of silence fronted by the popular entertainment industry was
nothing less than that—a conspiracy, deliberately crafted and reliant upon
a brand of mind control that would not look out of place in Orwell's *1984*:
"He hypnotizes you ten times a day and he even hires people to work on your
inner mind, while you are at work, at home, at play, at school, or asleep. He
uses music and songs as a weapon against you."[22]

As such recent scholars as Comentale, Richard Peterson, Elijah Wald, and
Pamela Fox have shown, the concept of "authenticity" is at best slippery and
at worst dubious when discussing any supposedly traditional form of music
in an age of mechanical reproduction, commercial or otherwise.[23] What
Comentale calls "the cagey markers of authenticity" often extend beyond the
music itself to the personae or masks of those who are known to write and
perform it.[24] Fox, for one, has examined country music as an arena "almost
exclusively associated with Southern white rustic or working-class imagery,
lowbrow cultural taste, and artists who convincingly represent both in their
personal histories."[25] The word "represent" carries great weight here, and by
any stretch of the imagination—regardless of the genre in which one attempts
to fit his songs—Guthrie's "representations" of himself fit this bill, particularly
in his "Woody Sez" columns, in his exaggerated Okie dialect for the Library
of Congress recordings, and in his personal relations with middle-class
colleagues from whom he wished to distinguish himself, such as the other
Almanac Singers. His biography reflects numerous challenges to such representations, be it *People's World* editor Al Richmond's charge that Guthrie "put
on like he was less sophisticated than he really was," Bess Hawes's recollection
of his carefully hidden "hyper-literacy," Moses Asch's portrait of him as a
"put-on . . . the actor acting out the role of the folksinger from Oklahoma" for
the Library of Congress sessions,[28] or Lomax's stated belief that Guthrie could
"write a ballad in five minutes that will fool a folk lore expert."

The question of "authenticity" partly accounts for Guthrie's increasing
discomfort with what he saw as an overly cozy relationship between the

recording and film industries. A Hollywood career was tantamount to a political sellout, at least for a folk musician:

> I feel good to see artists the flavor and stature of Earl Robinson, Burl
> Ives, Josh White, and others, being used in Hollywood, but I feel a
> bit sad when I think of the billions of dollars worth of uncounted
> good that these same three could have done by giving their days
> and nights to the workers that need them most. I did not especially
> think that the picture, "Smoky" in which Burl sang "Blue Tail Fly,"
> "Foggy Foggy Dew," and "On Top of Old Smoky" could be called a
> step forward for the working class. Hollywood will dish out some big
> piles of dough to put this idea into the heads of millions of workers
> that Burl is thusly demonstrating the daily life of the militant ballad
> singer.[27]

Yet, as a recording artist, Guthrie himself owed an immense debt to the film industry. His first studio album, *Dust Bowl Ballads*, which Wayne Hampton rightly calls "one of the most influential recordings in the twen- tieth century" and—perhaps on shakier ground—"the first serious produc- tion of social protest material," was effectively a spinoff "package" on the heels of John Ford's enormously successful film *The Grapes of Wrath*.[28] As Denning notes: "*Dust Bowl Ballads* stands as a counterpoint to *The Grapes of Wrath* in several ways. First, Victor agreed to record *Dust Bowl Ballads* to capitalize on the popularity of the film. Moreover, unlike most 'hillbilly' and 'race' records, which were released as single 78 rpm records with one song on each side, Victor packaged it as a double album: two three-record sets (twelve sides) with a booklet by Guthrie explaining the songs. Steinbeck himself offered a widely quoted endorsement of Guthrie."[29] *Dust Bowl Ballads* was one of a number of albums concurrently released in 1940 reflecting record labels' new trend in piggybacking off the popularity of film. Others included Josh White's *Chain Gang* (Columbia) and Lead Belly's *The Midnight Special and Other Prison Songs* (RCA Victor), both of which closely followed the release of the Paul Muni film *I Am a Fugitive from a Chain Gang*.[30]

For his part, Guthrie appeared ambivalent about his foundational debt to the Hollywood studios (as well as the studios' rendering of traditional music styles). As he explained to Lomax in a discussion of the song "Goin' Down the Road Feelin' Bad," which was used in Ford's film, "In the picture, they sing it pretty classical. I don't know whether the Okies and the hobos will recognize it or not, but then I'm not worried about that because I don't think that they'll be spendin' a quarter to get to see a bunch of grapes."[31] Guthrie in fact claimed that Ford had used the song on his recommendation:

> When I was out in California they was a shooting 2 of the Steinbeck pictures, "Of Mice and Men," and "The Grapes of Wrath." And they packed me off down there to the studios, I forgot the name of it, and they set me down on a carpet in a directors harum there, and said, Now what we want you to do is to sing a song, just don't even think, and without thinking, just haul off and sing the very first song that hits your mind—one that if a crowd of 100 pure blood Okies was to hear it, 90 of 'em would know it.
>
> This was the first song that popped to my mind, so without thinking, I sung it. They used the song in the picture, "Grapes of Wrath," which had more thinkin' in it than 99% of the celluloid that we're tangled up in the moving pictures today.[32]

Notwithstanding his ostentatious disrespect for Hollywood fakery (exempting, apparently, *The Grapes of Wrath*), Guthrie maintained that in writing "Tom Joad" he in fact owed more to the film than to the novel. It is unclear whether he even read the book. Ed Cray recounts a conversation between Guthrie and Pete Seeger:

> "Victor wants me to write a song about Tom Joad, about *The Grapes of Wrath*," Guthrie explained.
> "Have you read the book?" Seeger asked.
> "No, but I saw the movie."[33]

Cray claims that Guthrie was "downwind from the truth" in denying his debt to the book. What Cray relegates to a footnote in Guthrie's biography deserves to be magnified, for it sheds light on the possible dominance of film over literary fiction in Guthrie's estimation, as well as Guthrie's own keen desire to develop a profile in film: "Guthrie's hint he was basing the ballad solely on the movie is disingenuous, a bit of his playing the unlettered country boy. In a 1971 interview, Will Geer insisted, 'He read *The Grapes of*

Wrath. I'm quite positive he did. The picture wasn't out. He read *The Grapes of Wrath*.'"[34]

Guthrie insisted that any artist "who sticks any too close to the cut and dried Hollywood tradition" is part of "an actual outright conspiracy to keep the peoples culture away from them."[35] Yet if modernism's greatest desire was indeed for "communication and the many forms it took" (to repeat Goble), then, for Guthrie, desire for the cinema was even stronger than his desire for the telephone—a desire that began in his childhood. In one of the highly elaborated biographical jottings in his KFVD songbook, he positioned the impact of film against other sources of knowledge. The point to be made here is not about the truth or falsehood of his claim, but rather about the importance of cinema to him even at the earliest periods of his life: "Most of my education come from the picture shows. I figgered that was all right cause I didnt have a chance when I was young to learn much."[36]

Guthrie's objectification of Hollywood as a site of his own desires—which he took such frequent pains to deny—is abundantly clear. It is particularly instructive to examine his response to Lomax's question, on the Library of Congress recordings, about the bigotry faced by the Dust Bowl migrants in California. Lomax asks him, as an Oklahoman, "What did you have to fall back on, to kind of keep your pride up all this time?" First, Guthrie mentions "some of the biggest oil fields in the world." Then he turns to some of the other "things we've got down there to be proud of":

> First place, we've got some of the greatest movie stars in the world
> come from the state of Oklahoma. . . . One of the best-known movie
> stars in the world today is Kay Francis. She come from Oklahoma
> City. And another one that we got to be proud of is one of the most,
> I guess, one of the best-known and well-liked fellers in the whole
> movie star business that ever was, Lon Chaney. Lon Chaney come
> from Oklahoma, and we've got Lon Chaney to be proud of. . . .
> And to go just a little bit further, I think that Oklahoma claims the
> greatest and the best-known and the best-loved and best-liked movie
> star that ever lived on this earth.[37]

This was, of course, Guthrie's hero, Will Rogers, of whom he goes on to sing in the recording:

> We loved Will Rogers,
> We loved his smile,
> We went to the movies Will Rogers to see.
> We followed him now for many a mile
> From old Oklahoma to Los Angeles.[38]

Guthrie's choice of markers for Oklahoman pride indicates that not even he was immune to the cultural phenomenon of celebrity, which, as P. David Marshall notes, emerged "from the twinned discourses of modernity: democracy and capitalism." Celebrity movie stars, Marshall points out, are ordinary individuals with varying degrees of talent who have emerged into wide public consciousness not only through their appearance on celluloid but also, and perhaps more importantly, from the "staging ground" of publicity. The publicity machine works to one ultimate goal: "enlarging the meaning of any actor in the public sphere and expanding the audience's knowledge of the celebrity's personal life."[39] Even more than Will Rogers and the other stars of Oklahoma, the epitome of movie-star allure for Guthrie was the Swedish actress Ingrid Bergman, upon whom he fixated in a highly creative manner. Billy Bragg and Wilco first brought to light Guthrie's highly sexualized, double-entendre-driven ode "Ingrid Bergman" (1949), which they recorded on the first volume of *Mermaid Avenue* and which draws on the decision by the Italian director, Roberto Rossellini, to cast Bergman in his film *Stromboli* (1950):

> Ingrid Bergman, you're so perty,
> You'd make any mountain quiver.
> You'd make my fire fly from the crater,
> Ingrid Bergman.
>
> This old mountain, it's been waiting
> All its life for you to work it,
> For your hand to touch the hard rock,
> Ingrid Bergman, Ingrid Bergman.[40]

Guthrie was clearly captivated by the hysterically publicized scandal involving Bergman's affair with Rossellini, which ended her marriage to Swedish doctor Petter Lindstrom and led to her being condemned on the floor of the US Senate as "an apostle of degradation."[41] The orchestrated intrigues of the Hollywood gossip machine prompted Guthrie to moan into his notebooks:

> It's Ingrid, Sweet Ingrid,
> Make up your pretty mind;
> One way or the other, decide, decide!
> One day its your Doctor,
> Next day your Director—
> I sit here and itch in my britches
> I scratch my head till my skin turns red!
> Ingrid, make up your sweet mind![42]

Guthrie's *Sunday Worker* article "Me . . . and Ingrid" reveals the most about his ambivalence toward Hollywood, even in the context of his fixation on Bergman. After contradicting his claim elsewhere that most of his "education come from the picture shows" (he now says: "I didn't have the money when I was a kid in Oklahoma"), he explains: "I was on the road too much singing Union songs on the West Coast, then I sang all over New York for a year or so and was always too lost to think about movies" (another untruth revealed through his other writings, which indicate that he thought quite a lot about movies in these years). If he is to believed, his most consistent periods of film-watching were during his merchant marine tours ("seen the movies they showed aboard the troop ships") and in the army ("went most every night for fifteen cents to see an eleven cent show"). Upon his discharge he "came home, and somehow, kept on going to the movies." His marriage to Marjorie had meant that, while she was rehearsing or teaching dance, he was subject to "lots of waiting," causing him "to drift into lots of show houses. Picture shows, we call them where I come from. I guess you New Yorkers would call them Bergman Houses."[43]

Guthrie turns to Bergman as a synecdoche for the blanket coverage of Hollywood over all of America, not that he is wholly opposed to it. Far from it:

> I used to throw an ice pick at the movie list and go to the one it stuck
> in, till I hit Bergman in *Saratoga Trunk*, then, *Notorious*, then, *Joan
> of Lorraine*, and one alongside of Bing which I forgot the name of.

I tied a red bandana around my eyes and walked for one hour straight, then going into the Bergman that was nearest where I stood.

One night I found myself in a worse twist than the Republican Congress with no program. I took off my blindfold at 42nd and Broadway and seen her name in lights on four different movie shows. I counted nine average citizens who had gone into fits of indecision, the worst of which, I guess, was me.

You have seen pictures in papers showing jaywalkers getting run down by walking through thick traffic looking whapper-jawed and crooked. Well, both the pedestrian and the driver in several sample cases have confessed that they were looking at Ingrid lights when the wrecks took place. I doubt if things have cleared up much even to date.

It is not until his conclusion that Guthrie makes his political point—not only about the workers owning and controlling "their own movie sets and studios . . . their theatres and radios," but also about the critical waste of talent in the Hollywood machine:

Ingrid Bergman is one of the best, I can't doubt that, but I've seen her in oodles and gobs of pictures now, and this one play. And I say she never has had a part that frees her enough to make full use of her gifts and talents.

I doubt if I'll ever see her in any parts as real or as honest as the slum pictures that Sylvia Sidney did a few years back. The movies are sewed up too tight by our bankers these days to fight or to ridicule our landlords. No star the brand of Sylvia Sidney, Greta Garbo, Merle Oberon, Louise Rainer, or Ingrid is going to be hired by the big lords to speak out against the lords themselves.[44]

In spite of such diatribes (and even before the iron grip of McCarthyism on the film industry), Guthrie was certainly aware that some of his strongest and closest political allies were to be found in Hollywood, including the actors and activists Will Geer, Eddie Albert, and John Garfield (the latter of whom once pulled down Guthrie's trousers in a "mock tussle" at a public benefit for Spanish Civil War veterans, revealing to "a fair number of

Hollywood's elite" that Guthrie wore no underwear).[45] Guthrie recalled how he and Geer had "organized caravans of Hollywood people" to join picket lines, "and we hauled the strikers and families into big Hollywood sets and studios, and staged a big country dance demonstration on the set of *The Lost Horizon* and *Hurricane*, as well as to house parties of naked vulgarity to win the passionate souls of the Hollywood businessmen."[46] Indeed, as a committed political activist based in Los Angeles from 1937 to 1939, Guthrie was immersed in a progressive milieu of major dimensions, centering on the film industry. Denning points out that "Hollywood studios were without doubt the central cultural apparatus on the West Coast," with the California labor movement dominated by the CIO, "left-wing artists, writers, and craftspeople in the Hollywood studios."[47] Not for nothing would the sinister tentacles of the House Un-American Activities Committee make their first reach for these same studios in 1947.

For all Guthrie's anti-Hollywood ranting, he maintained a degree of faith in the capacity of film to inspire new generations of progressive political activists. After a disappointing evening watching Betty Grable in *The Dolly Sisters* (1945), he wrote to Marjorie of his "big hope for the salvaging of our stage and studio," with their "Grableized delusions of dangling pretty bodies in the eyes of hungry souls." His vision for the cinema was as utopian as could be expected from the architect of the "better world a-comin'" who looked to the "new theater and dance groups of a real progressive kind" to infiltrate and ultimately win over the Hollywood studio system: "Me, personally, I find that I have two faiths, one is that the film makers have gone as far as they can go in this bad hypnotic aimless direction and the people will yowl and yell and stay away from such shows. And my biggest faith is in the new crop of show folks that have not yet eaten all of the fuzz off the boss man's rug."[48]

It was with such faith in store that Guthrie boasted in 1944 to Marjorie's mother, Aliza Greenblatt, of a potential project to have "several short movies (12 minute) films to be used in schools and over television programs."[49] No record has emerged of this project's having come to fruition, but Guthrie was still setting his hopes on inaugurating a major film profile two years later when he pitched a proposal to the producer-director Irving Lerner, who would go on to work on such productions as *Muscle Beach*, *Spartacus*, *Custer of the West,* and *New York, New York,* as well as the television series *Ben Casey.* Guthrie had appeared briefly in Lerner's film *To Hear Your Banjo Play* (1946), a short documentary written by Lomax, narrated by Pete Seeger, and shot under the working title *Banjo Pickin' Boy.*[50] (It is open to question whether Guthrie had drooled over Lerner's previous documentary, *Swedes in America,* starring Ingrid Bergman.) Seeing a preview of *Banjo Pickin' Boy* had "opened up all kinds of new hope" in Guthrie, as he told Lerner: "I always did hope, somehow, that I would live long enough to see this very thing done with the camera and the mike, and all of the other tools of your trade."[51]

Guthrie's proposal was a film to be called "Greasy String," with its protagonist a wandering ballad singer like Guthrie himself, traveling "from coast to coast" across the landscape of American modernity to the musical backdrop of "some simple ballad, like 'Goin' Down This Road,' or 'This Land Is Made For You and Me' . . . up and down the skid rows across the streets from packing plants, the biggest factories, up and down the streets of the biggest industrial cities, and the little dots not big enough to be fly specks on maps." Whether or not he was consciously aware of it, Guthrie was effectively proposing the cinematic treatment of *Bound for Glory* that would not appear on the screen until thirty years later: "He would travel by box car, by cushion, by ferry, by truck, by limousine, jalopy, by shoe leather, and would cross fields, orchards, rivers, mountains, swamps, and all of the uplands and the lowlands and the downlands. When by himself, the fight would be against the weather itself and against every kind of bug, animal, germ, and his own feelings of the lost kinds and the found kinds."[52]

Most importantly, Lerner would have at the ready a main character molded out of the mythic clay that Guthrie, Lomax, and Guthrie's other image-makers had been fashioning for at least the past seven years: "a mystery to everybody except his own self," popping up almost magically "at strikes, on picket lines, at workers meets . . . and the very next time you see him he is out walking along with his old penny pencil and his sweaty nickel tablet again." Crucial to the characterization would be the protagonist's incorruptibility in the face of financial and material temptations: "He is lectured to on the silliness of living such a footloose existence when the doors of studios, stores, and fancy restaurants, etc., can be constantly opened to him. He does not say why he goes on, why he passes all of these things by."[53]

In sum, it was a story positively aching to be caught on celluloid, incomplete in its transmission as a novel, and deserving of wide dissemination as a film to be crafted by "more expert scriptmen" than Guthrie. He offered Lerner a wealth of cinematographic and directorial possibilities:

> You can see here the thousands of good chances to bring in your
> flashbacks and pannings. Your mike and camera would be free to
> bring in all of the sounds and echoes of a whole people living in a
> world of work, sweat, tears, and rejoicings. . . . I am writing you this
> because I've always wanted to do something like it. With your ear
> and eye and sense of visioning, the parts I've left empty could be
> filled in. The actual script would almost have to write its own self as
> we shot and sung from place to place.[54]

Guthrie's envisioned film treatment was never realized in his lifetime, although as early as August 1960, Sid Gleason—who had taken to hosting the ailing Guthrie and his folksinging acolytes in her New Jersey apartment— was reporting to an English correspondent that a film script of *Bound for Glory* was in circulation (she hoped the main role would go to Jack Elliott).[55] In the end, the Hal Ashby film starring David Carradine was released in 1976, winning Academy Awards the following year: Best Cinematography and Best Musical Adaptation. (This film also marked the industry's first use of Garrett Brown's Steadicam technology, which has made possible the smooth filming of action sequences across uneven terrain.)[56] In choosing the television actor Carradine to play Guthrie (Carradine was widely known for the hit series *Kung Fu*), Ashby bypassed a range of established Hollywood film actors including Dustin Hoffman, Jack Nicholson, Robert De Niro, Richard Dreyfuss, and Al Pacino, as well as musician-singers such as Kris Kristofferson, Johnny Cash, Glen Campbell, James Taylor, Art Garfunkel, and even Guthrie's son Arlo. (Apparently Bob Dylan "declined the part but offered to direct the film.") Carradine had to work extra hard to convince the United Artists brass that a television actor could do the job.[57] While Carradine in fact already had a major film under his belt—Martin Scorsese's *Boxcar Bertha* (1972)—as well as considerable stage experience, his association with television proved a real obstacle.

The history of television's stigma is long and complicated, but it is a subject that is also germane to Guthrie's fraught engagement with the mass media. As with so many facets of Guthrie's life, not many people are aware of his intense interest in the developing medium of television, another source of great ambivalence for him. As a futuristic certainty, television was in Guthrie's mind as early as 1940. Among his precious few writings on the subject are the notebook entries indicating that already he was envisaging the hijacking of the technology, with all its educational promise, by the hegemonic forces of the corporate class: "Two schools of flash would start up I reckon and there'd be one that showed you flower pots and fruit bowls and 5th Avenue shop windows and one that showed you . . . the Ghetto and the Skid Rows and the kids crowding the trucks off of the streets a trying to find someplace to play." He was already attuned to the potential for media manipulation of the democratic process, the broadcast industry's part in the buying of elections—and perhaps teleportation to boot: "Yes I look forward to television. I look forward to the day and time you can sell your vote by television and lose a election by it and I bet they already got it to where television will work but you just ain't got the money to get it with. . . . Say talking about this television, I look for it to put the busses and r.r. out of business. I'm dickering with a electric booth you can stand in and broadcast yourself wherever you want to go—just quit being there and be here—or vice virtue."[58]

In spite of his skepticism, Guthrie was by 1949 clearly smitten with the prospect of launching a joint career with Marjorie in television. His fingers were crossed for her, as he reported to his Oklahoma family: "Marjorie is trying out for a Television job today, and she will get a Couple of Hundred a Week if it goes through. She will be in charge of a bunch of dancers, to make up new steps for them, show them how to work on the stagespace available, and work out new dances with them every week." His own sights were set on a purely commercial comedy—apparently of the kind that would later emerge as the long-running country music review *Hee Haw* (1969–93): "I'm trying out tomorrow (Friday) Afternoon for the leading role in an Ozark Mountain Country Store Hillbilly Comedy in one of the lighter veins. (Hope for me). I'm holding out for $300 a week if it goes through the Acceptors Offices. . . . I'm an old store owner that plays a fiddle. I don't know my own name in the thing, yet, so far. Visitors come around the store every week, and I josh with them and shoot the bs in general."[60] To his mother-in-law, Guthrie elaborated on what such an opportunity would bring both to his financial security and to his development as an actor, a prospect that was obviously dear to his heart: "It will pay good if I get the part, and I will play the leading role, which will give me a chance to show people that I can get out of the mob scenes and backgrounds, and play closer up towards the lights and cameras. I love this kind of work better than a dog loves fresh meat. So I hope, and everybody around here is hoping that the thing comes through."[60]

For whatever reason, the thing never came through. Had it done so, it might have proved to be one of the most chilling descents in the history of American folk music. It would also have demonstrated that even the most nominally incorruptible are not always immune to the seductions of celebrity and the remunerative rewards of modern corporate broadcasting. In any event, Guthrie's television profile must remain, like so much else, in the realm of speculation over the unrealized possibilities in a productive, creative life cut brutally short.

8

Dance around
My Atom Fire

If Guthrie's thoughts on Ingrid Bergman, filmmaking, and television have proved an eye-opener to those who thought they knew the Dust Bowl Balladeer, there are more surprises in store. "I am in favor of the use of the Atom Bomb," Guthrie wrote to Marjorie from his army base at Scott Field, Illinois, on August 9, 1945—the day of the Nagasaki bombing. "We have dropped all sorts of notes to tell them ahead that their city has got to be wiped out, so take to your high places."[1] This may come as an unpleasant shock to many not familiar with Guthrie's biography—to those, for instance, who continue to circulate on Facebook the iconic memes of Guthrie the pacifist supported by a caption taken from his "Woody Sez" column: "I would like to see every single soldier on every single side, just take off your helmet, unbuckle your kit, lay down your rifle, and set down at the side of some shady lane, and say, nope, I aint a gonna kill nobody. Plenty of rich folks wants to fight. Give them the guns."[2] It may be unpleasant to those who have recently been enjoying one of the latest of Guthrie's songs to have emerged from the archives into wide circulation:

> My peace, my peace is all I've got and all I've ever known,
> My peace is worth a thousand times more than anything I own.
> I pass my peace around and about 'cross hands of every hue;
> I guess my peace is just about all I've got to give to you.[3]

And it will *certainly* be confounding to those self-declared patriots who have slandered Guthrie with the epithet of "draft-dodger," as great a historical inaccuracy as any that has been purveyed.[4]

139

Peace was certainly not all that Guthrie had "ever known." His relationship to warfare was so conflicted that it presents one of the muddiest threads in his biography, but it must be recognized as at least partly the result of the enormous and sometimes rapid-fire technological and political changes that marked the mid-twentieth century in the United States and abroad. His initial response to the atomic bomb put him on the same page as someone he would soon grow to despise, President Truman. As he explained to Marjorie, "The Atom Bomb and a short war will kill fewer men on all sides than TNT and a long war."[5] Some possibly unwelcome attention has already been paid to the rhetorical violence that he frequently employed—in contrast to his slogans for peace—particularly in his wartime writings.[6] Committed songwriters, Guthrie said, were "like guns and cannons" needing to be "polished, oiled, loaded, and loved."[7] As he boasted in his notebook in 1944:

> MY BIG GIBSON
> GUITAR HAS GOT A
> SIGN I PAINTED ON
> IT, SAYS, "THIS MACHINE
> KILLS FASCISTS."
> And it means just
> what it says too.[8]

Two important developments in Guthrie's private life appear to have compounded his war ardor, in addition to the about-face of the American Left in the wake of Pearl Harbor. The first was his marriage into a Jewish family and the second was the birth of his daughter Cathy into a world menaced by the rise and advance of Nazism. As Guthrie wrote to Marjorie, he was determined to inject "hate and murder and killing" into his songs "by the truck loads. I think of what fascism is trying to do to you and to your relatives, to me and mine, and seeing what they've done and are doing in the nations they've already overrun, it makes me even fuller of hate for them."[9] He told Marjorie that any money *he* made would go to buying "lots of guns and tanks and bullets" for their daughter.[10]

The years 1942–45 saw a snowballing effect in Guthrie's writing as he focused increasingly on the part that murderous technology would play in delivering the world from the grip of fascism. He recycled in song after song his jeering threats to Hitler, Mussolini, and Hirohito. Whether they took the form of "All You Fascists Bound to Lose," "Round and Round Hitler's Grave," or "You're Gone, You Fascists, You're Gone," the instruments of victory were still the same:

> Machine guns are barking in fox holes around
> And the bombs are busting all over the ground
> Our tanks are plowing and rolling along
> And it looks like you Nazis are [a] long time gone.[11]

In essays he laid out patiently the process by which the democracies were marching toward the glories of victory: "Guns in soldiers hands win it foxhole by foxhole, hand grenades and shells win it inch by inch, foot by foot. Planes bomb our way clear. Bombs plow our road on ahead."[12] In daybook jottings at sea he muttered about the need for more advanced war technology: "Ships must be built to go faster and carry more."[13] In letters home from shore-leave ports in Europe, he mocked the inferior state of Axis materiel: "Been seeing lots of torpedoes and Flying Bombs! (They're a joke / But vicious and terribly mean.)"[14] Guthrie's embrace of the god of war had, as ever, everything to do with the ultimate uses to which the lethal technology would be applied:

> The guns that roar and spit out
> fiery death
> The planes and ships that plant
> their seeds of death
> Have been used wrongly lots of
> times before
> But when we win them they
> will miss no more.[15]

Guthrie came to the conclusion, as he wrote in June 1942, "This is a good war and is bringing good changes."[16] But it must be said that the closer he got to scenes of actual wartime destruction—firsthand, as in bombed-out Sicily and London—the darker his descriptions became, and the more effort he was compelled to expend in justifying the rain of fire. A remarkable record is his unfinished novel "Palermo," begun in 1945 and taking up three of his notebooks. The narrative, which sometimes shifts between the first- and third-person point of view as he experiments with perspective, casts Guthrie as a seaman named Pat. Jim Longhi, his real-life companion, becomes "Tony," while the third of the "seamen three" (as Woody called the inseparable wartime trio), Cisco Houston, initially keeps his first name, but by the end of the draft has become "George."[17] A fictitious Sicilian woman named Gracia is also a major character whose main narrative purpose is to convey a militant hatred for the Nazis and fascists on behalf of the Sicilian people.

In Pat's first shipboard view of Palermo, beneath the spectacle of a dogfight between a Luftwaffe Stuka and an RAF Spitfire, the emphasis is on the destruction of a once-beautiful city, made stark by the slanting rays of the setting sun:

> A late afternoon sun was at his back, but it struck down on the front side of the buildings. Fell down on the fronts of crooked, cracked, shelled and bombed walls. The walls, some of them, still stood up as proud as they could. They stood alone and lonesome. Not a house anymore, not even a building anymore. Not even a little room for people here anymore.
>
> Piles of rocks, slabs, iron, lumber, decorations, old statues, had slipped and fell sideways to the ground.
>
> Nothing looked like it meant anything anymore. Everything was a pile of twisted, paralyzed junk.[18]

Walking through what is left of the city, the three seamen are initially confronted with more ghostly images of total destruction. But the people are still there, as Guthrie introduces into the scene what might well be reflections of his own new family of Marjorie and Cathy, transposed onto a canvas of European wreckage: "A man and a woman stood in their bedroom and touched its walls, floors, and searched for things. Pat watched through a shell hole in the wall. They were not old. They were young. The dirt from the room was on them. They talked low and in Italian. By the tones of their words he tried to guess what they were saying. They found a picture of a little baby, torn to pieces, and together they squatted down on the floor to put it together again."[19]

Indeed, children play an increasing role in the narrative, from a filthy little girl with "an old look on her face" playing at adulthood, her eyes "bright with tears as she cried and washed the face of her dolly in the cradle," to the "herds" of little ones flocking around the trio in the street, begging for candy, soap, and cigarettes. Guthrie's description of the Sicilian children—so eerily reminiscent of those he had described in the Hoovervilles of the Depression—unmistakably links them to his own American experience, as does the stench invading Pat's nose. Only this time it is the stench of destruction, of unmaking, rather than the industrial progress—the building up—with which he had normally associated it: "He had smelled this sort of dust before around rock quarries, tunnels, highways, or on other jobs, where there was blasting and firing. The odor is of burnt powder, fine dust, and a funny sweet chemical smell."[20]

However, underlying all the acknowledgment of the terrible price paid, in both human lives and earthly infrastructure, is Guthrie's repeated assertion that it has all been worth it. It is asserted through the description of the resilient children themselves, the joy of the wider population, now liberated from the yoke of fascism, and above all in the gleeful, vengeful fantasies of Gracia, who, with Pat, stumbles on a box of personal trinkets, letters, and postcards abandoned by a fleeing German soldier:

"Hey, flop down here an' help me sort stuff! Here's one from Hamburg!"
"Ballooom!" She pooched out her cheeks.
"Luxemborg!"
"Baloom!"
"Berlin! Hey! Berlin!"
"Booom! Balooom!" She went on. "You keep calling them off. I am dropping big bombs on them. Berlin? Ah! Balooom!" She held her arms out like airplane wings and danced around me as I talked out.[21]

It is Gracia who most explicitly establishes the connection between military destruction and the building of a new, progressive world:

"I could see everything as my bombs exploded! Everywhere!"
"Hmmm."
"I could see the rich people who paid Hitler to fight and kill the workers."

"Some plane you got."

"The bombs made great fires, fires bigger than our whole country here. In their light I could see the whole business! I could see the war in Spain and Franco killing millions of farmers and workers. Just for a penny or two. A little penny or two."

"Another postmark here that is smeared out. Some town." I squinted at the letter.

"Hitler will find all of his factories and all of his cities . . . all smeared out. This is what that post mark is a sign of. And we will smear out all of his robbers, too. I saw all of this in the flash of my bombs." She looked over four or five of the letters and let them drop down across her breasts.[22]

Thus, by the time Guthrie had learned of the unleashing of the atomic bomb, he had seen enough firsthand evidence of what conventional weaponry could achieve. His belief (and relief) that the atomic bomb had shortened the war was shared by many who, like him, would come to revise their opinions upon further reflection. But for now, with Guthrie still in army uniform, the bomb was a subject fit for poetry, for eulogy, as in "Freedom's Fire," which unequivocally beatifies its destructive power:

> We shined our light of freedom on the town of Hiroshima
> We shined our flame on Nagasaki the same
> We melted fascist warlords down from the ice of Yokohama
> I won my world for freedom when I found my freedom's fire.[23]

Not until a redrafting, this time titled "Dance around My Atom Fire" and dated 1948—three years later—did Guthrie offer an explicit injunction against the application that he had previously celebrated so passionately:

> Leader: WARFARE IS NOT THE SETTLEMENT,
>   BLOODSHED IS NOT THE ELEMENT,
>   SHAKE HANDS AND MIX ALL COLORS
> All: DANCE AROUND MY ATOM FIRE.[24]

It is difficult to speculate on what precisely had been working on Guthrie's mind between late 1945, when he was still nestling—sometimes uncomfortably, it must be said—in the bosom of the US Army, and 1948, by which time he was a demobilized veteran gazing into what had become the Cold War. Certainly by March 1946 he was still happy to play with the fascination of atomic physics, as he described the speed with which he, Pete Seeger, and their colleagues in the newly constituted People's Songs organization were able to ship out their introductory letters and bulletins: "This was action of the highest kind, it was fast action, fluid drive, jet propelled, and atom powered with plastic trimmings all around."[25] Exactly a year later, however, the situation had clearly changed. On March 21, 1947—on the same flight to Montreal during which he wrote of the fields below looking like "maps of victory"—he applied the benefits of aerial vision to another song, "My Eyes Do See All over This World," in which he castigates the atom for doing the same work that he had applauded in 1945:

> I see the buildings of our
> United Nations
>   Ten million brothers and
> sisters, boys and girls,
>   I saw our atom wreck
> our civilization
>   My eyes did see yes, yes,
>   All over this world.[26]

Guthrie had also been absorbing paranoid talk of a new menace to pile on top of the atomic woes: germ warfare, which in the heightened atmosphere of the Red Scare was becoming a useful rhetorical tool on both sides of the Cold War (with the United States and the Soviet Union trading charges, countercharges, and threats on an almost daily basis). Only the previous year, in January, the US public had learned that their army's Chemical Warfare Service had been developing biological weapons for the past three years at Fort Detrick, Maryland, in a program "cloaked in the deepest wartime secrecy, matched only by the Manhattan Project for developing the Atomic Bomb."[27] Two months later, Winston Churchill had delivered his "Iron Curtain" speech, effectively declaring that a new enemy—communism—had replaced the one formerly held in common by

Guthrie and the US military, fascism. Meanwhile, in the USSR, fearing a US invasion, Josef Stalin—himself no stranger to paranoia—ordered the development of an intercontinental ballistic missile system aimed at western Europe and the United States.[28] Already talk of a third world war was in the air as Guthrie jotted into his notebook on a plane: "I say about this atom + germ World War III that whichever country does the invading is going to lose out."[29]

By the end of the year the nascent space race was underway, born directly out of the arms race, with both the United States and the Soviet Union pointing their captured German V2 rockets skyward (each with the help of captured Nazi rocket scientists), experimenting with payloads carrying everything from rye seeds or fruit flies to—within another year—rhesus monkeys.[30] Guthrie may or may not have known of this, voracious news reader as he was, but he certainly reflected an upward, expanding zeitgeist as he envisioned yet a new aerial perspective:

> That moon told me
> tonight that it used to
> have some pretty good folks
> up there on it, just about
> like me and about like you.
> Then they figured out some
> way to have a big war with
> atoms on it and everybody
> got burnt up and blowed
> away.[31]

The defeat of the Progressive Party candidate, Henry Wallace, in 1948, the election of Truman to a four-year term, and the establishment of NATO through the Atlantic Pact of April 9, 1949, filled Guthrie with a mixture of dread and loathing, prompting a flurry of atomic-focused writing. On NATO, he snarled: "I'll not fly one atom bomb / To blow down the Russian towns!"[32] In July he wrote—and most likely never sent—a snarky letter to Truman himself:

MY DEAR MR. TRUMAN:

If you ever so much as lay a small claim to be a human with a brain, a soul, a heart, a mind, a feeling you could call the warmth of the blood of man, please, good sir, take a good look at the bills you are signing to make more high explosives to blow us all off of the map. Your face will look a whole lot blanker if the little atoms blow our world away and all of your pals and kinfolks along with the rest of us.

I'm not ready to blow just yet.

Your old buddy,

Woody Guthrie[33]

And he allowed himself a brief moment of hope that ran hard against the current of Cold War suspicion and the militarism that in the space of four years he had come to reject completely:

> The hour cometh when you must worship
> In brotherly love, yes, in truth and spirit.
> I saw my vision where the world turned ashes,
> And friends and enemies did hug and kiss.[34]

Wherever this hugging and kissing was going on, it was not on the other side of the planet, in Semipalatinsk, Kazakh Soviet Socialist Republic, where Stalin detonated the USSR's first nuclear bomb in August 1949. And there was certainly no hugging and kissing going on across the 38th Parallel, where by June 1950 the North Koreans had embarked upon their "Fatherland Liberation War," which China—with Soviet approval and military input—preferred to call the "War to Resist America and Aid Korea." Truman was urging the United Nations to sanction what he called a "police action."[35] On June 27, 1950, the UN Security Council, unmoved by a Soviet boycott, obliged him. A few hours later, Truman sent in the troops.

Guthrie's responses to the Korean War must be seen in the context of his dashed hopes for progressive America in the immediate wake of World War II. He had, after all, had a vision—a paradoxical vision, to be sure, born of the conviction that the combination of modern, deadly war technology and the commitment to progressive politics would result in a world deserving of the human sacrifice and the best that socialism and labor could produce. It was the vision that had cost him his *Ballad Gazette* program on WNEW:

> I lifted your shells and dropped your bombs
> And I saw this town and other towns blowed down
> And I talked to every Joe in the Kingdom Come
> Told him everything I'll do when I get home.[36]

To a great extent, Guthrie's vision had been filtered through a rejuvenated commitment to communism, prompted in part by a sense of appreciation for the efforts and sacrifices of the Red Army in the defeat of Germany and Japan.[37] While the Taft-Hartley Act and the targeted postwar purging of radicals from the labor movement depressed and infuriated Guthrie at home, he saw a ray of light in China with the progress of the Maoist juggernaut in 1949. As he wrote in a note below the manuscript lyrics to a song he called "People's Army," "I guess I was just waiting for the Chinese Eighth Route Army, and all of the Peoples Armies in China, to melt up together and roll down towards Chiang Kai Check."[35] Undercutting Guthrie's satisfaction over the pending defeat of the Kuomintang in China was the growing nuclear standoff between the United States and the Soviet Union inaugurated by the Soviet atomic bomb test of August 1949. He wrote a number of songs in quick succession devoted to his nuclear fears, beginning in October 1950 with "World's on Afire," an ironic, wistful love song set amid the ashes:

> My angel, my darling,
> When that atombomb does come;
> Let me be your pillow
> While this world's on afire.[39]

Although he had celebrated the deployment of the atomic bomb in Japan only five years previously, he now began to play with fearful scenarios based on the vaporizing of US cities. He wrote to his friend Stetson Kennedy in August 1950: "Well, I've been reading about the atombomb that hit Hiroshima and Nagasaki, and I've been to a whole string of movie shows that tried to show how bad it was, and none of them can come within ten miles of telling you how terrible bad that abombomb and its blasts and its burn were in real life." Guthrie dismissed the bullish programs he had been hearing on the New York radio stations, which had been assuring citizens that the city's health system would rise to the challenge of any nuclear attack. He imagined "500 thousand or half a million souls" in the "radius of the flame and burst and pressure and radioactivity of the bomb," concluding that New York was "absolutely unprepared and not ready for any atombomb to bust down on it."[40]

Over the next four years Guthrie returned frequently to scenarios of domestic destruction, with the chickens of Hiroshima coming home to roost in Brooklyn ("Not one brick on top of any other brick do I see left standing here to answer to the name of Brooklyne Towne").[41] Likewise Boston:

> A cloud of
> dust hit Boston
> town this morning
> one cloud of dust hit
> Boston town
> last evening
> Big atom cloud come
> up and rained the funniest
> rain I ever seen fall
> Atom rain damn
> near killed my town of
> Boston[42]

He threw himself behind the nascent campaigns for nuclear disarmament and test ban treaties. The alternative would be the end of the modern world, as he argued graphically in "Talkin' Atom Bomb":

> Gonna tell ya what to do when th' bomb goes boom;
> When th' flash an' crash and th' big fire comes;
> If your fone don't work and your traintrack's broke,
> If your highway's gone and your tunnel's all stuck;
>> And when you and your whole family
>> get knocked up about nine miles;
> Be a little bit complicated findin' a hosspital.

Just as the torpedo had settled all poker debts at sea during the war, the atom bomb—even for Guthrie—did the same in the contest between communism and capitalism:

> Only way ta save yer skin from this big bomb blast
> Is ta outlaw th' bigbomb and I mean fast;
> I don't care if y' haul my goods from factery t' home
> Down a Kapitalist Highway er a Communist Road.[43]

But even were the atomic bomb to be negotiated out of commission, there would still be other, more modest modes of destruction to worry about:

> Check those blinders
> Tell my sleepers
> Atom bomb's outta date
>   Germy bombs are cheaper.[44]

Having committed himself comprehensively to the peace movement by June 1950, when the Korean hostilities began, Guthrie had joined a slandered and much maligned fellowship. W. E. B. Du Bois, in his capacity as chairman of the Peace Information Center in New York, defended his organization and the peace movement at large from the US Justice Department's predictable and ridiculous charges that antiwar activists should "register under the provisions of the Foreign Agents Act." Du Bois declared: "The desire for peace cannot be made an 'alien' sentiment when the fathers and mothers of America's children read daily of impending atomic devastation in their own cities. Branding those who work for peace as 'foreign agents' will not stem the tide for peace in America."[45] Such sentiments coincided with much of Guthrie's immense songwriting output on the Korean War, amounting to a total of at least fifty songs written between 1950 and 1953, far outnumbering both his Dust Bowl and Columbia River offerings.

Korea, for one thing, was twinned in his mind with "Chorea"—the Huntington's disease—that was conclusively diagnosed in 1952. Understandably, he wanted to be free from both:

> Korea and me!
> Korea and me!
> You must agree!
> You've gotta agree!
> Both gotta get free!
> Both gotta get free!
> Korea and me! Korea and me![46]

But beyond the connections with his neurological affliction, Guthrie saw the Korean War from a number of particularly domestic vantage points, as if to confirm Du Bois's argument that the exertions of the peace movement were on behalf of all Americans, as opposed to any nefarious foreign powers. From the outset of the war, Guthrie challenged the presumption that US interests could have anything to do with a geographical boundary line halfway around the world, as he made clear in a defiant rant called "Thirty 8th Parallel":

> I'll never march across this 38th parallel! olel!
> Never march across this 38th parallel!
> I'll step across to shake my enemy's hand!
> But I'll drop my gun at the 38th parallel![47]

Anticipating such Vietnam War–era songs as Pete Seeger's "Waist Deep in the Big Muddy," Guthrie foresaw a fathomless swamp awaiting the young, ignorant troops sent into Korea by the politicians and generals in Washington:

> Korean Quicksands
> You stuck me good!
> You stuck me good;
> Yes, you stuck me good;
> Korean quicksands,
> Mudholes of blood;
> Korean quicksands of blood.[48]

Playing with a variety of musical genres, he invited doomed young couples to dance to the "Korean Waltz," to hop to the "Korean Quickstep," and to boogie to the "Korean Boogy" ("Ruther'd boogy with you / Than ta drop jelly bombs all nite").[49] He moaned to the "Korea Send Me Home Blues," the

"Korea Boggyhole Blues" ("If I never get outta this dam shock ward / Sweet girl I've done the best I could"), and the plain old "Korean Blues" ("No blues as blue / As my Korean blues. . . . Radio activity got my stockings / Germ warfare took botha my shoes").[50]

He cast Korea in a host of feminine representations, an Oriental princess resisting violation by the arms and boots of the invading Western forces, and he implored his "Korean Honeybun," "Korean Angel," "Korean Kewpie doll," "Korean Honeybunny," and "Korean Sungirl" to "shoot me home" and "boot me home."[51]

Home-front absenteeism—which Guthrie had vociferously condemned during World War II—was now gleefully celebrated in "Goldine Grain," with a pastoral vision of seed planting and harvesting overtaking the din of the munitions factory:

> I won't show up at my war plant job,
> When that death whissle toots again;
> My back'll be bendin' 'cross Peaceful Pastures
> Rackin' y'r goldine grain![52]

To some extent, Guthrie's contrariness to the political grain in the early 1950s—particularly his ostentatious crowing over real or imagined American defeats in Korea—can be put down to his outrage over the increasing restrictions on the freedom of thought and expression that characterized the worst of Cold War repression. He explained his own incorrigibility in his free-verse "Ponta Delegata," written in October 1952 as he threw in his lot with the community of doggedly unrepentant artists, many of them blacklisted, banding together in solidarity around Will Geer's embryonic Theatricum Botanicum in Southern California's Topanga Canyon. Guthrie's own defiance rings through the verse:

> I dont care today
> How senseless and how idiotic my words here sound in tone to
>   some of ye rich here; I know just one thing and that
>   one thing is this: This voice of this rebel tongue in
>   me does not fear any boundary line you try to invent or
>   to draw here around it (or me).[53]

But more critically, Guthrie clearly felt that his optimistic vision of the postwar world, so confidently and hopefully expressed in songs like "When I Get Home," had been betrayed by the prevailing markers of the Cold War—not only the Korean intervention but also the general fear-mongering, union purges, Jim Crow racism, and anti-Semitism (the latter two of which often went hand in hand with anticommunism, as had been proved during the Peekskill Riots of 1949). Guthrie's monthlong voluntary commitment to the "raving ward" of Bellevue Hospital in the summer of 1952, just prior to his fatal Huntington's diagnosis, only added to his sense of a world gone mad—hence his "Name Wanted," the miserable soliloquy of an overworked psychiatric nurse trying, and failing, to complete her rounds in a "GI breakdown ward":

> Crackups, breakdowns; flight deckers; G Severners; warshocks;
> Psychoneurotics;
> Bustdowns;
> Pile ups; psychoes; neuroes;
> I hear ten thousand different kinds of names for you.[54]

What the World War II veterans had come home to, Guthrie wrote, was nothing but a "post war junk pile":

>   ... to
> Come back here and to open up my eyes to see racey hate, jimcrow,
>   and all of that crazy damn shitty stuff right back here on all
>   of your faces
> And flying exactly like it ever did only a little bit smoother and
>   a little bit worser than it ever flew before;
> And me with no kind of a job and with no kind of a paycheck and
>   no kind of anything that you told me I was winning out yonder on
>   that firing line ...
> Its a big wonder I have not broke down and done a good deal worser
>   than I've done so far.[55]

Naturally, Guthrie looked to Korea as a shabby adventure being fought at the behest of the arms dealers and Wall Street. When the Progressive Party—barely clinging to life after the resounding defeat of Henry Wallace

in 1948—put forward the antiwar candidate Vincent Hallinan for the presidential election of 1952, Guthrie threw himself into the campaign, writing
songs and musical skits on behalf of Hallinan and his running mate, Char-
lotta Bass (the first African American woman nominated for the vice presidency), as well as the party's candidate for the California senate, Reuben W.
Borough.[56] But the Progressives, along with Adlai Stevenson's Democrats,
were trounced by the Republicans that November. With Eisenhower now in
the White House, Guthrie launched into a series of bitter musical recrimina-
tions such as "Ikey He Lye":

> Old Warboy Eisenhower stoled home base, folks;
> Better watch 'im awful close he'll steal y'home and all;
> I knowed 'im fromma good ways back; yesss,
> Knowed 'im frumma way on back.
> CHORUS: Anda he lye lyedee, he lye! lye!
> He lo lody he lye![57]

In January 1953, Guthrie was serenading the new president in a talking
blues called "Dear Mister Eisenhower," in which he pleaded for executive
clemency in what he called the "frameup Rosenberg case" (Julius and Ethel
Rosenberg having been convicted and sentenced to death in 1951 on the
charge of providing the Soviets with the atomic secrets that had enabled them
to develop their bomb in surprising haste). Guthrie argued, "We aint quite at
war with the USSR / I cant see what we got sa meny dammm seecrits for."[58]
As the Rosenbergs' date with the executioner approached, Guthrie's flippancy
turned to a more sober reflection on the implications of the death penalty.
Six years earlier, he had finished writing his cycle of songs about Sacco and
Vanzetti; now the nightmare of judicial murder was being repeated in the
name of Cold War hysteria, as Guthrie signaled in his poem, "Hot Seat":

> Did the Rosenburgs get the
> hot seat?   Did the Rosenburgs
> get the hot seat?   Did those
> Rosenburgs   get the   hot seat
> like Sacco [and] Vanzetti did?[59]

In sentencing the Rosenbergs, Judge Irving Kaufman had gone so far as to declare that their alleged act of treason had been directly responsible for the Korean War, in that the Soviets' successful atomic bomb test had bolstered their determination to commit "Communist aggression in Korea."[60] Ironically, Guthrie came close to agreeing with Kaufman, and he did not attempt to deny that the pair might have given the secrets to the Soviets. On the contrary, he declared:

> I hope you did
> I'm hoping you did pass them on over yonder across. . . .
> Because you Rosenbergs did more than any other pair I know
> of to keep my United States here from flying over and laying these
> atombomb eggs on the tables of every other nation in this world
> When you put that top secret atombomb plan into the hands of
> two or three hundred millions of my fine Soviet peoples like you did.
> I guess I can always love the name of Rosenberg because of that.[61]

Nevertheless, even the acknowledgment of possible treason and guilt was not enough for Guthrie to countenance the sentence of death, as he wrote in "Last Mile," his final comment on the Rosenberg case, written in March 1953, three months before their execution:

> Freedoms out crawling its last mile
> Love done went its last long mile
> If you kill my Rosenburgs now.[62]

One other death preoccupied Guthrie that same month. Josef Stalin had died on March 5. Immediately Guthrie committed to his notebook an elegy that, in defiance of all credibility, betrayed no awareness of Stalin's part in the nuclear arms race and the ratcheting up of Cold War tensions. As far as Guthrie was concerned, Stalin had, if anything, been responsible for keeping American nuclear belligerence in check, as he argued the Rosenbergs had done:

> Joe Stalin went on today
> To close one eye and to
> Open up his other bigger eye
> To rest one hand

And to work even harder

Toward that worldly peace

I know he worked his life towards.[63]

Thus with this brief, benighted elegy, Guthrie placed himself somewhere on the spectrum between childlike naïveté and outright self-delusion, leaving the most corrosive stain with which any custodian of his memory will have to reckon. For as Judy Kutulas makes clear, the Stalinist monstrosity—the show trials, the Gulag, the secret police, the murder of tens of millions through starvation, slave labor, and execution—had been a topic of open debate among "dissident Marxists" and others in the US communist movement as far back as the early 1930s.[64]

The Korean armistice was signed on July 27, 1953, after two years of attrition, military stalemate, and the serious consideration by the US Joint Chiefs of Staff, on more than one occasion, to use atomic weapons against the Chinese and North Koreans.[65] As the world breathed one of many temporary sighs of relief, Guthrie looked back at the two previous wars—one that had conclusively demonstrated American readiness to deploy the atomic bomb, and another that had come perilously close to repeating the demonstration—and surmised grimly, in April 1954:

maybe our

atoms and our

molecules has

got to run our

City back through

the dust a few more

times to teach us all a

few more little lessons

about human love + stuff[66]

Guthrie indeed had much to say about "human love + stuff," topics that, in the spirit of his age, dovetailed with modern concerns about warfare, science, and technology, as well as political theory. The interplay between the personal and the political in Guthrie's writing is never far from the surface—hence his powerful equations of political and personal breakdown that we have just seen. As the next chapter shows, Eros was, to Guthrie, both a scientist and an agitator, at work in the laboratory of the mind as well as the body—the body personal and the body politic. Apparently Eros, like every ethereal or physical particle in existence, was engaged in a process of struggle as relentless as that to be found on any picket line, military battlefield, or microscope slide.

9

The Science of Struggle

Early in 1943, Guthrie wrote to Marjorie proposing his "theory" that vene-real diseases were "the direct outcome of nervous frustration, and fear, that either weakens the system so the germ can take hold, or gets the body in such a nervous state that it can't fight back like it ought to." Since "three fourths of not only our sexual diseases, but all bodily sicknesses" were "based in the soul," there could be only one sure and certain medical prescription: "Do away with neurotic laws, rules, fogey customs, narrow minded marriage and divorce and clinical laws, and create a job and a time for leisure, a home and time for work and rest, love and all that goes with it." As if to block any incredulous response, Guthrie took the pains to point out, "I'm not any sort of a christian scientist nor metaphysician, but it is through the mind that all things take place in the body."[1]

Thirteen years later, Guthrie appeared to have drastically changed his position on Christian Science. In August 1956, he wrote two of the last marginally coherent letters that he would ever send, one to Marjorie, now his ex-wife, and one to their nine-year-old son, Arlo. He was fully in the wasting grip of Huntington's disease and in spiritual extremis with the newfound conviction that Jesus was his only "doctor."[2] He instructed Marjorie to write up "some kind of a legal notice a legal letter of some sort givin alla my moneys over to my first church of Christe Scientist Boston Massachusetts."[3] To Arlo he explained that Christian Science was the world's "only greaty sure and certainty Science" and Jesus "my only greaty

greaty scientist I say that God ever did let live anyway."[4] While these unreliable instructions were never carried out, in a sense they were logically in keeping with two strong aspects of Guthrie's biography, namely, his reverence for Jesus the carpenter, as an icon of both proletarianism and Christian socialism, and his equal reverence for what he conceived of as "science."

Scientific worldviews were highly controlling forces in Guthrie's sensibilities and expression, as they were for his society at large in the 1940s and 1950s. After all, Guthrie and his fellow artists and writers were barraged by developments in a host of scientific areas—from physics to sexology, from psychology to psychiatry, from chemistry to ethnology and anthropology. As Paul Peppis has argued, "discourses of science" were highly influential on all artists grappling with modernity in both the nineteenth and the twentieth centuries, an influence reflected (for instance) "through tropes and popularized scientific concepts such as relativity, repression, [and] the unconscious."[5] Fully in step with modernity's elevation of science and scientific method, Guthrie threw himself wholesale into the celebration of the processes that—as witnessed in his song, "Atom Dance"—had enabled humankind to harness the very forces of creation:

> Evolution in all our blazes
> Back past the glacial ages
> Baboon and mental sages
> Warm by my atom fire.[6]

Even when he had come to the point of condemning the very application of nuclear technology that he had applauded at the close of World War II, Guthrie remained a steadfast booster of the technology itself and of its potential for good. Yes, he had seen "our atom wreck / our civilization," as he wrote in "My Eyes Do See All over This World," but he had also seen another vision on that same flight to Montreal:

> I seen our rivers, and ships
> upon the ocean
> I see our factory our
> bridge and power dams
> I see our atom at work
> to feed and clothe us
> When
> My eyes do see, see, see,
> All over this world.[7]

The same hope is manifest in Guthrie's perception of "Heaven," as he called an undated postwar lyric that begins with a phoenix rising from the nuclear ashes:

> It's after my work tired and weary, I lay down to rest my eyes,
> I see this world change in a whirlwind and heaven flies down
>   from the skies;
> I see rising up from my wreckage cities and mansions so bright
> I see my friends eyes and their faces lit up with a bright shining
>   light.

In this postwar utopia, workers are "singing at work as they watch all the wheels," there are no "smudge clouds of smoke" obscuring the green and pleasant valley, the streets are "laid in finest of plastics," and "the atom is laboring as well." On the "new road," there is "no death curve" where "fast cars collide" or "turn over," there is "no patrolman, no officer, policeman, to ride into crowds on his horse," no "bowery nor skid row of homeless." Sickness is unheard of, as are "profiteers" and "battles 'tween worker and boss." Tellingly, Guthrie's own musical labors are matched by those of the thinkers and scientists who have brought about this brave new world:

> I am sawing the finest made fiddle, I am touching the richest
>   skin drum;
> I am blowing the sweetest of woodwinds and blowing the
>   deepest of horns;

> I dance to my music I'm making, and the world joins in with my
>   dance;
> Science and hope cures the fevers, not one grain is blowing by
>   chance.[8]

Now that atomic power had "vaporized" such evil "trees" as fascism, Nazism, and "Jap militarism," there was even more noble work for it to do.[9] The atom's application for good or ill would come about (like every other human accomplishment) through the work of dialectical struggle, of pitting plan against plan, so that indeed "not one grain" should be "blowing by chance." Such, at least, had been Guthrie's position as far back as 1943, when he embarked upon a massive self-guided reading course in dialectical materialism as filtered through selected writings of Lenin, Marx, and Engels.[10]

At about the same time that Guthrie was immersing himself in his studies, American Marxist theorist George Novack published a summary resounding with all the confidence of an empirical scientist whose proofs were simply beyond debate: "Marxism is the scientific theory of the revolutionary proletarian movement which aims to overthrow the outlived capitalist system and erect a new socialist order in its stead. Dialectical materialism is the philosophical foundation of Marxism."[11] But what was it exactly, this "dialectical materialism"—and how did it work? Guthrie offered what turned out to be a fairly cogent explanation in an undated letter to Marjorie:

> The theory is that in all things, all life, visible, or mental, physical
> or psychological, progress evolves out of the contradictions in all
> things. Two forces conflict with each other, two ideas, two principles,
> or two elk or two soldiers, and in the course of time, the living and
> the growing and the moving comes out on top, and shucks off the
> old dead husks and foliage, and the old and the dead and the lifeless,
> not being really lifeless, falls back to the bottom again and appears to
> be filth and rot and acts as a fertilizer for the growing.[12]

If indeed a tendency to universalize was one characteristic hallmark of modernist thought, then dialectical materialism carried decidedly modernist assumptions. Novack proclaimed: "Dialectical materialism admits no . . . barriers to its field of operations. It has a universal character. It takes all reality for its province. The materialist dialectics applies to all phenomena from the most distant nebulae and the most remote time to man's most intimate feelings and elevated thoughts." It was a self-evident and self-justifying theory that brooked no opposition: "Just as the revolutionary proletariat aims to conquer the earth for socialism, so dialectical materialism, which is the philosophical expression of that movement, seeks to extend its sway over all departments of knowledge, contesting the right of rival ideologies to rule over them." If it were possible for human thought to have reached the end of evolutionary history, then dialectical materialism was the proof. It was what made socialism "scientific" in the first place: "As the scientific system of the Socialist movement, the most advanced tendency of historical development, Marxism has reached new heights in the understanding of intellectual as well as natural and social processes. It has created a distinctive theory of the nature and activities of mental life, its own method of thought, its individual logic. The Marxist method of thought is the materialist dialectics. The dialectical method of reasoning about material reality is the highest form of conscious thought."[13]

With equal certitude, Guthrie would often couch his own political statements in terms of evolutionary struggle. As he saw it, socialism would indeed mark the logical end of evolutionary development, and it was the responsibility of "workers + scientists + artists" to pave the way for it.[14] Not least, the artists: "We are all waking up to the fact that we are all great artists—for in order to find your way up the ladder, through the hurricane of evolution, in order to grow out of the ooze and slick slime, from a dumb fish, bird, or lizard, or animal, upward into a human being, you must become a worker, an artist, a creator in life's own image."[15] Through a self-made system of empirical observation, he drew a host of conclusions linking biology, art, and struggle in terms of the dialectics that had become his guiding "scientific" principle.

The observations began in his own home, with his children as the objects of analysis. His conclusions were also informed by his musings on the world of modern dance introduced to him by Marjorie:

> I have watched little infants and babies labor and strain to teach the
> power of life to work in their muscles, to lift a leg, a head, or a finger,
> to cause the little hand to reach out for a ball or a toy, and all of this

work was a dance. It was not simply like a dance; it was a dance. It was the fight to overcome wild energy and to master it and put it to a higher form of mental and bodily work, and no man or woman ever outgrows this fight. This wildness is in you in vast quantity and you struggle each moment to put it to use. This battle, this conflict is the dance, because you must overmaster your wildness before you can portray life to others. The body itself is the dance, the people are the music, and the world your stage.[16]

Struggle, Guthrie argued, was at the basis of all comfort, whether secular or religious: "Nature is highly dialectical in the way she makes good use of her billions and trillions of conflicts. It is up from out of these conflicts in all of their forms and shapes that she chooses who amongst all of us is going to find that secret word of every religion, tenderness."[17] To some extent, Guthrie's fetishizing of scientific method came from his conviction—expressed in the midst of the war against Hitler—that "the least taint of mysticism . . . is not worth spending one single second on." On the contrary, as he wrote to Marjorie, the planned, scientific organization of "work, leisure, play and loving" would be the greatest lesson to come from the ashes of the war.[18] Both the military and the ideological struggles of the war, he implied, were between two competing methodologies or "plans": fascism versus cooperation. Fascism was "a scientific plan for murdering millions and millions of people," in deadly combat against another plan based on a moral "that said the weak had a right to work and to live and to produce and to build and to love and to learn; and that the strong should help the weak and the weak help the strong." While the fascists had been brutally eliminating all those they deemed degenerate or "weak," in advancement of their super-race, the "allies, being taught to help each other, and to help the weak ones, found out that the 'weak' ones physically, could help in a million other ways to work and wage a war and fight harder . . . in scientific or mental fields, all kinds of engineering, and office and clerical work."[19]

Thus, to Guthrie, struggle was everywhere, even in the molecules that had combined to produce the woman he loved, as well as the very love that bound them together. As he declared in the free verses of "Our Kitchen" in late 1943:

And her love for her people gives her energy for her work

Energy is a thing made out of its own opposites, it is the power
which loves the overcoming of any obstacles

This is distilled in the blood the same as liquor, a fuel, or a
perfume

This energy is in all of us and I have seen it in the muscles
of soldiers, seamen, merchant marines, all kinds of farmers and
builders,

And yet I did not see this power work its best till I lived with
Marjorie.[20]

As it was for love, so it was for music, which Guthrie addressed at the
same time in a brief observation he titled "All Artists," a reflection that
strains to undercut romanticism with the rigor of scientific analysis (quite
paradoxically, given Guthrie's own romanticizing of scientific method):

Man is at heart a dancer, also, and the time will come in a freer
world when the gift of hearing music from the mouth of nature will
not be considered as superstition or spiritualism, but a scientific
truth based on our keener understanding of the laws of vibrations,
harmonics, magnetisms, rhythm produced by the contradicting
clashes in the evolution of all things.

So when your friend takes a deep breath and says, "Ah! There
seems to be music in this very air!" of course you will know that he is
stating a scientific fact, and not a tender sissy's sigh, nor mystic grunt.[21]

Guthrie's scientism—for it can be called nothing else—was connected
to his overriding political mission of enabling the proletariat to realize
their rightful power and influence in a world that was "best controlled by
those who are up on the science of struggle."[22] Turning to what he called
"the doctrine of Marx and Engels," he declared dialectics to be "the only
science" capable of bringing into the light "all of the points in history where
we were led off track before."[23] It is true that a thoughtful evolutionary theorist like Stephen Jay Gould could cautiously view "dialectical thinking"
as one of many useful approaches offering "guidelines for a philosophy of
change." And for a "people's historian" like Howard Zinn (who had given

up shipbuilding for history after first hearing Guthrie's "Ludlow Massacre"), it would prove equally useful.[24] But for Guthrie, it went further than a mere approach, acquiring the status of a religious creed. Dialectical materialism—"the science of struggle"—had

> brought us
> past the last
> jail window
> of superstition
> and romantic
> individualism.[25]

To be fair, Guthrie could sometimes make light of his own admitted infatuation with his pet body of theory. As he wrote, "One of the best things about dialectical materialism is that the most ignorant people are soon able to scratch several pages of it down every day and to create poems and dances all with dialectics oozing around the edges."[26] He played with it in song:

> I sing about work I sing about play
> I sing about dialectic wage slavery
> I sing about you + I sing about me
> I sing at my trade in a trade union way.[27]

At the same time, it is clear that Guthrie indeed yearned for the one process of thought that would totalize all others—a theory of everything that would allow all of the world's and his own exertions and conflicting emotions to be slotted into place and explained comprehensively:

> I guess
> each language
> has its words.
> But the struggle
> is everywhere.
> Even the atoms
> and grains of
> dirt struggle for
> social security.[28]

Out of the "struggle for social security" came Guthrie's conception of a social or political physics, which he articulated in a number of notebook entries. "Movement," he wrote, "is the only science there is because all of us are chasing the motions and movements of atoms and beer cases and furniture and rent money. The flow and the motions of greed we chase down in order to get a closer look at social security."[29] The progress toward true "social security" would be slow, muddy, and messy, because "no two particles of [matter] move at the same speed in the same direction."[30] Hence the ubiquity of struggle, which, in his groping toward a unified social theory, Guthrie saw as having been stacked in favor of the "bosses" since the dawn of capitalism:

> So
> our conflicts
> have been
> many more than
> they should have
> been
> because
> our bosses
> made
> our conflicts
> worse in order
> to make us
> stand apart
> and work
> cheap.
> And so
> the science
> of our conflicts
> got to be the
> head science
> of them all.[31]

Guthrie's wishful vision at the close of World War II had placed dialectical struggle at the heart of all political activity around the world:

> This is my essay to
> prove once and for
> all that dialectics
> in peace years is
> going to govern the
> election booths of nearly
> every country on the
> map.[32]

In late 1945—when still a soldier awaiting demobilization—Guthrie had as yet no sense of the thoroughness with which communist theory and activity would be eradicated from US politics as well as the labor movement, hence his optimism and assurance that communists' mastery of the "science of struggle" would ensure their victory in every immediate postwar election:

> It is the
> consciousness of this
> conflict that makes all
> communists communists
> and this is why they
> surprise the world in every job they
> do.[33]

Beyond the confines of dialectical materialism, Guthrie's scientism, his near-religious faith in the efficacy of scientific systemization, manifest itself in a variety of other areas, including the most surprisingly intimate, from the mechanics of self-satisfaction while alone on the road (confessing to Marjorie, "the hot spit in my tight hand was the best of all my systems") to an entire theory of sex between partners.[34] Sex indeed became a systemic preoccupation for Guthrie, especially at those times when his partner's dissatisfaction threatened the harmony of their relationship. A scientific outlook, he implied, might well save the day, even if it threatened to overpower the "wildness" and spontaneity of sex itself. As he complained to Marjorie in 1947: "I could see that in spite of your good trying, the business of sex for sex's sake wasn't felt very strongly in you. To me it was the center of everything. I wanted it to be intellectual, and beautiful, even scientific, but there was and still is a wildness that I would like to feel, a self forgetfulness, a more daring and thrilling, surprising something."[35]

Indeed, the conflict between the ethereal and the material became an increasing concern for Guthrie as he attempted to identify and possibly explain the causes of tension in his relationship with Marjorie. At one point, regretting that the passion of his letters to her had been unrequited, he built up a half-joking picture of finding a scientific explanation for it all:

> I might be airy, I might be watery, I might be etheric, may be
> electric and may be like invisible kinds of magnetism which you
> have a pretty hard job of just touching your finger to. But I am now
> spearheading several attacks in all of the realms of human thought
> to capture all of these atomic and neurotic outposts and to deliver
> them over into the hand of the material physical scientists. You see,
> you can fight, work, eat, shower, shave, shine, slumber and slurp with
> a husband for a goodly number of years and still not be able to define
> nor even to describe all of the parts that he is made out of.[36]

At more intense moments of crisis, however, the joking seemed to disappear altogether, particularly during that difficult period when Marjorie was first pregnant with Cathy and subsequently a new mother, living apart from Guthrie and still with her husband. It was a dark, bitter, and confusing period for Guthrie, punctuated by such notations on his correspondence as "TOO DRUNK TO WRITE"—but also replete with writings in which he begs for a system through which he might learn to cope with the jealousy, resentment, and frustration that marked the period. As he wrote to Marjorie in March 1943: "I suppose the only system I can figure out is to love you while I've got you and to hate you when you're gone."[37] At other, more confident times he used the moments of separation as numbered empirical proofs to demonstrate the soundness of their relationship:

> 19. It will let us stand off and size each other up for faults and good
>   and bad habits which can be discovered and brought to light now
>   and possibly avoid trouble later.
>
> 20. It will temper and make flexible our whole acquaintance and
>   prove to our satisfaction that our meeting and loving was on a basis

that can and will stand forever. We can really prove that our affair
is as sane and sound as any in the world. It is a good thing. We can
prove to our own minds that beyond a doubt life for us should be
travelled together.[38]

Guthrie also committed to his notebook some addresses that he might
have wished to make to Marjorie's husband, Joe Mazia, appealing to scientific reasoning as a means of rationally discussing the emotionally charged
situation in which these three had found themselves:

> Our affairs have never been any other than to create for ourselves
> and for everybody concerned what we scientifically discussed and
> decided upon—not in a hurry—not in a wolfing way—but only
> slowly and after as much foresight, sight, insight, and hindsight as we
> possessed.
>
> We knew very well that a time would very soon come when a
> choice of one kind or the other would definitely have to be made.
>
> The relations everybody carried on with each other were
> positively trials as scientific as any laboratory could produce—
> trials—experiments—in view of a hundred complications—to say
> how—when—and where the whole thing would work itself out.[39]

Mazia was in fact a *real* scientist, a metallurgist on a high-security wartime contract at the Frankford Arsenal in Philadelphia, which perhaps put
Guthrie at a disadvantage in his own attempts to argue on a level scientific
playing field: "I dont entertain the least doubt but that we will use the most
intelligent means of creating a better life for both of us—all of us—because
this is a part of our work as scientists, as thinkers, and as good people."[40]
Under the circumstances, the terms with which Guthrie asserted his love
for Mazia's wife were fully in keeping with his hopeful, decidedly overplayed
scientific discourse: "Personally, I know that my love for Marjorie is as big as
it can possibly be—and I'd argue that all week—I can prove it by logic or by
science or even by psychology or mathematics—but I suppose—I know that
you feel the same way."[41]

Out of this appeal to science came one of the most remarkable documents
of this period: a notebook-length essay, addressed variously to Marjorie and

Cathy as well as Mazia, entitled "Lessons in Human Engineering." The subject was obviously looming large in Guthrie's mind, as one playful notation for Marjorie, written shortly after Cathy's birth, tells her: "Everything you lay a hand on is brung into its proper place in this mixed up world whether it's a diaper or a baby or a man, or a whole bunch of people. You are really a Casey Jones when it comes to this business of human engineering."[42] In spite of its title, the essay indeed appeals more to railroad engineering than to any other kind:

> Many people fall almost "too much in love" and idolize their mate
> so much that it sets up a kind of nervous anxiety that burns up too
> much fuel, overheats the pipes and the boilers and causes the engine
> to run too fast, wear itself out, and lose its steam too quick. An
> engine doing this would run too good and too fast for its own good
> and could only make about half of the trip. A smart engineer and
> fireman would talk it over, figure it out, and decide it would be better
> not to allow this to happen, but to take it a little slower and pull the
> whole load to the other end of the line.[43]

Inevitably, a range of other scientific (if not pseudoscientific) paradigms fell into Guthrie's view, and he used them as a means of reflecting upon both public and private issues. Readers of *Bound for Glory* will recall the brief period in Pampa when he cast himself as a lay analyst or "trouble buster."[44] Years later he looked back on that episode of his life with considerable satisfaction, having concluded: "All that any analyst can do for you is to back up with his science your own decisions to break your way out of your jail."[45] He recalled in his notebook one particular consultation in which a "patient" had asked for advice to cure a bout of premature ejaculation. Guthrie advised that he "get some kind of a system worked out":

> "See that radium phosphorescent wrist watch you've got on your
> wrist there?"
>   "Yeah."
>   "Take it off and lay it on your pillow tonight when you go to bed."
>   "Yeah?"
>   "And when you've got started making love to your wife—look at
> that watch. Concentrate your mind on it. Every single thought about

it. The metals its made out of. Who dug the ore. How the dial shines
in the dark. The funny whitish green colors. What makes it glow?
Where you got it. Who gave it to you?"[46]

As far as Guthrie was concerned, such a "system" of "not letting your mind
run away with you" could be mastered as easily as learning "how to fix a leak
in your roof."[47]

Even later, after he had voluntarily committed himself for psychiatric
observation—having gone from analyst to analysand—Guthrie continued
in his artistic ruminations on the science of psychiatry. In October 1950 he
created a scenario in which he appears to be introduced to some of the fundamentals of Freudian theory:

> I went to the psyko man
> To try to understand
> Where 'bouts I'd lost my mind
> And to save the pieces.
> He could tell by the way I walked
> He could tell by the way I talked
> That I could never find my mind
> Nor save the pieces. . . .
>
> I begged him, "Doctor please,
> Try to save some pieces!"
> Then the psyko doctor said,
> "Down in your empty head
> There's an ego chasing an id!
> I can save the pieces!"[48]

Soon the struggle between the id and the ego became as welcome a subject
for Guthrie's pen as any other sexually inflected process:

> Every time I see you shakin' it around'
> Every time I see you jiggle it around,
> My blood runs hot
> And my words freeze cold;
> My id starts chasin' my ego 'round.[49]

In October 1952, after being misdiagnosed as having "elements of schizophrenia, psychopathy and a psychoneurotic anxiety state," a bemused Guthrie tried to make sense of the new psychiatric landscape onto which this window of analysis had, rightly or wrongly, been opened."[50] He wrote in his notebook:

> I'm a schizofreenick extravert, yes, yea;
> A schizofreenick exxtraverdt, hey hey;
> It means I'm always putting on a show
> I'ma schizzofreenic extravert, good news.[51]

Guthrie's comical skepticism may well be an indication of another thread running parallel to his faith in scientific method. It is clear that by the end of the 1940s, in concert with his growing disillusionment over the prospects of political progress in the face of Cold War repression, Guthrie's faith in utopian science had also taken a beating. His euphoric boosting of atomic power was undercut with a more skeptical outlook that expressed itself in a variety of registers. It might be a wistful love song such as "One Thing the Atom Can't Do":

> You can drop an atom pill
> In the gas tank on your car
> It will roll you round this world, and shine your shoes 3 times
>   a day;
> It cant show me how to court nor kiss
> Nor ask my sweet to marry;
> Thats one thing the atom cant do.[52]

It might be a raunchier recitation, such as "Old Atom Hunter":

> Newtron Nelly she's a kuteyfool;
> Radioactive, kute little fool;
> Kissed her this mornin' on h'r toadstool;
> So, gittback, move back, stinkymy pooh.[53]

Or it might be an exasperated free-verse letter addressed to Marjorie's mother, Aliza, in which the complexities of atomic science are no match for those of renewed fatherhood:

I've been reading a
whole big
    stack of books
All about

                      Atomic Bombs,
                 Atomic Energy,
               Atomic Factories,
             Atomic Houses—
               Cars—
             Planes—
           Ships—
     And all of these sound
dumb and little
   And small
       Compared to
        Fixing
         Arlo
             Dybuck
                Davy
     A good
        tight nipple
      in the
        dark
         barefooted.[54]

By far the most comprehensive account of the waywardness of Guthrie's love affair with the atomic "science of struggle"—arguably the defining scientific *and* political paradigm of his age—is to be found in a densely packed notebook, a "welcome book" dedicated to the newborn son of his brother George, Christopher Gwynn Guthrie, begun in October 1952 and completed in December that year, as the Korean War raged and the world seemed to be careening toward thermonuclear Armageddon. Guthrie announces to his young nephew that his primary focus will be on the

> Little
> Teensy   Bitty
> specs
> of this
> dagum
> atom stuff

that is the basis of all life and—perhaps—imminent death. Effectively, Guthrie hands to his nephew's generation all the hopes that had been confounded and betrayed by his own in the misapplication of technology, nuclear and otherwise:

> I know
> you can
> figure out how
> to   stop and how to
> start
> all   of   our   atomic
> and hydronic
> and nuclear
> energies
> and planetary powers you'll
> dig up . . .
> which me
> and my
> tribe . . .
> had
> To try to do
> for one another
> as best we
> could
> by
> thrashing around
> with wood and coal and
> steam and gas engines
> and electric sparkles

we

done

perty well

with

But   not   good

enough to brag much about.

His euphoria of August 1945 completely forgotten, Guthrie infuses with regret his admission of a lost opportunity:

I want   to   learn

all   I   can   learn   about

how   to   pick   up   from

these   old   broken

Pieces   and   old   burny

ashpiles

and learn   all   I   can   learn

about

Saddling   my   nuclear   and

my spacial

and   all   of   my   planetary

powers   to   make   or   to   teach

you   and   me   how   we   can

love   one   another   more

and   work   together   lots

better.[55]

In the end, Guthrie appears at a complete loss to explain the place of science in the equation for social justice and happiness. Once—and not too long before, August 1950—he could write a playful song about one of his heroes and introduce it with the note: "You know, Professor Albert Einstein told me one day when we was riding the boxcar. He said he was gonna invent a theory that would do away with race hate and race fightings and race bombings and all this Jim Crow stuff."[56] Now, in his welcome book to his nephew, it appeared to be anybody's guess as to what good, if any, science would do, as he implied with stoic resignation:

    I   dont know   so   plain
just what kind of a
    Chemical element
    That   peace
and   libertad   and   freedom
    Is [57]

In 1944, he had marveled in a daybook entry, "How many scientific discoveries await the mind of man inside a can of garbage? Acids. Plastics. Paints. Gasses. Drugs. Dyes. Moulds. Bacteria."[58] But the abstracts that were dearest to his heart—"peace," "libertad," "freedom"—were perhaps more fit for the analysis of artists, dancers, and songwriters than the technocrats of modernity's brave new world. Indeed, the same could be said for the abstraction that preoccupied him the most throughout his writing career, that elusive entity he called "Union," to which we now turn.

10

A Unity of Disunity

Marshall Berman describes one of the great contradictions of modern life: the simultaneous sense of connection and disconnection that accounts, at least in part, for the ambivalence with which many observers, Guthrie among them, have recounted their experiences of modernity. Berman writes in one of his most celebrated passages:

> To be modern is to find ourselves in an environment that promises us adventure, power, joy, growth, transformation of ourselves and the world—and, at the same time, that threatens to destroy everything we have, everything we know, everything we are. Modern environments and experiences cut across all boundaries of geography and ethnicity, of class and nationality, of religion and ideology: in this sense, modernity can be said to unite all mankind. But it is a paradoxical unity, a unity of disunity: it pours us all into a maelstrom of perpetual disintegration and renewal, of struggle and contradiction, of ambiguity and anguish. To be modern is to be part of a universe in which, as Marx said, "all that is solid melts into air."[1]

For all Woody Guthrie's efforts to outline, describe, and contribute to the foundation of an earthly union, he was forced time and again to reflect upon, and often replicate, the cleavages, dissociations, and alienation that were—and still remain—intractable hallmarks of modernity. Whether in terms of class, politics, gender, nation, region, or race, the forces of disunity hammered constantly at the barricades of unity erected in Guthrie's mind and upon his pages. This was perhaps inevitable, in the sense that the very concept of struggle relies on a cleavage, a positioning of "us" against "them," a perpetuation of contending forces. Guthrie's fealty to the "science" of dialectical materialism would require nothing less, given his understanding of it.

As the world knows, the "us" he chose was the proletariat; the "them" was the "rich men" or the "bosses," a division most forcefully articulated by one of the organizations that Guthrie most admired, the Industrial Workers of the World (IWW), in its preamble: "The working class and the employing class have nothing in common. . . . Between these two classes a struggle must go on until the workers of the world organize as a class, take possession of the earth and the machinery of production, and abolish the wage system."[2] But such a neat binary opposition between "us" and "them" was harder to perpetuate in reality than on the printed page (or indeed in song). On the ground, the divisions between—and among—contending forces were much muddier. While it was easy enough for Guthrie to simply blame "the fascists" for implementing the strategies that "divide, scare, separate, frighten, and confuse people in order to draw lines between them," it was much harder for him to square the demands of dialectical struggle with the desire for universal union.[3]

In part, this desire grew out of Guthrie's sense of union as a practical solution as old as human history itself, "wrote down in the Book of Ages" and "carved in the solid rock"—from "Jesus of Nazareth" telling his people "you must join the Union Army" in order to overthrow Roman imperialism to Abraham Lincoln calling for the union of "white man" and "dark man" for the overthrow of American slavery.[4] These were practical strategies leading to empirically verifiable outcomes. But in his review of Guthrie's union songs, Wayne Hampton correctly identifies a perceptible progression from the more practical "organizing songs" of the late 1930s to the "utopian," "mystical," and even "escapist" union songs of the mid-1940s and onward.[5] This progression was an inevitable outcome of Guthrie's glorification of labor as a rhetorical strategy in the dialectical struggle against the "bosses," which underlay the creation of so many of his working heroes, from Jackhammer John to the Great Historical Bum to the Union Maid to the multitasking

Everyman of "Hard Travelin'" and "Talkin' Hard Work." This glorification also contributes to the popular misconception of Guthrie as a well-seasoned manual laborer, a myth he was happy to perpetuate, if not inflate to legendary proportions.

In point of fact, Guthrie's most extensive and sustained period as a manual laborer—aside from his youthful period as a sign painter—was his year in the merchant marine (June 1943 to July 1944), when he worked as a cook and mess man. The pressures of having to prepare meals and clean up after three hundred seamen, three times a day aboard a pitching "Liberty ship" in the North Atlantic, enabled him to experience a profound connection with his fellow workers aboard ship and beyond:

> On a ship you work
> You enter into the feeling of work
> You sweat, move fast, think;
> You work
> Your sweat makes
> Your mind get bigger
> And you see all the
> Work plainer,
> All the work in the world.
> You feel the inner spirit of work.
> Your hopes are in your work
> And you feel a part of
> All the work everywhere.
> You feel united with it all.
> Your sweat is your connection
> With all the rest.[6]

Later, with his seaman's papers revoked and his subsequent drafting into the US Army as a teletype operator, Guthrie—already an expert touch typist since high school—wrote enthusiastically to Marjorie about the enhancement of his skills, which might enable him to stake a claim to remunerative white-collar membership in the future: "I see in my mind all the lessons, notes, lectures, the codes and kinds of messages I will send when I get to be a real operator. I see myself in a high office at work when you walk in with a sandwich and a malted." Guthrie conveyed to Marjorie the same sense of pride and belonging that he would inscribe into all other forms of labor throughout his oeuvre: "I'm not an expert teletypist by any means. But I really believe that I felt the pride, a good sample of it, that you take in the machine that you operate your best. I think that for a few short minutes here I felt like you feel at your work."[7]

Guthrie's identification with the proletariat had less to do with his fleeting experiences of manual or administrative labor than with his status as a "cultural" or "mental" worker. As Michael Denning has pointed out, Guthrie's proletarianism can be usefully viewed in the context of the Popular Front period when the communist movement was issuing its first appeals "to the 'brain workers' of the United States to join the 'muscle workers' in building a new civilization."[8] Guthrie stood squarely behind this objective, which had such great implications for himself as a bona fide member of the proletariat. As he argued to Marjorie, "It is a fact that the poet does not hammer nor climb, lift nor load, lay bricks nor paint your wall"; nonetheless, "he is no more and no less than any clerk, teacher, good worker."[9] They all had a part to play in the development of an oppositional workers' culture: "Whether you are trying to get your boss to pay you 20 bucks instead of 15, for pounding a typewriter all week long, or whether you are a cab driver or a grease monkey, it is out of your own humor, and hopes, and fights, that you've got to make up your songs."[10] The elimination of the distinction between manual and mental labor—the amalgamation of the blue and white collars that was still a relatively novel concept in Guthrie's lifetime—would enable labor itself to emerge as a unified entity, as the IWW had envisioned. And, as Guthrie wrote to his newborn daughter Cathy, labor—"work"—no matter what it was, would be at the basis of her own identity—her "identification": "It might not always be the same kind of identification the FBI will ask you for, but it will be your own identification to keep your own mind clear and your head level and your chin in the wind."[11]

Guthrie argued strenuously that labor was the very antidote to mysticism, that "work has got to take the place of superstition and hokus pokus."[12] He vowed to Marjorie: "If ever you and me . . . let any sort of a South Sea Island sleep come over us and either one gets lazy or droopy or quits turning out work, I had rather see the other one get up and leave than to keep living together and not working."[13] In spite of such muscular declarations, however, when it came to his conceptions of "Union," it was ultimately mysticism that ruled the day. One of many indications would be his margin notes scrawled into his copy of Vernon Louis Parrington's *Main Currents in American Thought* in December 1944:

> Republic of Jesus
> no ranks no caste
> mystic union[14]

Picket lines too were holy, mystical sites for Guthrie, as he implies in the unpublished "When the Pickets Start to Marching":

> I have gone across this country now
> A dozen times or more;
> I have sung in richmans mansions
> And the slums from door to door;
> I have sung in padded studios
> And the networks of the air;
> But when the pickets start to march
> My soul is there.[15]

And with a highly illuminating, quite possibly deliberate spelling error in his manuscript, "Hard Hitting Songs by Hard Hit People" (ca. 1941), Guthrie writes of "the Union hall" as "the soul [*sic*] salvation of real honest to god American culture."[16] Similarly, it was the contested "soul" that was at stake in a strike by "sodie jerks," "perfume gals," and "cleanup guys and girls" against the United Cigars stores in 1947—a forgotten three-day conflict that Guthrie inflated to a spiritual struggle "sung and fought and heard all around this planet":

> United Cigars can't buy our soul
> Slick talk can't wreck our CIO
> Local Eleven Ninety Nine is solid gold
> And so is the Union spirit.[17]

Guthrie made the religious connection explicit when he went so far as to propose to Marjorie that the "thing of 'unionism' is the only lure and bait that any religion has really held out for anybody and their best slogan has been 'love thy neighbor'—(work and think and plan along with your fellow worker)."[18] Countless examples of his union writings overflow with a fervor and spirituality that could well match that of any evangelist out to rack up his tally of saved souls: "It comes to me like it has come to thousands and to other millions of people everywhere. Some call it religion, spirit, a holy spirit, or a higher frame of mind, something. I feel it plain when I am doing my work as best I can."[19] In short, "Union" was to become Guthrie's grandest narrative.

For a time at least, "Union" might underpin Guthrie's whole conception of creation, including the biology of humanity. Witness the undated welcome poem on the subject, addressed to Cathy around the time of her birth in 1943:

> The body itself is all union.
> The greatest union in this life is a
> human body.
> Every drop of blood, spilt or unspilt, is
> union blood, every drop mixed in with every
> other drop. Every little
> vein, corpuscle, or blood vessel, all are
> united—they are really not a lot of separate
> veins chasing off different directions, but one
> vein and one direction—always on and on.
> No two parts of the whole body
> Try to stand up alone
> But every part stands up together and
> works together.

And even death has its basis in union with new life, as Guthrie asserts in a passage which, in spite of his frequent attempts to discourage reviewers' comparisons between himself and Walt Whitman, resonates with the faint echoes of *Leaves of Grass*:

> And if it comes to Death
> You are crumbled back to the start
>
> again
>
> Back to the wind and the rain again
> Back again
> To the soil again
> and to find a union with the grass
>
> again.[20]

For Ella May Hamlin in *House of Earth*, the realization of union constitutes a moment of epiphany, whether or not clarified by a temporary state of
madness during her hallucination in the midst of a prairie blizzard: "And the
people are all born from one and they are really all one. The people are all
one, like you and your baby are one, like you and your husband, both of you
are one. And all of the upper north plains are one big body being born and
reborn in and through one another, and those also of the lower south plains.
All of those of the Cap Rock. This is the greatest one single truth of life that
takes in all of the other works."[21]

Guthrie's Palermo narrative betrays a similar outlook, one that would be
contested by most enemies of essentialism. In Sicily, "the land and sky" looks
"the same as we've got in the States." So do "the buildings and the houses," as
well as the people: "They might as well have been in my own country because
nobody could have told us apart. All people to me look like one big mixed up
family finding it out. I have seen and tasted all colors of grapes and people.
To me it is all one big something. One big life. One Big spirit. One big bunch
of us. One big job. One big union."[22]

Reductive as such conclusions might be, Guthrie was not alone in resorting to such totalization and essentialism. This characteristically modernist
appeal to the universal underpinned the projects of many of his contemporaries. David Hollinger has examined some of them:

> In the name of a mystical "humanity," the prophetic Hoosier
> Wendell Willkie proclaimed *One World* in which farmers near
> Kiev deserved our sympathy and respect because they were just like
> farmers near Kokomo, Indiana. In the name of *The Family of Man*,

Edward Steichen and the Museum of Modern Art exhibited a series of photographs displaying what we now recognize as a sensibility common to male American liberal intellectuals of the period. In the name of an essential "human nature," Freudians and behaviorists offered prescriptions designed for the entire population of the globe. In the name of species-wide fraternity, advocates of esperanto sought through a distinctly European synthetic language to mitigate the divisive effects of linguistic diversity throughout the world. In the name of an ostensibly universal capacity for spiritual experience, religious ecumenists sought to neutralize sectarian conflict through the claim that "we all believe in the same God," which turned out, of course, to be the God of liberal Protestantism.[23]

Guthrie's similar visions of unity, of totalization, naturally extended to his conceptions of the place of music in a progressive society. Yet music in Guthrie's mind was also a site of schism, of conflict between an "us" and a "them"—namely "authentic" folk musicians versus the corrupt, sold-out purveyors of Tin Pan Alley. As in all other spheres, the victor in any musical contest would be revealed through the exertions of dialectical struggle. Guthrie's soaring rhapsodies on the unifying power of music are reflections of his dedication to the cause of unity in all walks of life, in spite of his opposing commitment to the eternal evolutionary struggle between the "authentic" and the "phoney." As he wrote to Marjorie and Cathy during one of his sea voyages, music was central to this struggle:

> As a general rule, any activity of the mind which tends to show us the real "oneness" of all things is great. The more a song shows this oneness the greater is that song. This is the highest activity of your mind and heart, this oneness. To see and to feel and to know of this oneness. This Union. To see the relation and the connection between all life's objects, forces, peoples, and creatures. To see the clash, conflict, the opposition of these great forces. To see the fight, the outcome, the new organization of the new groups that arise out of the old ones. To see all of this in nature and in people, this was what caused the Hebrews to write psalms. It caused the Negroes to sing their work songs.[24]

During the same voyage Guthrie envisioned for Marjorie and Cathy a worldwide event that could not possibly be realized until later in the twentieth century with the development of a global broadcasting infrastructure and satellite technology. As he imagined it:

> Think for a minute how many musical instruments there are in the world. All kinds. All sorts. Reeds. Strings. Brass. Wood winds. Drums. Bells. Lots of others I guess. They are in every jungle, on every desert, every street, every house. There are as many as we have windows and doors. I wonder if all of these could be collected together to play some one big symphony, sort of a world symphony . . . get all of these instruments to play the same piece on the same day and see if we can hear it all around the world.

But Guthrie's spiritual hope was clearly subdued by his realization that the current state of broadcast technology would not allow for such a unifying project; for there would always be benighted places on earth where the blessings of modernity had yet to arrive:

> No, we couldn't hear it. We couldn't hear it in all of our hills. It wouldn't carry across our mountains nor through our canyons nor over the deserts. No. It wouldn't even fill all of our streets and cities.
>   It would be mighty loud, but it would not fill all of our vacant spaces.[25]

Technological infrastructure notwithstanding, Guthrie viewed the unifying potential of music—*his* music, of course, folk music, the "real old honest to god songs of protest against mean treatment"[26]—in direct proportion to his strident belief in popular music as a corrupt agent of division and distraction, the province of "the big bands and the orgasm gals" singing for "a few pampered pets who have not yet evolved upward to the plane of a real human being."[27] With as wild a brush stroke as he could paint, he declared: "A folk song tells a story that really did happen. A pop tune tells a yarn that didn't really take place."[28] In Guthrie's mind, the dialectical struggle between his conceptions of folk and popular music were reflections of the broader evolutionary struggle between the "living" and the "dying"—there were "two kinds of singing and two kinds of songs. Living songs and dying songs." Needless to say, the latter were "the ones about champagne for two and moon over Miami"—the ones "on the juke boxes, in the movies and over the radio."[29]

What Guthrie was slow to appreciate was that, already by the mid-1930s, activists in the American communist movement had been turning, as Robbie Lieberman has observed, from a relatively narrow "commitment to proletarian culture" to a wider "interest in mass culture, with a focus on Broadway, Hollywood, and big-name writers who endorsed antifascism."[30] As we have seen, courtesy of Michael Denning in particular, Hollywood was in fact a major center of radical activism during the Popular Front years. As for Tin Pan Alley and the popular recording industry, Denning also observes what would have caused chagrin to Guthrie and other folk purists: "The latter-day success of the folk music revival—of the music of Woody Guthrie, Huddie Ledbetter and Pete Seeger—has often led historians and cultural critics to assume that folk music was the soundtrack of the Popular Front. This is not true: the music of the young factory and office workers who made up the social movement was overwhelmingly jazz."[31]

This put Guthrie at odds with his natural urban allies, for in his more combative moments he would mistakenly damn what he called "jazz" as the music of the fascist opposition. He recalled a young boy singing a rousing folk song in the Arvin, California, migrant camp he had visited in 1939: "It leapt out of this boy's mind like a young mountain lion, and the road was lined with cops in their big black sedans, laughing, grunting, and talking, and listening to jazz music on their radios."[32] Meanwhile, Seeger was actually being advised by New York activists to hang up his banjo. David Dunaway writes that a Communist Party official took Seeger aside at a fund-raiser and said, "Pete, here in New York hardly anybody knows that kind of music. . . . If you are going to work with the workers of New York City, you should be in the jazz field. Maybe you should play the clarinet."[33]

Eventually, however, Guthrie demonstrated a welcome capacity to modify his more strident beliefs pitting folk music against other popular forms—at least intermittently. By 1946 he had joined the board of directors of People's Songs, in association with the likes of Marc Blitzstein, Oscar Hammerstein II, "Yip" Harburg, Leonard Bernstein, and Lena Horne, among other figures from the realms of Broadway and popular music.[34]

He was obviously committed to the organization's mission to promote—in Seeger's words—"every kind of musical expression . . . folk, jazz, popular, or serious cantatas."[35] In 1947 he would even write an appreciative review of an album by the avant-garde composer John Cage: "I've been around at several dance gatherings and musical houseparties here in New York City where I heard John Cage overhaul the family piano in his own way and play some of his choked down odd and unusual kinds of things. I've heard him work with [a] roomful of tomtommers and drummers on first one stage and then the other one, and not only did I feel that this sort of piano music was really a keen fresh breeze, but a welcome thing in the way of a healthy change from the old ways you hear the average piano played."[36]

Clearly, by this time Guthrie had come to accept that the world of music was in fact a world of musics, and that in the tonal realm, as in every other, he would inevitably have to embrace a sort of "unity of disunity." He signaled as much in one refreshing, undated notebook entry:

> Music talks, and it speaks differently in you than in me, because we
> are the same mirror, yet our reflections are not the same. If you and
> I were twins and had never lived apart a moment in our lives, still we
> would have looked into different corners and out different windows
> and our eyes would have seen the same room, yet different colors
> of paint and furniture, we would have looked at the same trees and
> seen different leaves, and when music brings your old hopes back to
> you and my own back to me, there would be spaces and distances
> and differences in us.[37]

Such a realization enables Guthrie to emerge even further from the relatively narrow pigeonhole of "folksinger" or "Dust Bowl Balladeer" into much broader territory, where he can be seen interacting energetically with the various and often conflicting dimensions of American modernity. We have seen so far that these dimensions have included the artistic, the theoretical, the technological, and the political. The next chapter proposes a further dimension, a gendered one in which Guthrie's progressivism was in constant struggle against certain reactionary tendencies that he himself was unable to reject.

11

I Say to You
Woman and Man

In discussing modernism's "transformation of gender relations" in the early twentieth century, Michael Denning points out some of the defining aspects of this "generational revolt"—the "refusal of the patriarch" that marked the challenges to Victorian values in Guthrie's early years. "The first two decades of the century," he writes, "were a high point of the women's movement; these years were dominated by the struggle for women's suffrage, by the emergence of a 'new woman,' and by the invention of a new term—'feminism.' There were close connections between women's rights, sexual radicalism, and the artistic renaissance: indeed, in 1917, the New York *Evening Sun* was noting that 'some people think women are the cause of modernism, whatever that is.'"[1]

Yet, for all the associations of modernity with progress and emancipation, the "refusal of the patriarch" was a long time coming in both the socialist and proletarian arenas (if it has in fact yet arrived). In his early study of factionalism within the American Left, Milton Cantor pointed out that prior to the 1930s "there was scant mention of women among socialists," with "the woman question" seen only as part of the larger "labor question"—if it was addressed at all.[2] During the mid-1930s, when Guthrie and many of his radical associates were emerging into the public sphere, cultural discourse was still marked, as Denning observes, by "the belligerent masculinism of the proletarian avant-garde and the militant labor movement" as well as "the sentimental maternalism of Popular Front representations of women."[3]

It is correct, though certainly not enough, to say that Guthrie was a product of these times. An examination of his fraught engagement with the half of the human race that he—quite tellingly and provocatively—called "womban" indicates that he clearly embodied many of the progressive and counterprogressive, even reactionary, currents that marked the struggle against both patriarchy and its bigoted cousin, homophobia, in modern America. Indeed, Guthrie's relationships with women as individuals and as a class have prompted some of the most trenchant criticisms of his life and his legacy; his previously unpublished pronouncements on homosexuality and abortion will no doubt prompt more.

Guthrie's champions have pointed to a handful of powerful writings to demonstrate the path he apparently walked from misogyny to enlightenment, such as the extensive notebook entry from June 1942, which Billy Bragg and Wilco recorded as the song "She Came Along to Me":

> Ten hundred books of
> just this size I could write
> you about her
> > Because I felt if I could
> know her I would know all
> women and they've not been
> any too well known
> > For brains and planning
> and organized thinking—I'm
> sure the women are equal
> and maybe ahead of men.

This ode of Guthrie's to Marjorie's progressive influence in the context of the war against fascism declares outright that any such war could not be won without female energy and commitment. Guthrie envisions a world blended into one race through miscegenation—perhaps "ten million years from now"—with racism thus eliminated and with "the fascists out of the way":

> But it never never
>
> never
>
> > Never
> >
> > Could of
> >
> > Been done
> >
> > If the women hadnt
>
> entered into the deal.[4]

Bill Nowlin has argued that, although Guthrie "wasn't unlike most other men, having grown up in a patriarchal society that regarded women as keepers of the home and center of the family," he nonetheless "evolved over time." Nowlin reprints Guthrie's faintly Whitmanesque lyric from August 1947, "I Say to You Woman and Man," a call for a woman "to come out from the confines of home and become a wild dancer"—clearly marking Marjorie's influence on his thinking:

> I say to my woman dance
> out of our home.
>
> Dance out and see fighting.
> Dance out and see people.
> Dance out and run factories.
> Dance out to see street meets.
> Dance out in the deep stream.
> Dance out to your vote box.
> Dance down to your office.
> Dance over to your counter.
> Dance up your big stairs.
>
> If your husband gets jealous
> dance out to new lovers.
> If your man keeps your
> heart tied dance out
> and untie it.
>
> Dance out to sing equal.
> Dance up and be pretty.
> Dance around and be free.[5]

This would appear to be Guthrie at his most enlightened. Yet only three days before writing these echoes of Whitman, Guthrie wrote what was more likely an attack on Whitman's homosexuality than any charge against his perceived marginalization of women:

> I got to steer clear
> Of old Walt Whitman's
> Swimmy waters
> He didn't find a woman
> In all of his
> Leaves of Grass.[6]

Guthrie's engagement with homosexuality is, like so much else, a conflicted one. Bryan Garman has extensively discussed the homosocial images of *Bound for Glory*, with its bonding hoboes, in an echo of Whitman's "I Sing the Body Electric," both physically and emotionally replaying the "embrace of love and resistance" performed by Whitman's male wrestlers. For Garman, Guthrie's images sometime "obscure the rigid line that separates the homosocial from the homoerotic."[7] When another of Guthrie's recent champions, singer-songwriter Jonatha Brooke, released in 2008 an album of unpublished Guthrie lyrics set to her music, entitled *The Works*, she chose the title based on a notebook entry that had profoundly impressed her for its progressive outlook on sexuality: "Your own people will sing loud yells about Woody Guthrie being two sex maniacs. But if I took the other road these same several yellers would scream that I'm a queer. I fully aim at this time, dear lay man and lay woman, to walk up and to run bare back down both of these trails and to get my soul known again as the two, both, the sexual maniac, the saint, the sinner, the drinker, the thinker, the queer. The works. The whole works."[8]

Yet for all Guthrie's desire to "get [his] soul known again" as "the queer," some uncomfortable, hardly progressive episodes in his biography suggest otherwise. Guthrie—for whom the words "sissy" and "sissified" were epithets of choice—held highly conservative views about what constituted proper sexual relations between men and women, and between men and men. (No archival sources have yet been unearthed documenting his opinions on lesbianism.) In a letter to Ed Robbin, he complained of Carl Sandburg's supposedly effete delivery of folk songs: "Because old Carl has been somewhere doing something that's made him sound like a monosexual dulcimer player having a cross between an opium dream and a wet nightmare. It hurts me to play these records of his. It would hurt the whole labor movement to mistake this for anything virile, living or American—not always the words or the content, but goddam that kind of singing that sounds like two men sleeping together too long."[9]

Apparently, even toward the end of his life, after years of immersion in the bohemian world of Greenwich Village and New York City at large, Guthrie's homophobia had not softened. Ed Cray recounts how, at Greystone Park Hospital, "Guthrie became proprietary about Ward 40. When two 'hemosexual' lovers embraced in the bed next to his, Guthrie 'pointed out the pair of unnatural lovers' to the ward attendant. The lovers were placed in separate wards."[10] Of course, this critique must be placed in the context of Guthrie's times. Even his close friend and political mentor Will Geer was obliged to keep his homosexuality hidden, and it is unlikely that Guthrie ever knew of it.

Often women fared little better. In his moments of cultural purism, particularly when defending folk music against the pernicious tide of popular culture, Guthrie would cast women as the willing agents of a sexual anesthesia, in stereotypical representations of the Jezebel figure hired by the venal producers of Hollywood and Tin Pan Alley to sap the soul of the American workingman: "Yes. He hired his women and they sang you off to sleep. They had sex orgasms over microphones. They brushed their bellies in your face. You smelled her hips. You tasted her eyes. You sucked her lips. You felt all of this. Yes. All over a movie screen. A phonograph record. A magazine snapshot. A radio program."[11]

The point of these comparative examples is not to criticize but rather to establish Guthrie's highly conflicted nature with regard to sex, sexuality, and women's emancipation. Any discussion must take into account the fact that, in his most productive period, Guthrie was poised on a fault line, where, as Denning notes, America was experiencing a "shift from modern to postmodern gender relations and household formation."[12] Guthrie's own output to some extent documents this shift, although by no means in a consistent fashion. There are perceptible moments of advancement and retrogression, depending often upon his personal relations with women as well as a sexual "disinhibition" commonly associated with Huntington's disease.[13]

Guthrie in fact produced a variety of representations of women in the labor struggle, running from helpless victim to mere auxiliary figure to outright leader. Of all his representations of women, the most widely known will no doubt be his song "Union Maid," partly inspired by the activism of Oklahoma union organizer Ina Wood and partly by the anti-union victimization of African American sharecropper and activist Annie Mae Meriwether.[14] In the most popular versions, Guthrie's "Union Maid" serves predominantly as an inspirational figure, a proletarian version of the French Revolution's Marianne, whose primary aim is to "organize the guys." It is unclear what, if any, is her own area of labor (although it is implied that she is a factory worker). Intriguingly, the one released recording of Guthrie singing "Union Maid" (with the Almanac Singers) is merely an excerpt in which he sings an unflattering verse actually written by Millard Lampell:

> Now you gals who want to be free
> Take this little tip from me;
> Get you a man who's a union man
> And join the Ladies Auxiliary;
> Married life ain't hard
> When you've got a union card,
> And a union man has a happy life
> When he's got a union wife.[15]

This is in keeping with Guthrie's apparent acceptance of women's supporting role in a labor sphere dominated by men. As he slyly avers in "She Come Along to Me," women may indeed be "equal" or even "ahead of men" in terms of "brains and planning / and organized thinking":

> Yet I wouldnt spread
> such a rumor around
> Because one organizes the
> other.[16]

Guthrie's output is indeed peopled intermittently by inspirational women whose main purpose is to "run the men / that run the world," rousing the union spirit of hesitant workingmen, often highly individualistic figures nearly collapsing under the weight of their own machismo.[17] Hence one of many variants of his "Girl in the Red, White, and Blue," who uses her sexuality to spur on the male workers in the service of war production:

> She pointed out the window
> To the 48 States,
> Said, "If you want to win my hand,
> Take your axes and your engines and your jackhammer, boys,
> I'll marry the hard workingest man."[18]

This is by no means to say that Guthrie offered no representations of women playing equal and even leading roles in the various struggles to which he was committed. The "fair maiden" in Guthrie's "The Ranger's Command" not only encourages the cowboys to "hold a six shooter, and never to run" from predatory "rustlers," but also rises "from her warm bed with a gun in each hand" to join them in the fight to keep what they have rightfully earned through their hard work.[19] Likewise, in "Miss Pavilichenko," Guthrie eulogizes the legendary Soviet sniper, Lyudmila Pavlichenko, scourge of the invading Nazis:

> Miss Pavilichenko's well known to fame;
> Russia's your country, fighting is your game;
> The whole world will love you for a long time to come,
> For more than three hundred Nazis fell by your gun.[20]

Of all of Guthrie's fighting women, however, it is undoubtedly Harriet Tubman who stands out as the strongest in comparison to her male companions. Guthrie first sets her bravery against the faintheartedness of her husband and her brothers:

> In 'forty-four, I married John Tubman.
> I loved him well till 'forty-nine;
> But he would not come and fight beside me
>
> So I left him there behind.
> I left Bucktown with my two brothers,
> But they got scared and run back home.
> I followed my northern star of freedom;
> I walked the grass and trees alone.

And it is Guthrie's Tubman who—in the song as well as in historical fact—
uses the threat of deadly violence to combat male cowardice along the
Underground Railroad:

> One slave got scared and he tried to turn backwards;
> I pulled my pistol in front of his eyes.
> I said, "Get up and walk to your freedom
> Or by this fireball you will die."[21]

Indeed, Guthrie implied that for every celebrated figure like Pavlichenko
or Tubman, there was a brave unknown who, in her anonymity, was no less
courageous in challenging not only the financial exploitation but also the
unwanted advances of her male boss. Hence his "Tuccumcari Striker," an
apparent calypso written in 1953 (well in advance of the "calypso craze" that
was to hit the United States three years later):

> I live in Tuccumcarri
> I think my name be Sary
> My picket sign I carry
> I'ma leetle too young to marry.
> > I work for boss name Barry
> > I work his goddam dairy
> > I squeeze all day the cows teattz
> > I'ma leetle too young to marry.
> My damnd old Bossman Barry
> He use t' own a quarry
> He pinch my legs I'm wearry
> I'ma leetle too young to marry.

In the end, the Tucumcari striker pits herself against the repression of the
police force and vows that she will work until she and her union can bring
about the dictatorship of the proletariat:

> Deputy pull gun big hurry
> > Tell me to leave Tuccumcarri
> > I come walk picket line, sir,
> > I'ma leetle too young to marry.

> I think my name be Sary
> My picket sign I'll carry
> Till I own your Tuccumcarri
> I'ma leetle too young to marry.[22]

All the above examples serve to indicate the various points on the spectrum—from reactionary to progressive, from misogyny to hero-worship—where Guthrie engaged with issues of gender equality. There is ample evidence that he indeed wrestled with the learned misogyny that so often threatened to undermine his own progressivism. But he never quite escaped from under the more traditional views of domestic partnership that he inconsistently maintained in his life, at least when it came to the comparative liberties, as well as the respective responsibilities, of the men and women in a relationship. In spite of his own notorious failure to provide for his wife and children during his first marriage, he could confess to Joe Mazia (at least in the confines of his notebook) his wounded sense of masculinity on the eve of his second marriage, due to a similar failure to provide for Marjorie, with Cathy in her womb: "My position here has not been one that would make any man feel like a man. And all of your outlays in a financial way have come as blessing to you and, to me, they have been curses."[23] Moreover, if it was acceptable for men to spread their sexual warmth around, it was apparently not the case for women—at least so Guthrie felt in the early stages of his desire for Marjorie. As he wrote to her before she had finally left Mazia for good: "I just aint able to reason out how you can sleep with Elmer and write such nice love letters to John."[24]

There is no way to fully examine Guthrie's representations of women's activity and activism without dealing with the issue of his own sexual desire. In this, he was to some extent filtering the currents in popular culture and their impact upon images of women, even within the spheres of progressive activism. As Denning notes in his discussion of the groundbreaking musical revue *Pins and Needles* (1937–40), the Popular Front was most likely to throw up a revolutionary heroine "caught between the world of wage labor and a popular culture saturated with fashion, consumer cosmetics and beauty products, Hollywood stars, romance magazines, and the love songs of Tin Pan Alley."[25] Guthrie's own conflation of progressive activism and sex is reflected in the admission he made in his 1946 blues parody, "Revolutionary Mind":

> One hand on my pillow;
> One hand on my head;
> I want some picket line walker
> To strike out for my bed.[26]

Bryan Garman does not overstate the case when he argues that for Guthrie, like Whitman before him, "political and sexual union are closely related and the democratic ideals on which the United States was founded have the potential to be regenerated through sexual activity."[27] Garman notes that, in fact, Guthrie's difficulty in "adhering to Communist Party discipline" was at least partially due to his refusal or inability to "toe the line when it came to issues of sexuality. For him, the politics of the body and the body politic, the politics of the bedroom and those of the union hall, were inextricably linked."[28] Guthrie's own declarations on sexual emancipation seem to bear out this impression; in Garman's words, they underscore "the connection between economic and sexual repression by implying that those who govern sexual mores control and destroy the bodies and spirits of the people in much the same way that capitalists exploit the bodies of workers."[29]

Such a connection underlies Guthrie's melancholic free-verse disquisition, "My Teeneager Girl," written in April 1952, three years before his erstwhile radio colleague Nicholas Ray finished directing the film *Rebel Without a Cause*, one of the decade's signal responses to the heated debate on teenage freedoms. Prompted by the vision of a teenage girl "out here walking and talking along with your / other buddies of bobbysox pals in your schoolgang," Guthrie surmises:

> I know that you're
> Walking along talking about all of the good sensible natural
>   hopes and plans and dreams and other like things that you
>   have every right to expect to happen to you in your world.

But, thanks to "the whole profit system . . . cocked and primed / and set against you as a person," these young people are doomed to be kept "just as far down, just as lowly down, just as longly down" as the culture requires:

You are not allowed to do any one natural action
At the time when it's most natural for that act and action to be
     done; you are always forced to do this in some way that is so
     bad and so unnatural . . . doing everything with
your lovermate or along with your gang, as they all turn down
     this twisted and unnatural road(s) to get the kicks, or to try
     to revolt, or to try to get a bit of your spite back on your
     parents because they in their worst ignorance lied to you and
     misled and misguided and misinformed you, mistaught you in
     every
way possible to humankind(s).[30]

The forbidden "natural action" is, of course, the sexual expression or experimentation policed not only by parents, schools, clergy, and courts of law, but also by a capitalist ethic that, with its emphasis on the drive for material success at the expense of all else, represses or distorts the natural sex drive. Sexual repression of any form, Guthrie warned, would ultimately and always mean the return of a disruptive, vengeful Eros, never to be denied regardless of societal or economic mores:

The full and terrible world shaking orgasm is being tracked down
by people of every race, creed, color, faith, and political belief, on
account of, well, they have passed it by in favor of gaining more of
prestige, profits, or some new hold on a social position. Many decide
it wasn't too awful important after all. When the orgasm matches
wits with the publicity people, the hopes of fame and of fortune,
the orgasm is forced to take a back seat. It raises all sorts of hell and
kicks holes in its coffins as fast as we try to bury it or to give it some
other name.[31]

Still, in spite of what may appear a refreshing advocacy for sexual openness, these excerpts may make for some uncomfortable reading on a number of fronts. While Guthrie does not specify the age of his "Teeneager Girl," his disquisition raises natural concerns about the proper age of sexual consent and the age difference between the observer and the observed (Guthrie was forty at the time of writing). One's concerns may be further amplified by a knowledge of Guthrie's biography, which included many casual couplings at the emotional expense of his partners, the relative neglect of the children from two of his three marriages, a predatory sexual voraciousness—in part driven by Huntington's disease—that resulted in a conviction for sending obscene letters, and at least one abortion (to which he was opposed).

Indeed, in his staunch opposition to abortion, Guthrie rejected and ridiculed the progressive rationale of a woman's right to choose, which still accompanies the debate. In a disturbing notebook entry from 1952, entitled "Baby Knocker," he describes accompanying Marjorie and an unnamed woman to a doctor's office and his attempts to talk the woman out of an abortion:

> But she said she was being more politically revolutionary
> And broadminded, and modern minded, and everything, to
> Not allow the baby to see the lights of this
> Insanely crazy hopeless dirty filthy rotten generation
> Of foney baloneys, and she feared that it might grow
> Up to suffer in the same disorganized fashions as all
> Of her friends and enemies had grown up to suffer;
> And I told her that maybe her baby might grow up to
> Turn out so many new kinds of useful creatings that
> Its lifetime and span would (could) maybe put the
> Last finishy touches on this very system of profit worshipry
> That all of us hate and wish to see dead;
> But I saw that Dockman go ahead there and knock
> That little baby.[32]

Ed Cray adds: "When one woman he impregnated asked him for money to help pay for an abortion, Guthrie refused. His seed, his 'creation ore,' was too precious to be squandered; the woman found a cooperative doctor without his help, and ended their affair."[33]

Add to these factors the troubling issue of Guthrie's homophobia, and Garman's conclusion carries some weight: "His gender politics were, like the society's in which he lived, far from egalitarian."[34] Much of Guthrie's inconsistency should be considered in the larger context of his idealization of women, not only as sexual partners (when not mere sexual objects), but also as mother figures, which in turn fed into the "left-wing pronatalism" that Denning (after Paula Rabinowitz) describes as having vanquished any feminist stirrings in the Popular Front years—an almost holy maternalism represented, for instance, in the images of Ma Joad and Rose of Sharon in *The Grapes of Wrath* or Dorothea Lange's *Migrant Mother.*[35] Guthrie's own claim in *House of Earth* that childbearing was "the world's greatest work" is part of the same strain.[36]

However, if it was through parenting that Guthrie betrayed some of his most conservative impulses, his tragically brief child-caring role during his marriage to Marjorie also brought out some of his most progressive ones. It was particularly during the years of Cathy's short life (1943–47), as well as the formative years of her posthumous siblings, Arlo (born 1947), Joady (born 1948), and Nora (born 1950), that Guthrie was most expressive in his writings on children and the impact of child-care responsibilities on him personally. From the time of his army discharge in December 1945 until his initial hospital commitments in early 1951—a period that, from the death of Cathy onward, was increasingly punctuated by the confusion, separations, and violence brought on by the entrenchment of his Huntington's disease— Guthrie spent fitful periods at home, caring for the children, while Marjorie taught and practiced dance. There is evidence that he had psychologically been preparing himself for this role as early as Cathy's first year, when—still at sea—his thoughts on child care began to dovetail with his pseudoscientific and political preoccupations: "To live a married life, to keep a home, to care for and teach children, this is as much an art and a science as learning how to perform or to operate machinery."[37]

Accompanying the prolific outpouring of Guthrie's children's songs and albums was a host of observations on the transformative powers of child rearing. Immediately upon Cathy's birth he wrote a manifesto, purportedly from her own little hand: "Men have enjoyed an artificial superiority over women for several centuries. I have got to work and do all I can to break the old slavery idea of the woman being chained to her house which, in many cases, certainly isn't a home."[38] Given the immense outpouring of his writings on the wondrous inspiration provided almost daily by his children, there is no reason to doubt Guthrie's claim:

If

my kids

didnt show

me how to live

every day I'd

already been

almost nearly

dead.[39]

But perhaps inevitably, Guthrie's celebrations of child rearing were also undercut with bursts of exasperation over lost opportunities—complaints that women in the domestic straitjacket had been making for centuries:

> I didn't get to bathe
> not a bit today already.
> I had all of my brats
> latched onto my eyes and
> my hands all full already.[40]

In the midst of his domestic obligations, Guthrie confessed to his notebook that he saw little chance of keeping up with the intellectual and creative competition:

> I guess I'm too busy
> having kids to read
> so many books as you.[41]

It is no accident that Guthrie's increasingly jaded notations on the institution of marriage should have coincided with such fits of domestic exasperation, magnified intensely by both his and Marjorie's grief over Cathy's death and the strain it placed on their marriage. August 1947 appears to have been a particularly difficult time, with Arlo a month old, Cathy six months dead, Guthrie's novel *Seeds of Man* underway, and, lurking behind it all, the embryonic, disorienting signs of Huntington's disease. That month, Guthrie's highly personal frustrations led to a range of negative conclusions on marriage. Clearly he was sexually frustrated (and it could hardly have been otherwise, with Marjorie's exhaustion, her grief, her renewed motherhood, and the burden of her responsibilities both at home and at work):

> I never would have done
> Half of the mean things
> And the nervous things
> And the blind things I done
> If I'd been able to make
>> my woman see how she'd
>> ought to make love
>> to me.[42]

He resorted to a crude recycling of the "Madonna/Whore" complex that has preoccupied theorists from Freud onward, implying in his "Whores and Wives" the wistful desire to integrate the two opposing images but leaving no hope for such an integration in his current marriage:

> I don't really believe in
> whores, whore houses, nor in
> whoredom.
>> But I'd like to be married
> to some good pretty woman
> that had enough sense to
> know how to give me all of
> the fancy works that a whore
> does.[43]

Out of this fierce frustration came a series of abstract ruminations on the process of marital breakdown, with one partner growing "tired and sick of the whole marriage set up" and stepping out "toward another mate to ease the revolutionary mind."[44] Guthrie rationalized his own sexual wanderings in an apparent appeal to equal justice—after all, women had done it to him: "I have had more than one mate stand up and tell me that the firing had ceased in her female soul for me. We did not always part nor separate at the first stop sign, but coasted sort of slow and easy along with our eyes ahead and our hands out the window, looking, reaching, feeling for someone else to try to fill our empty places."[45] He appeared to be paving the way for an inevitable rupture, with an increasing advocacy of divorce as a social blessing—"the only remedy that will even partly cure the sickness or the sicknesses that sprout up out of the very dust when the care was not tender enough for tenderness to grow."[46] Guthrie turned to his trusted old scientific analogies as a means of justifying his increasing sense of marital repulsion:

> It is a crime and not a virtue to pretend for years that you are maritally all right when both of you are suffering the hell of unsatisfied love or the hell of incompatibility. The brave thing and the proper thing to do is by all means to be as scientific about human hearts and minds as you are about minerals and metals.
>
> There are alloys and metals and all kinds of chemicals that mix together very well, but there are others that actually destroy each other if kept together.[47]

The knowledge of Guthrie's marital crisis adds a somber hue to the otherwise liberating exhortations of "I Say to You Woman and Man"—written, as it was, in the desperate month of August 1947—for it came from the depths of a marriage undergoing a slow, painful disintegration. Guthrie's call to "Dance out" was not solely a cry for women's liberation in the abstract; it was meant for both women *and* men—for Marjorie and for himself:

> And if I just had this
> one thing to say to
> a husband it would
> be these words
>
> Go dance
> That's all
> Just jump up and let
> go and dance.[48]

In fact, Guthrie was not through with his exhortations to "Dance Out and Grab," as he urged Marjorie to do in another fragment, written as much to facilitate his own freedom as hers:

Law knows,
Marjorie,
If we do have to bust up,
which I think
we might,
Law knows
you can dance out here
and grab you a man
Lots more to your liking
Than I ever was,
And you can
Grab him
In nothing flat[49]

In spite of all Guthrie's yearnings for stability and an anchored home life, the double-edged sword of marriage was always cutting both ways. Thus, in a rueful entry written for his three-month-old son Arlo in October 1947, he cast the institution of marriage as an insufferable drag on a man:

Don't let marriage slow you down, Arlo. Don't let a marriage slow you down. If you hit a good marriage or if you hit on a bad marriage, Arlo Boy, don't let marriage mess you up.

No man could be married onto a prettier mama nor onto a better mama than your mama Marjorie is. But, Marjorie and me see the world from such different cliff tops that I doubt lots of times if we see eye to eye and puss to puss.

But when you do grow up, Arlo, and bite down on yourself a wife, just remember what I'm saying to you here, this morning, Oh, Arlo, don't ever let a marriage slow you down.[50]

Guthrie's marriage to Marjorie lasted until October 1953, punctuated by frequent separations and reconciliations. Following their divorce, which had been advised by doctors concerned about the welfare of the children in a household ravaged by Huntington's disease, Guthrie married his third and last wife, Anneke Van Kirk Marshall, who was pregnant with their daughter, Lorina:

Wife Number Three! (Pore girl!)
I done drove two (Pore girl!)
Just crazy as you! (Have mercy!)
Wife Number Three.[51]

Two years later that marriage would end in divorce, spurred on in part by
the debilitating impact of Guthrie's disease on his capacity as a provider and
caregiver, which left the young and unprepared Anneke exasperated beyond
hope.[52]

In the end, it was obviously more than sexism or rampant masculinism that had wreaked such havoc with Guthrie's marriages; they were also
challenged by a political vision of liberation ever at war with a conventional
desire for security and stability, as well as the ravages of neurological disintegration. That Guthrie and Marjorie remained in love until his death, there
is no doubt. As he wrote to her from Greystone Park Hospital in October
1956, with his appreciation shimmering through the warped expression of
his illness: "You did live with me on thru all my daily worker days and all my
Almanacy Singing days all the real merchant Mariana days You stuck by me
in all my Army carby Ar[med] forces days."[53]

Their marriage could not, in the end, withstand all the strains that had
been placed upon it. But it has left a powerful legacy, not only in the form of
their progeny and the vast Woody Guthrie Archives launched by Marjorie,
but also in the Huntington's Disease Society of America that has grown out
of Marjorie's Committee to Combat Huntington's Disease. The latter is itself
a product of her determination to find an explanation and ultimately a cure
for the affliction that destroyed the man she loved and that still threatened
their children. Through her lobbying and her tireless commitment, Marjorie Guthrie became the patron saint of Huntington's disease research, one
outgrowth of this conflicted marriage battered in a contest between desire,
tradition, and all the crosscurrents of modernity.

12

Blacks + Jews = Blues

One further outgrowth of Guthrie's marriage to Marjorie is worth exploring in the context of the huge demographic shifts associated with American modernity. His integration into Marjorie's Jewish immigrant family in the 1940s inevitably transformed both his racial and his political awareness. Just as his journey away from Okemah and into the urban centers of Los Angeles and New York had enabled him to reconstruct his entire worldview of African Americans and other non-Anglo groups in the United States, so did his immersion into a bohemian Left substantially driven by urban Jewish activists—in the context of both World War II and the establishment of the state of Israel.

Guthrie's prior years in Oklahoma, Texas, and even California had been marked by a casual, thoughtless racism that has already been the subject of some study. Certain well-known milestones along the road to his racial enlightenment included a public berating—and his own heartfelt apology—for his use of the "N-word" over the radio; the antiracist tutelage of such political mentors as Ed Robbin, Will Geer, and Alan Lomax; his wartime experiences with Jim Crow in the military; his immersion in the fight against racial segregation alongside black musical colleagues—the likes of Lead Belly, Josh White, Sonny Terry, and Brownie McGhee; and his witnessing of the virulent racism that drove the Peekskill Riots, which he would record in song.[1]

It must be said too that for all his good intentions and his unquestionable commitment to racial justice and equality, Guthrie could not wholly shake off the resonance of white paternalism that sometimes marked even the most sympathetic expressions of his times. Mark Goble has paid attention to the "primitivist conventions"—the "fantasy of nature and sensuality that uses race . . . as one of its essential mediums in U.S. modernism."[2] Guthrie himself was not immune to such primitivism (in spite of his contempt for the equation of folk music with "the primitive"). It shows, for instance, in his description of American slaves as "simple in heart and spirit" and living "directly and closely in contact with an unseen Something or Other that we call Inspiration, a something too many of us are too busy to pay any attention to."[3] Guthrie was clearly tapping into what Ronald Radano calls the "rhetoric of romantic 'jungle' primitivism that had extended from the era of African colonization." Radano explains the progressive cultural intentions that often lay behind such admittedly essentialist "rhetoric" on the part of both black and white practitioners in the first half of the twentieth century, beginning in the 1910s: "As racialized as they were, these depictions sought to challenge assumptions of racial inferiority by exalting the qualities of distinctiveness that were thought to express the essence of the Negro race."[4] Such of Guthrie's "appeals to a romantic Africa" (Radano's phrasing)—as well as other sites beyond the US border—were clearly reactions to the frenetic pace of modernity that had presumably cut off white Americans' access to that "unseen Something or Other." So Guthrie would attempt to reestablish the connection, sometimes through such ill-judged measures as the romantic minstrelsy (and excruciating dialect) of the aged Mexican shaman Rio in *Seeds of Man*, or even in the intimacy of his love letters to Marjorie: "Lets not let anything keep us from having every drop and every ounce of joyous wildness that the freest couple in the African jungle will ever have. Let's be just as modern as we know how and just as old and primitive as anybody anywhere."[5]

However, such tainted expressions are aberrations in an otherwise uplifting story of racial awakening and change. To the extent that there is any inconsistency in Guthrie's rhetoric of race, it can at least be partially put down to his positioning on yet another historical fault line—the "racial realignment" that Michael Denning assigns to the 1940s, with its "central cause" being "the massive migration of white and black southerners to the war-industry cities of the North and West . . . the largest internal migration in US history."[6] There is evidence to suggest that this "racial realignment" had in fact begun before the 1940s and that Guthrie was directly caught up in it. As his Library of Congress recordings make clear, Guthrie was fully aware that, in terms of political and labor activism at least, nonwhite groups had been at the vanguard of progress, even before his arrival in California in 1937. John Steinbeck had kept hidden behind the Joads and other poor white Okies the multi-ethnic activism that had inspired *The Grapes of Wrath* in the first place (Denning notes that the novel's "roots . . . lie in the great 1933 strikes of Mexican, Filipino, Chinese, and Japanese farmworkers").[7] But Guthrie was up front about it, however much his expression was marred by unfortunate wording at the expense of the Japanese:

> All of these Japs—they formed them an organization. They
> unionized. The Japs and the Chinese. The Chinese, they done the
> same things; they kinda unionized—and the Filipinos, they finally
> got to where they had a little better jobs than getting out in the fruit
> and in the crops and doing all this hard work. They finally got to
> where they was taking care of most of the apartment and rooming
> houses and the buildings of that kind around over California. And
> so there was just one bunch left, and that was what's called the Okies,
> that fell into that country.[8]

Peter La Chapelle has paid the most attention to the quasi-racial stigmatizing of the "liminally white" Dust Bowl migrants in California and its impact on Guthrie's own racial enlightenment.[9] In particular, La Chapelle focuses on Guthrie's aim, through his "Woody Sez" columns as well as his KFVD broadcasting, to forge a "kind of multiethnic, class-based coalition" linking the Dust Bowl migrants, "antifascist Spanish guerrillas and exiles, and dissident diasporic Jews."[10]

One of the least known chapters in Guthrie's history is his deepening engagement with the Jewish diaspora. Of all the world's oppressed peoples, it was the Jews of twentieth-century Europe who best enabled Guthrie to reimagine the concept of "refugees" on behalf of the Dust Bowl migrants, just as it was the Holocaust—perhaps even more than American slavery—that ultimately enabled him to identify racism as a defining mark of a particularly homegrown American fascism. Guthrie's relationship with

Judaism, one of the richest sources of inspiration for him, began years before his immersion into Jewish family life and politics through his courtship and marriage to Marjorie. Within months of his arrival in California, he had met Ed Robbin, who opened his eyes onto another world. Robbin had lived four years in Palestine, writing for an English-language newspaper in Jerusalem and living on a kibbutz. It is likely that it was in Robbin's presence that Guthrie first listened at any length to arguments for and against the establishment of a Jewish homeland in British-mandated Palestine. Guthrie was present during an argument between Robbin and his Arab-American friend George Shibley, an attorney who would go on to represent the Mexican American defendants in the Sleepy Lagoon murder case (which sparked the Zoot Suit Riots of 1943) as well as later defending Sirhan Sirhan at his trial for the murder of Robert F. Kennedy. As Robbin recalled, things had gotten "really hot" with Shibley that night:

> He maintained that the Jews had no place in the Middle east—that this was Arab land the Jews were stealing, and that the Jews were being used as imperialist pawns. I went into the historic right of the Jews to this small plot of earth, and said that Jews had bought and paid for the land they occupied. The debate that night got somewhat bitter. So I called a halt to it and asked Woody to sing some songs. As he tuned his guitar, he started talking in his slow drawl: "I don't know much about the politics in those countries way across the seas, and I don't know whether Ed or George is right. But I got a song that says it all, because wherever there are people, the struggle is much the same. It ain't nation and nation or one color and another. It's always been the rich squeezing the poor. And it's the same in those lands where the prophets from Isaiah to Jesus preached the same thing."[11]

In Robbin's reflection, Guthrie evaded any further engagement with the issue by singing "Jesus Christ." However, it appears that very soon afterward Guthrie was implying almost a familial connection with the Jewish refugees from Europe, noting that his own cousin had "built him a shack in one of those flood basins out there . . . a big packing box that he got down at the water front and all over it was painted the name of a family of people that managed to get out of Germany just as the Nazis were taking over. My cousin called it his Hitler Box."[12] In 1937, as he began to ruminate on the possibilities of adobe as a solution to homelessness (which would be most fully expressed in *House of Earth*), Guthrie wrote to a new friend, actor and activist Eddie Albert: "You see old adobe brick houses almost everywhere that are as old as Hitlers tricks, and still standing, like the Jews."[13]

Upon his arrival in New York in 1940, Guthrie and the Jewish diaspora were well primed for a mutual embrace. As Irwin Silber later speculated, "There was the heart of America personified in Woody. . . . And for a New York Left that was primarily Jewish, first or second generation American and was desperately trying to get Americanized, I think a figure like Woody was of great, great importance."[14] This was certainly borne out in Marjorie's initial conception of Guthrie, before actually having met him. Upon hearing *Dust Bowl Ballads*, this American-born daughter of east European Jewish immigrants had imagined Woody Guthrie as a tall, "Lincolnesque" figure wearing a cowboy hat.[15]

Through Marjorie, Guthrie found his most powerful and intimate connection to the rich and mortally threatened world of European Jewry: her mother, Aliza Waitzman Greenblatt (1885–1975). As Susanne Shavelson notes, Aliza, who had arrived in the United States from Bessarabia (in today's Ukraine) in 1900, "was among the first to organize the American Jewish community and raise funds toward the establishment of a Jewish national home." Upon her marriage to fellow Bessarabian immigrant Isidore Greenblatt (which would produce four children besides Marjorie), Aliza became active in both socialist and Zionist circles, establishing the Atlantic City branches of both the Farband, a socialist charity, and the Zionist Organization of America, as well as raising funds for Hadassah and the Jewish National Fund. In 1920, Isidore had spent a year attempting to establish a canning factory in Palestine; in the 1950s, both he and Aliza would attempt another year of living in Israel before returning to the United States permanently, having been defeated by the "material conditions under which they lived." By the time of her death in 1975, Aliza had established herself as one of the foremost poets and lyricists writing in Yiddish, having published "five volumes of poetry and an autobiography, *Baym Fenster fun a Leben* [A Window on a Life], all in Yiddish."[16]

And just as Aliza's younger daughter Marjorie would be instrumental in furthering research on Huntington's disease, so would she be a major force in the preservation of Yiddish literature through her inspirational role in the establishment of the Yiddish Book Center in Amherst, Massachusetts. Aaron Lansky, the founder of the center, recalls a conversation with Marjorie and her daughter Nora following Marjorie's donation of Aliza's Yiddish library to the center—a conversation that reveals much about Guthrie's adoption and enthusiastic immersion into the world of American Jewry:

> After the boxes were safely loaded we sat down with Nora and Marjorie at the kitchen table. Nora served up fresh coffee and homemade cookies, and Marjorie began to speak about her own childhood and her lifelong relation to Yiddishkeit. Although Woody was not Jewish, she said, he always struck her as having a *yidishe neshome*, a Jewish soul. For one thing, he was a voracious reader: "One time my father gave him a copy of a tractate of the Talmud in English translation, and he read it over and over, highlighting the passages he liked with different colored inks." He was also unusually helpful around the house. "Our Jewish neighbor used to watch Woody as he wheeled the carriage or helped with the chores. She was so impressed with his domesticity that one morning, while he was carrying out the garbage, she came up to him and said, 'Woody, you're a regular Jew.' Woody said it was the nicest compliment he ever received."

Lansky also recalled Marjorie's reflections on Guthrie's relations with her parents:

> Although Woody's relationship with his father-in-law, Izzy, had been stiff, he and his more literary mother-in-law had gotten along famously. They were, of course, very different writers: Woody was folksy, vernacular, and political, while Aliza tended to be lyrical and refined, writing more about nature than about people. But they shared a love of words, and they both wrote a great deal for children. According to Marjorie, Woody enjoyed Aliza's work and actually learned the Yiddish words to [Aliza's] "*Fort a fisher*" and other songs,

which he performed in public. But he never stopped chiding her for not being more political. "'Enough flowers and butterflies!' he would say, 'What about the working masses?'"[17]

The concept of the promised land became increasingly important to Guthrie during the war years, and just as California had proved wanting for the migrant children of the Dust Bowl, so, he feared, had America proved wanting for the Jewish exiles from Europe. One ugly moment hit Guthrie and Marjorie in the face, as they were confronted by a sign posted outside an Alton, Illinois, swimming pool, in 1945: "No dogs or Jews allowed."[18] He had previously written to Marjorie: "I think of what fascism is trying to do to you and to your relatives, to me and mine, and seeing what they've done and are doing in the nations they've already overrun, it makes me even fuller of hate for them."[19] And now such anti-Semitic fascism was neatly wrapping itself in the Stars and Stripes. Guthrie's incredulity was further stretched to the breaking point when he learned in 1948 that, at the behest of the US commander of occupied Germany, General Lucius D. Clay, the life sentence of the so-called Beast of Buchenwald, Ilse Koch, had been reduced to a mere four years. In a fury he spewed onto the page a snapshot of the genocide in a series of terse six-syllable lines, casting himself as both Jewish victim and witness:

> I'm here in Buchenwald.
> My number's on my skin.
> Old Ilsa Koch is here.
> The prisoners walk the grounds.
> The hounds have killed a girl.
> The guards have shot a man.
> Some more have starved to death.
> Here comes the prisoner's car.
> They dump them in the pen.
> They load them down the chute.
> The trooper cracks their skulls.
> He steals their teeth of gold.
> He shoves them on the belt.
> He swings that furnace door.
> He slides their corpses in.

Yet by the single wave of an American hand "old Ilsy Koch went free."[20] If ever the Jews needed another Moses and a new promised land, it was now.

It is perhaps difficult for the most recent two—or even three—generations raised on the increasingly bitter Israeli-Palestinian conflict to appreciate what the prospects of a Jewish homeland would have signified both to Jews and gentiles of Guthrie's generation and that of his in-laws. The Greenblatts had been among the roughly 2.75 million eastern European Jews fleeing the Russian pogroms between 1881 and 1914.[21] By 1945, both they and the Guthries, along with the rest of the world, had begun to learn the full extent of the Nazi Holocaust, by far the most perverse manifestation of industrial modernity yet seen—the genocidal triumph of bureaucratic efficiency, technological advancement, and scientific rationalism (in Zygmunt Bauman's words, "the deadly logic of problem-solving").[22]

There is, of course, no way of determining how Guthrie's allegiances over the Israeli-Arab conflict might have shifted over the ensuing decades of the struggle, especially after the Six-Day War of 1967—the year in which he died—which saw the first expansion of Israeli territory beyond the borders established in 1948. There is no record of his response, if any, to what the Arabs have called al-Nakbah (or "catastrophe"), the flight of up to 750,000 Palestinian Arabs and successive generations of refugees, now numbering over five million in the West Bank, Gaza, and elsewhere—an inescapable fact and factor in the struggle for Israel's right to exist.[23] What we can say is that, in August 1947 at least, in the waning days of British control, Guthrie's allegiance lay firmly with the Jews against "perfidious Albion," resulting in an intense outpouring of words and visual imagery, much of it produced on the same day—August 4.

August 1947, a stressful and depressing enough period in Guthrie's personal life, seemed to promise few uplifting moments in the wider political realm, not least with regard to the anti-imperialism he championed. Hence his bitter excoriations of the British Empire, whether in the context of the Greek Civil War ("King George of Greece he don't want nobody free; / And Churchill is in sad company"),[24] in India ("The kid from India told me, 'I don't want to see England love our country so much that they send in armies and keep us in cages and feed us less than animals'"),[25] or in the Holy Land. Guthrie, a preternaturally avid news reader, would have been satiated with reports of the empire's war against the Jewish Resistance Movement, its interception and seizure of Jewish immigrant ships such as the *Exodus 1947*, its executions of Jewish resistance fighters (with retaliatory kidnappings and executions of British officers by these same fighters), and its barbed wire internment camps—not only in Cyprus but, unbelievably, Germany, where thousands of European Jews were imprisoned after thwarted attempts at mass immigration to Palestine.[26] To Guthrie, the British Empire was tacking bewilderingly close to Nazism in its treatment of the Jews in Palestine:

> Old Churchill is
> smearing my Jew blood
> long as he can.[27]

All of Guthrie's wartime affection for Britain appears to have dissipated. Now the simple image of Aliza Greenblatt's discarded peach pit, sitting in Guthrie's ashtray in Coney Island, sparked a whole chain of vicious associations at the expense of the British, along with a defiant vision of a new Jewish nation rising like a phoenix from the ash piles of Auschwitz and Buchenwald: "Grandma's wet peach seed here on my ash tray makes me remember how bad the rich British are treating my poor Jews. You Nazis, you fascists, you world cager British have whipped my bare skin down to sad ashes but my seed left here in my ashes will tear your caged zoo ship into ten thousand little pieces."[28]

It was thus against the backdrop of the bitter fight for a Jewish homeland that Guthrie immersed himself deeper and deeper into the world of Jewish culture, not least through his unsolicited reviews of Moses Asch's recordings for the Disc and Folkways labels. In November 1947 he wrote to Asch praising a new Disc release, *My Father's House*, from the Hazamir Singers and Children's Chorus of Tel Aviv. Noting of the album's six folk songs that "Marjorie sings several of them in her Mother's native tongue, Yiddish," Guthrie declared: "This singing will rust down and wear down and tear down every barbed wire pigpen that our empire dreamers can ever build up around our songs, or around our hopes for one big human family singing and dancing, working, all the roads and trails around the world."[29] With the establishment of Israel in May 1948, Guthrie launched into an intense period of research and writing a cycle of Hanukkah-themed songs, annotating a host of newly acquired books on the holiday and its historical origins.[30] Over the next year he produced a raft of songs including "Happy Joyous Hanuka," "Honeyky Hanuka," "The Many and the Few," and "Hanukkah Dance," the latter two of which he recorded for Asch in 1949 but the majority of which remained unheard until the New York–based Klezmatics recorded them in 2006 and 2009.[31] Yiddish phrases and endearments appeared in some of his children's songs, such as the lullaby "Headdy Down," in which his sons Arlo and Joady are urged, "Keppy down, Kepula" ("lay your little heads down").[32]

Most importantly, Guthrie's Jewish-themed songs indicate his continued striving to establish political connections between Judaism and the wider world. Thus could his "The Many and the Few," for instance, resonate with the history of outnumbered Jews resisting not only the imperial tyrannies of Assyria, Babylon, Persia, and Macedonia, but also, implicitly, the British Empire. Indeed, broadening his focus, Guthrie positioned Jewish folk music as a counterforce to all of the modern imperial powers jockeying for influence in the postwar global carve-up. As he wrote to Asch upon hearing the Folkways release *Music of the Middle East* in 1949: "The blank spaces in all of our United Nations broadcasts, between the long pauses of some of its delegates, ought to be filled in with songs such as these from the scrubby sprigs of Israel (as well as all other tribes and lands which your plastic records catch so warm and so plain)."[33]

It is clear that by the early 1950s, the knowledge of the Holocaust and the struggle for a Jewish homeland had forced Guthrie into yet another reassessment of the concept of "refugee," even broader than that which he had imagined back in the 1930s connecting the Dust Bowl migrants and the exiles from the early Third Reich. Already there were ample signs that Guthrie's postwar promised land, which he had hoped to see built upon the ruins of a vanquished fascism, had remained as elusive as before the war and as contested upon the streets of New York or Alton, Illinois, as upon those in Jerusalem or Tel Aviv. Indeed, if Guthrie had begun to perceive a shared fellowship between "post-Holocaust" Jews and African Americans—both "strangers in the land" (in Eric Sundquist's words), in spite of their vastly different experiences of oppression and victimhood[34]—he had witnessed it just a stone's throw from New York City, during the riots against Paul Robeson in the pleasant Hudson Valley town of Peekskill, in Westchester County, New York, in 1949.

This signal manifestation of postwar American racism had tarnished the reputation of New York and its environs as bastions of northern progressivism and enlightenment. Guthrie had seen firsthand the angry mobs of Peekskill screaming racist epithets while waving US flags. "I've never heard such cusswords as they spit off from their lips," he wrote in his song, "Peekskill Golfing Grounds"—"Jew bastard. Wop. Hey nigger. Kike and Commy."[35] Like his People's Songs colleague Mario "Boots" Casetta, he had heard them chanting "'Hey, you white niggers, get back to Russia' and 'Jews, Jews, Jews'"—all of which was caught on tape and incorporated into the documentary song "The Peekskill Story," which included music by the Weavers and narration by Howard Fast and Paul Robeson.[36] If ever there was a natural fellowship between victimized blacks and Jews, it had been crystallized at Peekskill. If ever the absurdity of a "color line" had been revealed, it had been in the indiscriminate branding by the mobs of Peekskill, for whom the phrase "white nigger" held no irony whatsoever.

In the wake of Peekskill, and with the chants and violence of the rioters still ringing in his ears (and reverberating in his songwriting), Guthrie and his family moved into a new apartment in the Beach Haven development in Brooklyn's Brighton Beach in October 1950. There Guthrie found that even the discriminatory practices on his own home ground could prove the underbelly of the monster that had been unleashed at Peekskill. The Guthries were among the first to move into the Beach Haven development only recently completed by Fred Trump, the real estate mogul whose son Donald would come to epitomize for many the extremes of architectural arrogance, celebrity hubris, and the naked avarice of American capitalism. (It was Donald Trump's candidacy for the US presidency that first prompted my publication of Guthrie's Beach Haven writings in January 2016 under the title "Woody Guthrie, 'Old Man Trump,' and a Real Estate Empire's Racist Foundations."[37] Candidate Trump's outright targeting of Mexicans and Muslims, as well as his tweets and dog-whistles against Jews and African Americans, had Woody Guthrie sounding the alarm from beyond the grave.)

Frederick Christ Trump has earned a qualified reputation in some quarters as a champion of public housing, due to such co-operative developments

as Beach Haven and Trump Village, built off the back of contracts from the
Federal Housing Authority (FHA) in the early 1950s. But Trump was no
altruistic saint, having resorted—as noted by Coney Island historian Charles
Densen—to "dubious means to reap windfall profits from federal contracts
and Title I developments."[38] In addition to cozying up to the mob in order
to smooth the way for his projects, Trump enthusiastically perpetuated the
"restrictive covenants" against minorities that had long been facilitated by
FHA contracts—in particular, the instructions to avoid "inharmonious uses
of housing," which, as Gwenda Blair notes, was "a code phrase for selling
homes in white areas to blacks."[39] Indeed, Fred and Donald Trump would be
jointly prosecuted by the US Department of Justice in 1975 on the grounds of
racial discrimination (with both the plaintiffs and the defendants claiming
victory after a highly ambivalent verdict).[40]

By the time he moved into Beach Haven, Guthrie had already witnessed
and criticized the racism and bigotry that had turned the sidewalks of Coney
Island—even his own beloved Mermaid Avenue—into avenues of the outcast:

> I watched your black feet
> > scuffle down along my
> > Mermaid Avenue sidewalks
> > tonight and a thing come
> > over my mind and said your
> > ten toenails have all
> > been looking glasses
> > full of your hurt face
> > watching your hands of
> > ten fingers cut your
> > toe nails.
>
> I asked that sidewalk why
> > do people all of your
> > same color stand along
> > my curb in the fronts
> > of my little stores and
> > wait for my filthiest
> > jobs at slow money?

I hate this fascist hat
  that puts you down and
  keeps you here scuffling.[41]

So much for the war that was to "settle the score once and for all, of all kinds of race-hate." Even before the move from Mermaid Avenue, Guthrie had signaled his nervousness about taking up residence in "Bitch Havens," in spite of the "Four rooms and a half" that would markedly expand his family's living space.[42] Less than two years into his residency at Beach Haven, he was lamenting the covenants that had kept his new neighborhood the province of the lily-white (as well as those not-quite-white others, such as Jews, who might pass in comparison with blacks and other, darker minorities). Optimistically, he looked to the Jews in the area as natural allies in his wishful scenario of smashing the color line to transform Beach Haven into a multiracial cornucopia of life, laughter, and love—a vision wholly in keeping with his euphoric predictions of the world following the defeat of Nazism and fascism:

> This old Jewish looking mother here walking back from the
>   appetizer store with her sacks full of bagels and loxes
>   and onion rolls and the morning's morning in your eyes,
>   you wouldn't care, would you, mother, if your eyes looked
>   up in these windows of every apartment and saw a sight
>   a hundred times more alive and living and as funhaving
>   and as colorstruck as Beach Haven could be if you saw a
>   face of every bright color laffing and joshing in these
>   old darkly weeperish empty shadowed windows all up
>   around
>   your (and my own) head here? Huh? Would you mind that
>   so much? No. No. I knew you wouldn't.

And in defiance of the bigoted codes of Trump and the FHA, Guthrie imagined himself calling out to a "negro girl yonder that walks along against this headwind / holding onto her purse and her fur coat":

I welcome you here to live. I welcome
you and your man both here to Beach Haven to love in any
ways you please and to have some kind of a decent place to
get pregnant in and to have your kids raised up in. I'm
yelling out my own welcome to you.[43]

Before long, Fred Trump himself came to personify for Guthrie all the viciousness of the racial codes that continued to put decent housing, both public and private, out of reach of so many of his fellow citizens, no less in the North than in the South. The association was indeed highly personal for Guthrie: "My worst enemy is my landlord that tries his best to make me and my family live a life of race hate just because he so sickly chose to live his own sad life that way."[44] The name of his "enemy" returns again and again in Guthrie's Beach Haven writings. "Trump, you made a tramp out of me," he snarled in an unpublished seven-verse diatribe:

You robbed my wife and robbed my kids,
Made me stay drunk and to hit the skids;
Yepsir, Trump, you made a tramp out of me.[45]

The robbery of which Guthrie accused Trump was, of course, symbolic: it was the robbery of his family's right to abide in a multiracial community based on mutual respect rather than profit-driven bigotry. As Guthrie lamented in a letter to Stetson Kennedy, the children of Beach Haven were being raised "under the skullyboned stink and dank of racial hate, jimmy-crack Krow."[46] And he declared where the culpability lay:

I suppose
Old Man Trump knows
Just how much
Racial Hate
he stirred up
In the bloodpot of human hearts
When he drawed
That color line
Here at his
Eighteen hundred family project

By the branch
of Beach Haven,
I suppose
Old Man Trump knows
How many drops
Of sad tears
And crazy fears
He caused my family
In and out of
Beach Haven to feel
And to fall heir to.[47]

And, as if to leave no doubt in anyone's mind over his landlord's personal responsibility for perpetuating black Americans' status as internal refugees—strangers in their own strange land—Guthrie reworked for a second time, after "I Don't Feel at Home on the Bowery No More," his signature Dust Bowl ballad "I Ain't Got No Home":

Beach Haven ain't my home!
I just cain't pay this rent!
My money's down the drain!
And my soul is badly bent!
Beach Haven looks like heaven
Where no black ones come to roam!
No, no, no! Old Man Trump!
Old Beach Haven ain't my home!

In his parting shot, Guthrie declared to his sworn "enemy": "We are crazy fools / As long as Race Hate rules! / No, no, no! Old Man Trump! / Beach Haven ain't my home!"[48]

Increasingly, Guthrie turned to fantasies of mass miscegenation as a surefire means of wiping out the racial separatism inscribed into the housing codes of Beach Haven and elsewhere—in a sense, his own brand of biological warfare. "God dont / know much / about any color lines," he jotted into his notebook in November 1952, noting that the defenders of "white southern womanhood" (and other such fictions of racial purity) were "way ahead of God" in their lynching and terror campaigns.[49] Again, America's white supremacists and Germany's Nazis had shared the same delusion: "You can't any more say it's white and southern [than] Mr. Hitler could say his nazis and his fascist gang were plumb the right kind of German nor any other right proper blend of a person."[50]

To be truthful, Guthrie's own fantasies of race mixing were not entirely free from the essentialism that he had set out to criticize as racist weaponry in others, even as he applauded the mixture—and the resultant characteristics of his children's bloodline—that his own marriage to Marjorie had presumably produced. He wrote to Stetson Kennedy in August 1950, reveling in his children's "sixway blood mixture that would outdo this whole world for fire and for deviltry and for passion and for fun and for action and for quick fighting spirits"—as though strains of blood could ensure any such thing.[51] But there is no denying that Guthrie imagined concerted race-mixing as a political project, a resistance campaign capable of overthrowing the raft of restrictive laws— and the violence through which they were enforced—underpinning Jim Crow:

> I know the million laws against mixed loving;
> And how the fight shapes up to make Two sides; one side the folks
> that love in the face of the law's pistol and hangrope. . . .
> And the second side is the rifles of the thugmen. . . .
>
> If there was only any way of knowing just how many bellies rub
> together in my 48 States tonite to turn out my big
> mixed race that'll win out over guns
> With love and hugs and winks and jokes alone. . . .
>
> That, in its way,
> Is destined to be one day known
> As my biggest of scientific miracles . . . this joking
> and this dancey rubbing which will outnumber atom
> bombs, deputy guns, all kinds of burny crosses,
> my miracles of being able to breed and seed and bear
> Six more of my hot blood
> to stand in the place
> you tried to kill with all your guns.[52]

While no evidence has yet emerged of Guthrie's actually having had an affair with a nonwhite woman, his interracial desire—which was as much political as erotic—is a matter of record. In the midst of the war, while at sea, he had written:

> I would not have
> A colorless woman
> To sleep with for a wife
> Where no color is
> There is nothing at all
> Because God uses paint
> To taint each skin its color
> If you aint got no sense
> You just aint.[53]

Such writings throw considerable light on Guthrie's contempt, his incorrigibility, his belligerence, and his defiance when it came to confronting the illogical and arbitrarily imposed barriers to interracial human interaction, whether physical or social. They illuminate, at least partially, his unrealized desire to form an interracial folk group with "some perty (negroid) girl" to compete with the all-white Weavers.[54] And then there was the moment in Jacksonville, Florida, that Kennedy recalled: "We were in the corner crossroads general store, one of those mom and pop things, and there were both black and white people in there shopping, just a handful. And Woody in a loud voice says to me, says, 'You know, I think little colored kids is a whole lots prettier than little white kids, don't you?' And it almost got us killed right there. We had to get him out of there."[55] Kennedy was aware too that the racist context of his times informed Guthrie's openly expressed (if perhaps never consummated) desire for interracial sex, his ostentatious pronouncements about planting his "seed" in the womb of a black woman—possibly, as Kennedy surmised, "one of the symptoms in the advanced stages" of Huntington's disease, "a preoccupation with four-letter words and sex"—but equally possibly an expression by "Woody the messenger, you know; seed, you plant seed and they bear fruit hopefully, and they fall on fertile ground hopefully—there's sort of a mix here, you could take it either as semen or ideology or both. That's all right with me."[56]

Certainly Guthrie could be seen at his most depressed and defeated when his race-mixing project was thwarted, even at the hands of the very labor movement to which he was devoted. Such was the case in December 1947, when the white members of a striking tobacco union in North Carolina boycotted his appearance because he had refused to cut a song with the lyrics:

> All colors of hands gonna work together
> All colors of eyes gonna laugh and shine
> All colors of feet gonna dance together
> When I bring my CIO to Caroline, Caroline.

As Guthrie recalled, "It cut me to my bones to have to play and sing for those negroes with no other colors mixing in."[57]

Conversely, his euphoria shone through when his project was accepted and championed, as when he recalled that same year, with relish, a metaphorical slugfest with his hated opponent, Jim Crow:

> I hit you a good lick
>> last night in old
>> Washington slums. It
>> was up in the boxing
>> ring there at Turner's
>> Arena. I hit you with
>> 3 songs. . . .

> I told my little joke about
>> the hounds holing the 2
>> rabbits up in the old
>> holler log and how the
>> lady rabbit told the gent
>> rabbit we'll just have to
>> hurry up and outnumber
>> those hounds.

> Those hounds are the fascist
> race haters. The rabbits
> are us working folks.
> Our hearts and our hands
> will outnumber all of
> your old spread hate.[58]

It need hardly be said that, in all likelihood, Guthrie's victorious rabbits would be of a mixed breed, a leporid representation of the ideal "rainbow blends" that he had fantasized in 1942, in the midst of his "good war" against Hitler:

> And the mixture is all
> of us and we're still mixing
> And all creeds and kinds
> and colors of us are blending
> Till I suppose
> Ten million years from now
> We'll all be just alike,
> Same color
> Same size
> Working together—
> Maybe we'll have all of
> the fascists out of the way
> by then.[59]

Guthrie's fantasies of an eventual mono-race can be seen, in some respects, as retrograde, harkening back to the eighteenth century, when "scientific monogenism" reflected a highly conservative, even fundamentalist view—that, "after the creation and the fall from paradise, Adam and Eve's descendants settled in different parts of the world and then lost, in varying and racially marked degrees, their moral and physiological prelapsarian perfection."[60] If Guthrie's race fantasies were indeed aimed at bringing humanity back to a mono-racial, monochromatic Garden of Eden, it was hardly a realistic or even desirable scenario. His vision was problematic in that it not only foresaw the elimination of white supremacy, but also all reasons for black pride in those cultural arenas that positively redefined modernism in the face of its racialist currents, challenging the white-supremacist overtones of Conrad, Eliot, and Pound with the glorious productions of the Harlem Renaissance and the wider "Black Atlantic."[61]

Having said this, Guthrie was at least aiming toward a symbolic way forward, away from the segregation and racism that had defined political and social life in both Oklahoma and Texas (even in his own home) and that he had not begun to interrogate seriously until his arrival in Los Angeles. That city, and New York after it, engendered in Guthrie a racially—and radically—modernized perception enabled by his firsthand immersion in the vast, energetic multiculturalism of urban America. The faces of Guthrie's city dwellers were not simply pale "petals on a wet, black bough"—the faces of Ezra Pound's ideal monochrome populace.[62] They were also the color of the bough itself, and the many colors between petal and bough. Pound, in his own fantasizing, could actually envisage his New York as "MY CITY, my beloved, my white!"[63] As the next chapter shows, Guthrie could (and would) do no such thing. For, whatever his faults—and whatever he still had yet to learn—by the time he arrived in New York, he had already learned and unlearned too much to ever succumb to such a contemptible fantasy.

13

Urban Centrifuge

Folk musician and photographer John Cohen recalled a late encounter with a disheveled Woody Guthrie in New York, sometime in the 1950s: "He was crossing from the center of Union Square, right through the traffic, towards where I was. Maybe he recognized me, I'm not sure. But to see him cross the traffic, like he was going one way and the traffic was going the other way, and he didn't pay any attention to the traffic. It was like, 'Get out of my way, get out of my way.' It reminded me of Charlie Chaplin trying to deal with life or something, *Modern Times*, and he was just Woody."[1] Chaplin's *Modern Times* (1936) is, of course, a quintessential document of American modernism in both form and content, and Cohen's linking of Guthrie and this particular film is highly revealing. The comparison with Chaplin points clearly to Guthrie's own modernity, his engagement with the technological and economic forces of the modern world in a predominantly urban setting, and—not the least important—an occasional impulse to turn urban anxiety into comedy.

Not all modernists have dealt with this anxiety comedically. A mere fifteen years before Guthrie arrived in Los Angeles to commence his own urban life, one of modernism's most howling *cris de coeur* was voiced:

> What is the city over the mountains
> Cracks and reforms and bursts in the violet air
> Falling towers
> Jerusalem Athens Alexandria
> Vienna London
> Unreal.[2]

Whether or not Guthrie ever read Eliot's "The Waste Land," he was certainly attuned to the urban angst that prompted it, be it reflected in the apocalyptic imagery of "My Name Is New York" ("I might boil and blow / And shake to the ground / And smoke and tremble / And blaze all around"), the divinely ordained urban destruction of the "Los Angeles New Year's Flood" that "swept away our homes," or the "mighty big earthquake" that "shook old Frisco down."[3] Modernist anxiety runs like a current through Guthrie's writings on the city, however much it also fueled his absurdism. From the comedic discomfiture of "Big City Ways" on his KFVD air check of 1937 to his later depictions of hard times on the subway, homelessness on the Bowery, the deaths of children "under car wheels and trains," and especially New York as the epicenter of capitalist greed in his "Woody Sez" columns, Guthrie's sense of the malevolent city could be a fair match for Eliot's.[4]

Yet, characteristically, there was a flip side to Guthrie's urban angst. Edward Comentale writes of the "giddy counterrepublic-cum-amusement-park" that is Guthrie's "Mermaid's Avenue," his "Technicolor" ode to the vibrancy and expanding potential offered by the city.[5] This vision—as opposed to that of the infernal city, with its "hooded hordes" of shady Jews and other nefarious foreigners who so unnerved Eliot and Pound as they had Dickens before them—celebrates the great awakenings and the electrifying connections that only New York could offer:

> Heard all that I came to hear here in Coney Island's Jewish air
> Heard reflections, recollections, seen faces in memory,
> Heard voices untangle their words before me
> And I knew by the feeling I felt that here was my voice.[6]

The road to the acquisition of that voice was by no means a straight one, beset, as it was, by inconsistencies and experimentation on Guthrie's part as he attempted to negotiate the paradoxical opportunities and degradations that marked the urban experience in early- and mid-twentieth-century America. It was a negotiation revealed in his earliest reflections on Los Angeles, his first urban home. In his KFVD broadcasts, Guthrie freely exploited the perception of what Lauren Rabinovitz calls "a 'culture gap' between the urban and the rural," using the caricatures of "the 'city slicker' and 'the rube'" that had permeated American popular culture almost since its beginnings.[7] Guthrie's strategy was designed to endear him to his audience of recently transplanted migrants from the South and the Midwest, hence his introduction to one KFVD song, "Better Stay in the Livery Barn": "But you remember, and so do I, when it was shore nuff true that a country boy thet come to town had to shore nuff watch his self, or the City Dudes and Slickers would hound him till they got every last penny he had. They used three deadly tools, Likker, Wimmen, entertainment."[8] The familiar markers of puritanical damnation of the city are there (wine, women, and song), showing Guthrie tapping into the timeworn opposition between pastoral innocence and urban decadence. Yes, he might occasionally sing of the "Bright and Shining City," lifting the familiar religious trope of the "Land beyond the Sky / Where the Soul shall live forever and be Free."[9] But in his earthly renderings of the city, at least, he would sometimes run closer to Thomas Jefferson, who, in *his* engagements with the onset of modernity, had imagined an ideal republic of farmers—"a chosen people of God"—to counter the degrading influence of the "mobs of great cities."[10]

From the moment of the air check that landed him his KFVD job in 1937—when he sang "Skid Row Serenade" along with the admonitory "Big City Ways"—Guthrie harped incessantly upon the supposed urban-rural divide, filling his programs with wistful songs such as "I'm A-Goin' Back to the Farm" ("Where a man's got elbow room") and "Left in This World Alone" ("It seems such a pity / As I roam thru the city / I am left in this world all alone")—all sung from the point of view of the defeated rural migrant in a heartless city.[11] Guthrie's Okies were outcast, homesick, wandering "along the beach at midnight / Listening to the wind that blows" and sharing, if any fellowship at all, only a most lonely one.[12]

Introducing the Carter Family's "Foggy Mountain Top" on KFVD, Guthrie slandered Los Angeles mercilessly—even hypocritically—as he set up a vista from "away high on top of one of these California Mountains" overlooking the city that had embraced him, nurtured him, politicized him, and immersed him in all its multicultural, multiracial glory, with its bookshops new and used, the museums and art galleries that he would frequent, the city that first prepared him for a lifetime of urban inspiration and opportunity—"the Big City—like a bunch of warts on yer hide, formin' and growin' like bacteria on an orange, and a spreadin' it's racket and noise and greed and heartbreaks and selfishness in every direction."[13] Of course Guthrie's strategy worked, for a while, at any rate. He received fan letters to confirm it: "It floats me away from these hectic days of rush and heartache and jazz into a green valley of rest and peace. I have never heard any program like it—two perfectly blended voices, quiet, restful, unpretentious, singing sweet old melodies of the past, to me, alone."[14]

Guthrie was well aware that Los Angeles had much more to offer him than noise, crowds, avarice, decadence, and temptation. Most importantly, it offered him a progressive culture—both artistic and political—with people and cultural practices that would help to transform his worldview and his output. Peter La Chapelle provides a snapshot of the musical milieu alone: "Country music, along with working-class-focused forms such as jazz, blues, *corridos*, Latin dance, and immigrant European music, changed the very foundations of cultural and economic life in the city, creating a local variation of what Michael Denning has called 'the laboring of American culture.'"[15] Denning himself has described the richness of Guthrie's Los Angeles, with its "many refugee writers and artists," "as internationalist a culture as any to have appeared in US history . . . [transforming] the ways people imagined the globe."[16] Guthrie was wholly immersed in this transformation, establishing firm friendships with the likes of Ed Robbin, Will Geer, John Steinbeck, and a number of Jewish immigrants and activists within the Hollywood studio community. Guthrie's Los Angeles was peopled by more than just the bankers, landlords, sleazy salesmen, confidence men, lousy drivers, and femmes fatale he caricatured in his KFVD songs.

Guthrie was still dragging the faded tropes of the urban-rural divide when he arrived in New York on February 16, 1940. His earliest New York output continued to perpetuate the clichés of rural innocence in its encounter with big-city decadence. Guthrie's persona of the "rube" encountering the sensory overload of the city for the first time (as though he had not spent the previous two years in Los Angeles) is most fully developed in the "Woody Sez" columns that he continued to file in New York for the *People's World*. His stock in trade was still the Okie naïf's bewilderment, a wide-eyed innocence undercut with sly critical barbs aimed at the "Capitalist cistern": "Boy, it really takes the nickels to live here. You can't get to first base unless you make 847446 fone calls, and take 85756 busses every day. You got to spend sixty cents in nickels to see about a dollar job. Then you got to spend the rest of the dollar to get to the right place at the right time."[17]

A glimpse into the reality of Guthrie's initial weeks in New York, behind the hillbilly "rube" façade, is provided by Nora Guthrie, who describes the bohemian, artistic, modernist milieu into which her father slipped almost immediately and quite effortlessly. Guthrie was soon rooming with Pete Seeger in the "top floor loft" of Harold Ambellan and Elisabeth Higgins on East Twenty-First Street: "Both Ambellan and Higgins were artists and political activists, creating sculptures and ceramic tiles as well as musical and literary works. They were among a new generation of young NYC artists who began combining their working studio with their living space." The timing of Guthrie's arrival into this milieu could not have been more fortuitous: "This loft-style living scene was becoming popular with musicians and artists of all fields in the 1940s. They opened their lofts for informal public performances and exhibits, drawing audiences from family and friends. Through these venues, they were able to gather and share their work with the public, creating a template for the next generation of NYC artists in the 1960s and 1970s."[18]

Just as Los Angeles had proved a mecca for an international brigade of immigrant artists and political activists heading for the Hollywood studios, so was New York like a magnet drawing a host of migrants from within and without the United States. There may have been a grain of truth in Saul Bellow's assertion that in 1940, the year of Guthrie's arrival, New York was "a very Russian city"—a reference to the communist movement that thrived there, driven largely by a cross-section of Jewish émigrés from eastern Europe and their American-born offspring.[19] But there was so much more to New York than this. The reverberations of the Harlem Renaissance were still to be heard in the early 1940s, not only at the Savoy and the Cotton Club, but also considerably south of Harlem itself—through the jazz and blues of Max Gordon's Village Vanguard and Barney Josephson's two defiantly integrationist cafés—both named Café Society—downtown at Sheridan Square and uptown at Fifty-Eighth Street. Guthrie soon became familiar with all of these venues.

Jorge Arévalo Mateus argues, "Only in a city like New York could Guthrie meet such a cross-section of uniquely talented and creative people as Lead

Belly, Sonny Terry, Brownie McGhee, Aunt Molly Jackson, Pete Seeger, Earl Robinson, Alan Lomax, Moses Asch, even Martha Graham, personalities that helped to form the person he became."[20] Other influential names can be added: Nicholas Ray and Henrietta Yurchenco, from theater and radio; Merce Cunningham, Sophie Maslow, Anna Sokolow, Jane Dudley, Margot Mayo, and, of course, Marjorie Mazia, from modern dance; the Ambellans, Rockwell Kent, and Jackson Pollock, sculptors and painters; John Cage, avant-garde pianist and composer; Charles Olson, modernist poet. A handful of these were native New Yorkers; the majority were not. Like Guthrie, they too had been drawn to New York as an artistic and political mecca, to become a part of the premier internationalist culture of the United States. There were others whom Guthrie met only through their works, and it is open to question whether he would have encountered them at all had he not immersed himself in the New York cultural front when he did. Certainly it is difficult to imagine him sending this letter from Pampa or even Los Angeles: "I went to the Almanacs to get my mail, and got a book of poems from Langston Hughes called 'Shakespeare in Harlem.' I read it around over the streets, walking or setting along cement steps, watching the people go by."[21]

The series of communal dwellings in Greenwich Village that Guthrie shared with his fellow Almanac Singers in 1941 and 1942 became some of the city's most important artistic sites, attracting such celebrated visitors as Rockwell Kent, Dashiell Hammett, Mike Gold, Elizabeth Gurley Flynn, Marc Blitzstein, Walter Lowenfels, and Charles Olson, among many others. Guthrie was entranced by the creative energy that surrounded him in the Village, as he recorded in his poem, "This Is the House Where the Almanacs Used to Stay." In addition to the "banjos, fiddles, guitars played" by members of the folk circle surrounding the Almanacs, there were:

> Some piano players with time to spare,
> Artists just plain, and some long hairs,
> Professors, teachers, saints, and nuns,
> And laundry men come on the run.[22]

Pete Seeger may well have once thought—as he recorded in his diary at the advanced age of sixteen—that the "greatest danger" to revolutionary thought and action was "the Greenwich Village type, the bohemian."[23] And now here he was, two decades later, with Woody Guthrie and the other Almanacs, living the Greenwich Village bohemian life and hosting a vibrant salon. Guthrie himself wondered, when he finally moved out of the collective dwelling, "Would, or could a thing like this Almanac House ever happen again in our earthly history?"[24]

But for all Guthrie's celebrations of New York—and there were many—they were not without their countercurrents, particularly in his later periods of stress and depression. His "ambivalence," as Arévalo Mateus observes, is a matter of record, with Guthrie marking New York as "the very worst / and best old town in the universe."[25] Periodically Guthrie would run from the city, seeking a reacquaintance with the wilds beyond; but he eventually took the pains not to demean it—or, indeed, modernity itself—against the "old, wild, unsettled bedrooms of mama nature": "I'm not sour on the city, nor mad at big houses and cities with rugs, pillows, bath rooms, soap, towels, sinks, stoves, radios, record players, nor gas connections, nor telephones nor sore at nurseries, schools, nor at colleges of wood, rock, brick, tile, sand, iron, cement nor marble. I'm not angry at trucks, cars, nor paved crooked highways."[26]

The city's association with Marjorie quite naturally resulted in some particularly tender-hearted outpourings, including a description of New York as "an old sweetheart's keepsake."[27] Guthrie's romance with New York, entwined as it was with his love for Marjorie, was at its height during those brief five years—1942 to 1947—when the prospect of a new family, with Cathy at its center, grounded him to the city that would be their home. The energetic wartime activity too, which saw New Yorkers banded together in the home-front fight against fascism, made the city all the more heady a place to be. In March 1943, Guthrie poured into his notebook a passionate, extended eulogy for the city that had captured and embraced him with its many arms. New York was elemental and, for all its undeniable foulness, a source of plenty and sustenance. Broadway might well be "the sex organ of New York" and the Bowery "the ass hole end of things," but its avenues and streets were still "the solid rock guts of the people," its buildings "glands and factories that pour this stuff out into the trucks and carts[,] and the trains run through the tubes and holes and blood veins." Guthrie explained his use of such starkly anatomical imagery:

New York is something that is alive to me. She breathes in her air
and puffs steam back out again. She eats her bread from the big table
spread out on three sides of her and all of your other towns eat off of
this same table. She washes herself in the clean upper end of the river
and uses the lower sides for the toilet and outhouse. She drinks her
water from the mountain tops and pulls her brass chain and dumps
her filth down her east river.

New York is her name and she knows no stranger and if you call
her by name she'll answer you by yours.[28]

In June 1943, Guthrie, Marjorie, and Cathy took up residence in Coney
Island, Brooklyn, the area that would inspire some of Guthrie's most ebul-
lient writings. As Marjorie later recalled, "Woody didn't want to live right
in the heart of New York because he said he needed open spaces and we
went out to Coney Island. The beautiful ocean in Coney Island and a lot
of beach is not too different from the wheat fields of Oklahoma."[29] Guthrie
may have indeed begun to feel a sense of suffocation in the garrets, lofts,
and narrow lanes of Lower Manhattan—as he wrote to Marjorie in July
1942, while she was still living with her husband in Philadelphia: "New
York is growing every year. It's not the same little horse and buggy town
that you left behind. 14th Street has grown so that everybody calls it 24th
now."[30]

But possibly there was something about Coney Island's carnivalesque
history—its decades-long reputation for abandon that had infuriated a
generation of uptight, godly reformers—that struck a chord in Guthrie.
His old KFVD characterizations of the city as Babylon were well behind
him, even though he had moved into a locus attracting such badges of
honor as "Babel gone daft."[31] And Guthrie *did* enjoy that carnival aspect,
the sense of fun and play that he associated not only with Cathy and her
peers but ideally everyone of every age: "Coney Island is a fine place to live.
You've got the beach and the sand, the boats and the bells, the people on
the boardwalk and a show of humanity playing all around you."[32] In the
residential areas behind the boardwalks and rides, something deep and
mysterious, both worldly and otherworldly, resonated:

Oh the streets are full of loud kids and strollers and I can hear lots of
folks talking—but above all of the noise on the streets there towers
the heads of the big buildings in all of their quietness.

They are all full of life's sweetness and full of life's sorrow and full
of life's strange contradictions.[33]

Coney Island's great multicultural humanity had dug itself in and taken
root, reflected not only in the mélange of American fast foods and *shtetl*
delicacies—"Blintzes and cheeses / Knishes and spam"[34]—but also in Marjorie's family, the Greenblatts, and the Guthries' other neighbors, "Russians
by accent, descent, and not just by accident."[35] And there was the politics of
Coney Island, born out of the coming together of such peoples, mixing on
the streets and in the low-rent apartment buildings and houses along Atlantic Avenue in Seagate and along Mermaid Avenue. As Guthrie surmised:
"It is no wonder that Coney Island has got a name for being progressive.
The folks there have had to think together in order to survive at all."[36] With
his sense of purpose grounded in the fight against fascism, the enthusiastic
reception of *Bound for Glory* in 1943, his baby daughter growing, curious
and healthy, and with the love of her mother, a devoted artiste par excellence,
Guthrie's life in Coney Island—particularly on Mermaid Avenue—was as
satisfying as it had ever been or would be again. There was every reason for
Guthrie to conclude: "Coney is wide open, above board, and needs lots of
fixing but I like it there."[37]

It is the great tragedy of Guthrie's life that so much should have combined to batter him just as he had come to this conclusion—just as he
had finally found a home after a seeming lifetime of restless wandering.
Cathy's death in February 1947 was the worst of it; and with the perverse
timing of fate, it coincided with the postwar gutting of radicalism from
the political sphere and the increasing entrenchment of his fatal illness.
Inevitably, even the idyll of Coney Island could not withstand the pallor of
death cast over it in Guthrie's mind. Cathy had died, as she had lived, in
Coney Island. Her father's elegy betrays the depth of the anguish that he
bore as he walked the same streets and sands that he had walked with her,
holding her hand:

> I've lost the best friend
> That I'll ever, ever have;
> Whistle, birdy, a song
> For my Cathy that's gone.
>> I'd sung for the strikers at Phelps Dodge that day;
>> Your Mommy left a note on our door that did say;
>> "The firemen were here and the ambulance, too;
>> We're at Coney Island Hospital waiting for you."[38]

He had said that Coney Island needed "lots of fixing but I like it here." Now, six months after Cathy's fatal burning, it was just "a stack / of old planks / Waiting here to catch afire."[39]

In the immediate weeks and months after Cathy's death, Guthrie did work, it is true, against his increasing depression to hold on to a vision of New York as a nurturing, life-giving force. "My New York City," written in April 1947, is one of his most romantic odes, both to Marjorie and to the city itself ("My New York City is the town where I found you"); but in addition to Marjorie, it conceivably addresses Cathy, whose face in Guthrie's memory seems to be reflected in the melancholic cityscape. The verses are repositories of absence and loss:

> I see your face there shining
> Where the kids play in the streets
> In a billion jillion windows that are New York Town to me.
>
> No matter where this train rolls
> I look out my window glass
> Your eyes shine in my tree leaves
> And my buildings that I pass
> I'd give my fame and fortune up
> To hold your hand today
> And go a billion jillion places that are New York Town to me.[40]

In spite of his efforts to maintain the optimism and sense of potential that had characterized his earlier impressions of New York, Guthrie's writings on the city from February 1947 onward grow increasingly dark. In November 1947, he wrote a chilling observation: "I looked over acrost the top of your

town and I heard things worse than death."⁴¹ Early 1948 saw him almost
perversely immersing himself in the degradation and squalor of the Bowery,
which he sought to rub into the faces of his associates in the People's Songs
project. Furious that Pete Seeger and Waldemar Hille, the *People's Songs
Bulletin* editor, had dared to suggest softening his lyrics, Guthrie exploded at
them: "There are not four good plain songs or ballads in all of your Peoples
Song files nor being sung around by any of us selfcalled Peoples Artists,
which truly or factually or graphically make plain . . . life like she's lived
just acrost over yonder a few short blocks from where we set and pass our
criticism on songs and ballads that poke too much fun at the very politicians
and office holders whose daily decisions put more or fewer tangled faces over
there to run that skiddy road called the Bowery."⁴²

January 1949 saw Guthrie again at odds with People's Songs, as he
unreasonably castigated them for what he saw as their part in ensuring the
defeat of Henry Wallace in the 1948 presidential election. In his scathing
seven-page postmortem, he pitted New York's softness and timidity against
the hardiness of West Coast activism. Once—eight years before—he had
praised New York as "about the revoltingest place in the country," where
"you'll see the working folks marching up and down the streets, having
meetings, talking, preaching, and always going the rest of the country just
one better."⁴³ Now the situation appeared the reverse: "The west coast peoples
are more migratory than the New Yorkers, the west coaster has been pushed
and herded around more viciously than the New Yorker, the hobo spirit is
more prevalent on the west coast than in New York. The west coast rank and
filer has missed and begged more meals than the average New Yorker. Thugs,
vigilantes, goons, ginkers, and foney law officers have cracked the head of
the westerner harder than the New Yorker." While offering no constructive
suggestions, he poured scorn on the People's Songs rallies and hootenannies
that had managed to do so little in the midst of the country's largest concen-
trated population: "Instead of patting ourselves too hotly on our own backs,
here in a city of 8 million people, we hooters had ought to be highly criticized
and analyzed for not being about to hold our Hoots more often than once
per month and to draw around 13 hundred head. By this time, by all the
laws of trial and error, we should have been pulling larger crowds twice this
regular and often."⁴⁴

It was an unfair criticism to make. In point of fact, neither the West Coast nor New York could withstand the intensity of the anticommunist onslaught against the unions and the wider public sphere. The Taft-Hartley Act of 1947 had virtually criminalized all aspects of radicalism in the labor movement, and the HUAC was in the ascendant, not only in Hollywood but also in New York. Even the People's Songs hootenannies, dwindling in number as they were, could be dangerous places to be. The dancer and activist Norma Starobin recalled their being "severely attacked by young hoodlums. . . . They got in there and just started to break our furniture. They must have been planted by either their church or the FBI."[45] For his part, Guthrie found that his union and Communist Party appearances—among his greatest sources of pride as a performer, as well as sources of sporadic income—had virtually dried up. People's Songs, on the verge of bankruptcy, was a pariah among all but the most defiant unions in New York, as elsewhere (it would limp on until March 1949).

As his professional profile declined along with his health, his family cohesion, and his political optimism, Guthrie began to treat New York with a cynicism that would have been unthinkable in the early 1940s, when *Bound for Glory* had won him the critical praise of the city's major papers. Sending a *New York Times* clipping with his photograph to his sister Mary Jo in April 1949, Guthrie sneered: "The hungrier you get up here in New York, the more they run your picture. After you starve clean to the rim of death they call you a professional, and after you die off they call you a great genius. And when somebody steps in and buys up all of your diaries and scribblings and songs and poems they call you the greatest feller which ever lived, so's your debtors and loaners can get rich off the stink of your dead bones and yaller pages of ideas."[46]

A brief moment of professional respite came with a commission from Alan Lomax to provide songs for Columbia University's venereal disease awareness program in the summer of 1949. The ten songs that Guthrie composed for the projected radio broadcast were important in that they enabled him to demonstrate that he still could contribute public service at a time when so many of his efforts would have been spurned amid the darkening political climate. But it is difficult to approach two of these songs in particular—"V. D. City," which sees Guthrie returning to the old binary of the pure celestial city versus the corrupt urban hell, and "Brooklyn Town," with its poisonous, city-based femme fatale—without appreciating their critical renderings of a degraded and degrading urban cesspit in the starkest of terms. In "V. D. City," it is as though Hieronymus Bosch had come to New York with a guitar slung over his shoulder, to sing of the dereliction of both the urban body and mind:

> There's a street named for every disease here
> Syph Alley, and Clap Avenue
> And the whores and their pimps and their victims
> Crawl past on the curb to my view. . . .
>
> Your eye is too festered to see here
> Worse than lepers your skin runs with sores
> Every window stands full of lost faces
> Human wrecks pile the steps and the doors.[47]

Meanwhile, the protagonist's outing to "some joints in Brooklyn town" leaves him with only an empty wallet, a memory of "one pretty, pretty gal" with "two big sparkling eyes, waving curls, and a great big smile," "a daze from that night," and a "soul . . . afire"—clearly, the burning corruption of syphilis.[48]

These examples are further indications of the ambivalence with which Guthrie treated what was, in the aggregate, a beloved city to him. While he would increasingly take flight from the city and hit the road during periods of stress and depression, he would return again and again. There was apparently only one fate that could permanently divorce him from New York, as he suggested in 1950:

> Around New York
> Around New York
> And around New York I go
> If an atom bomb
> Hits my New York
> It'll be New York no more.[49]

At one point—sometime after August 1956, during his commitment to the Greystone Park Psychiatric Hospital in New Jersey, with its expansive lawns and the "magicy tree" beneath which his children played—Guthrie declared to Marjorie in one of his last letters that he had no wish to return to New York, briefly reverting to the puritanical imagery now informed by the born-again Christianity that marked his final communicative years: "I like my low littel hills, my farmin lands my trees my flowers my birds my things I see all aroun me here better than I do at BSH [Brooklyn State Hospital] dropped like it is right off down so squarely there in that old dirty crowded farmless wicked city of Brooklyn. I just love love my any wide opendy land and country like this is here better than I love any man made land or city God knowes."[50] But Guthrie would still have three final New York addresses awaiting him: Marjorie's home on Eighty-Fifth Street in Howard Beach, Queens, where he was brought on weekends for family get-togethers; Brooklyn State Hospital until June 1966; and Creedmoor State Hospital in Queens, where he breathed his last on October 3, 1967.

The Atlantic Ocean off Coney Island became his final resting place, his ashes packed so tightly into a mortuary can that his children could not sprinkle them. Arlo was obliged to throw the entire can into the sea, out past the stone jetty establishing the boundary of Coney Island. The can sank beneath the waves, and it would take an expert in tidal movements to speculate where it may have gone after that.

But the can did not really contain Guthrie's final remains, anyway. They are, in addition to his published recordings and writings, the unpublished papers, notebooks, diaries, letters, paintings, sketches, and unreleased recordings housed in the archives started by Marjorie Guthrie and Harold Leventhal. For nearly two decades, the Woody Guthrie Archives were located in Leventhal's New York office on West Fifty-Seventh Street. But New York rents are high, and it costs money to maintain a temperature- and humidity-controlled atmosphere to ensure that precious documents—whether the first draft of "This Land Is Your Land" or Woody Guthrie's last letter—will not crumble into dust. Apparently no New Yorker could match or perhaps even attempted to match the $3 million offered by Tulsa philanthropist George Kaiser to buy the archives and house them in the purpose-built Woody Guthrie Center that was opened in 2013.[51] In that respect, New York let Guthrie slip through its fingers. New York's loss was Oklahoma's gain, just as Oklahoma's loss had once been New York's gain.

Oklahomans, Texans, Angelenos, and New Yorkers may well argue over who created Woody Guthrie. If Okemah spawned him and showed him his first familial joys and tragedies, it was Pampa that unlocked his musicianship and gave him the Dust Bowl, his first wife and three children, and the contents of its public library. If Los Angeles introduced him to the Popular Front, the CIO, and political broadcasting, as well as Ed Robbin, Will Geer, and John Steinbeck, it was New York that introduced him to Alan Lomax, Pete Seeger, Lead Belly, Moses Asch, and Marjorie Mazia, as well as an entire bohemian avant-garde. The Asch, Stinson, and Folkways labels distributed his records from New York; E. P. Dutton published his *Bound for Glory* in New York; and New York's Richmond Organization published his songs, followed by Woody Guthrie Publications, a New York firm. The city was indeed both a magnet and his final centrifuge, drawing him like millions of others into its center, spinning him around in the whirl of its modernity, drawing and separating his art from his inner thoughts, and dispersing it outward, all around the world. Like modern American culture itself, Woody Guthrie is now, to borrow Comentale's phrase, "deterritorialized." He is both nowhere and everywhere.

Conclusion: Constant Changer

In a recent article in the journal *American Communist History*, conservative historian Ronald Radosh noted that my previous scholarship on Guthrie had revealed him to be—"much to the consternation of the Guthrie family, I am certain"—"an out and out racist."[1] While I cannot speak for the Guthrie family, I would challenge Radosh's "certain" opinion. After all, as the earliest custodians of Guthrie's massive archive, his family will have been the first to appreciate the truth of Guthrie's own admission that he was "a constant changer." Had Guthrie ended his life as "an out and out racist," that would have been something to worry about. But as we know, he did not. As I had written previously, Guthrie "proved something uplifting. Racists are not born, but made; and they can be unmade."[2]

The potential for Guthrie to change raises a whole host of questions, never to be answered conclusively. His death at fifty-six robbed us of the answers. We know that he had "flip-flopped" (a signature expression of his) on a number of issues besides race—the New Deal, intervention in World War II, the atom bomb. Given time, would he have acknowledged the environmental damage caused by the Grand Coulee Dam? Might he have publicly renounced his support for Stalin, as his protégé, Pete Seeger, eventually did? With his heightened sensitivity to the plight of refugees, would he have called for an independent Palestine—even accompanying Seeger into the BDS movement against Israel? How would he have responded to the Equal Rights Amendment? Would he have retracted his homophobic utterances and stood up in support of gay rights and same-sex marriage? What would he think—and write—about September 11? The Bin Laden killing? A Donald Trump presidency? The Internet? We will never know. We might hazard an educated guess or two, but we will never know. Considering Guthrie's potential for change brings to mind the punch line of an oft-quoted joke by Kurt Vonnegut: "Keep your hat on. We may end up miles from here!"[3]

What Ricardo Quinones writes of James Joyce's modernist hero Leopold Bloom might well apply to Guthrie's output as well as his biography: "a perfect instrument for registering the variety, the flux, the interpenetration, the simultaneity and randomness of experience."[4] In spite of the vastness and variety of Guthrie's expression across a range of media, even the most well-meaning of his champions (not to say his detractors) have worked to preserve him in the amber of their own choosing. Peter La Chapelle rightly observes, "An unfortunate offshoot of the efforts to mythicize is the tendency of even respectable academics to reduce Guthrie's life and career to absolutism, ranging from leftish saintliness and romantic rebelliousness to profit-minded opportunism and unremorseful Stalinism."[5] The awareness of my own contribution to this potentially reductive enterprise—with the exclusively political focus of *Woody Guthrie, American Radical*—is one thing that has prompted me to write this book. Any narrowed focus, deliberate or otherwise, inevitably does a disservice to Guthrie's expansiveness. But paying attention to Guthrie's relation to modernity almost serves as a guarantee of his emergence as an artist of "the variety" and "the flux" described by Quinones.

The point of this book has been to argue the case for Guthrie as much more than the "anticipatory" modernist that Thomas Crow calls him, especially when considering him in the broader light of modernity as an experience as well as the narrower light of modernism as a mode of aesthetic response. Granted, Guthrie's visual artwork may not have been as relentlessly abstract as that of, say, Mondrian or Kandinsky; but the same might be said of Diego Rivera and Frieda Kahlo, although none would deny them their place in the history of modernism. In any case, modernist art encompasses much more than Abstract Expressionism, Pop Art, or Picasso. Beyond the painted canvas it is, among other things, literary, cinematic, tonal and otherwise sonic, kinetic (through dance), and—ultimately—attitudinal: how else can one speak of a "modernist sensibility" or "the modernist mind"? Guthrie was not simply or solely a visual artist, and it is cases like his that ask us to reexamine our own definitions of modernism and, as Christopher Butler urges us, to avoid making "any strict boundaries" for it. Edward Comentale in particular has done much to prompt such a reexamination, exploring Guthrie in both modern and modernist lights previously unconsidered—not only visual but also literary and sonic, not only artistic but also technological and commercial. It is through such studies as Comentale's *Sweet Air* that the boundaries between "modern life" and "modern art" are most fully tested and often breached. Thus, as he observes, even Guthrie's more nominally *traditionalist* output can be seen in the context of a modernist avant-garde, if considered for its strategic intention and effect as well as its form. Comentale writes, for instance, that "Guthrie's folk songs reflect the aesthetic strategies" of other modernist artists such as Rivera, Walker Evans, Ben Shahn, and James Agee: "Mistrusting the logic of folk authenticity and expression, this group pursued their work as a series of 'motivated forms,' at once motive and abstract."[6]

Immediately, if not sooner, some will raise the example of Guthrie's many strident pronouncements on "folk authenticity and expression" as evidence that he should *not* be included in this group of "mistrusting" avant-garde strategists. However, protean as he was, Guthrie himself provided some evidence to the contrary. His own preservationist mission was undercut with an intense desire to "make it new," even within the bounds of traditional genre—hence his defense of folk music against a published argument in 1946 that the "conditions that produced great folk songs have by and large passed on . . . because work is done by machines." Guthrie countered strenuously: "The machine has not choked off the birth of work songs, it has been a great help to their spread and growth, witness the millions of songs set to railroad and engine rhythms, and the same goes for trucks, cars, barges, ships, planes and everything else."[7] If anything, as he charged in yet another defense, "Our trains have had twice as many songs made up about them as you can find about horses."[8] His notebooks bristle with defiant barbs:

> I wouldn't bet a nickel on the hairs that grew yesterday
> I don't care how good the old days were for you[,] they're not
> good enough for me.[9]

THE

SONG

I SING

WILL KILL

SOME OLD

IDEAS.[10]

But the rub, of course, comes with Guthrie's ambivalence, even his reactionism, which accounts at least partly for those examples of formal conservatism that have prevented observers from appreciating his relationship to modernist art as well as modern life. For every assertion of his fealty to the avant-garde and his readiness to be the "constant changer" that he claimed to be, Guthrie would also claim, almost simultaneously: "I didn't come here to fight every thing that's getting old. I see some good old things I like."[11] Theorists of modernity are able to account for such retractions. Thus, for instance, Guthrie's expressed skepticism about the benefits of television (countered, of course, by his desire to be a part of it) is an outgrowth of what Steve Wurtzler calls "the process of technological change and the always contested emergence of new media forms."[12] Similarly, Guthrie's appeals to the slower pace of life outside the "mad rush" and "whirl" of Los Angeles and New York can be theorized in light of Hartmut Rosa's claim that, in the experience of modernity, "almost every surge of acceleration is followed by . . . the call for deceleration and the nostalgic desire for the lost 'slow world,' whose slowness first becomes a distinct quality in retrospect."[13]

Such "nostalgic desire" is evident enough in Guthrie's writings, as it is in the wider realm of American folk music and culture. As Richard Reuss noted, "Henry Ford, whose automobile sales did as much as anything to destroy the rustic past in the United States, garnered much publicity for his hobby of importing old-time fiddlers and folk dancers to Dearborn, Michigan."[14] Guthrie's own retreats, while not as unintentionally ironic as Ford's, were born of a similar modern unease. Newly arrived in New York, he told Lomax, for instance, that the kindliness of Oklahoma's folk hero, Will Rogers, would be harder to find "in the fast and nervous overworked and overrun and overindulgent east or North or New York or anywhere else." In Oklahoma, he said, "we take it just a little bit easier, go at things a little bit slower, maybe we might not get as many dates covered every day or as many telephone calls put in or as many bus rides, but then we'll do just as much on one bus ride and on one phone call and on one meetin' as a lot of people do on a dozen."[15] As his later "meetin's" and love-trysts with the telephone show, Guthrie demonstrated otherwise the more of a New Yorker he became.

But he would never completely shake off the suspicion that something had gone wrong with modernity, whether it was its "aesthetically blunting effects" (to quote Brian Jones), which drove him into more and more abstract renderings both in his writing and his visual output, or the increasing bureaucratization of simple, everyday existence.[16] As he wrote in 1943 in a notebook meant for his daughter: "In these modern times, Cathy, every time you make a move, you've got to furnish papers to show, prove, ascertain, and clarify your personal history plumb back to your very first gooing days, anyway."[17] Guthrie's consequent retreats into nostalgia were indeed noteworthy, demonstrating all the more his subjection to the crises of modernity. All his quick changes—his assertions and counterassertions, his giving with one hand and taking away with the other—are, at least in some respects, reflections of the overarching, defining crisis described by Marshall Berman: the "struggle to make ourselves at home in a constantly changing world."[18]

It is also important to view Guthrie's varied and often contradictory responses in the context of "modernity's broken promise of autonomy" as described by Rosa. In Guthrie's mind, autonomy extended to well beyond political or economic freedom; it was the equivalent of self-definition, the capacity to establish or determine one's own identity against a barrage of impositions, or would-be impositions, from without. One of Guthrie's notebook ruminations is particularly revealing. First, there is the obligatory dismissal, the requisite embarrassment that he, as a proudly unlettered Okie, should profess any interest whatsoever in this abstract thing that really does interest him:

> 1. Identity. Maybe that's too big a word for me. I never heard all
> of these big long words till I come to New York. Oh, I heard a
> few words that were pretty long, like "neurotic" and "homo" and
> "abnormal" and "sectarian" and "chauvinist" and the likes out
> around Hollywood, and Los Angeles, but the closer I got to New

York the longer the words seemed to get. So now I've heard the word "Identity"—

Then, we come to the crux, the explanation for much of what Guthrie wishes to establish about himself and the world's perception of him:

> 2. It seems to mean being able to know who you are. To me, it seems like you can't quite prove who you are till you can prove what you do. Your work is you. It's your identity. It's your self respect and your pride and your work and your people's work—and I just had a talk with a man that said he'd lost his identity, and it's a whole lot worse than losing your ration stamps or your social security card.[19]

This explanation makes all the more significant another notebook entry written in the dark month of August 1947, when Guthrie's domestic life seemed to be disintegrating along with his neurological system and the American Left itself: "If I'd not found the labor movement just when I did I'd have committed my own suicide looking for it."[20]

How, then, to maintain—to preserve—one's sense of wholeness and stability, one's identity, one's autonomy, in the midst of rapid and seemingly endless dissolution, formation, and reformation? Modernity also offers a few lifelines—not least, in Guthrie's case, the ability to preserve his output in concrete form. There were his records, which, stable as they were in form, could not always guarantee a shared response from their auditors. Hence Guthrie's extended annotation of his copy of the Asch album *American Folksay: Ballads and Dances* (1944), on which he had sung a number of songs. Hearing it for the first time had "scared" him, he said: "What will people think when they hear this wild scraping and scratching? I'm not lying an inch when I tell you that I actually hid this album of records in my house so my friends couldn't stumble onto it." At the time of his first listening, the record's very corporeality seemed a threat to him: "I felt ashamed because I had helped to make it. I wanted to melt the wax up and pour it back to the factory and my hands ached to grab all of the records off the market and toss them back to their moulds." But after subsequent listenings, there was a dramatic change—helped along, initially, by a technological breakdown that had managed to slow the passage of time:

I went around lots of places and saw other people who had bought the album. I heard them say some pretty good words about it but I kept quiet. Then my phonograph was broke for about a week and I didn't hear many records of any kind. I tinkered and worked and finally got the machine to where it will play again now. The past couple of days I listened to this album several more times.

It was like a young kid of mine. It was wild and fiery and rough and tumble but I kept looking for a few good things in it and I got to where I like this kid better than my quite smooth ones.[21]

Guthrie's preservationist urge was thus one of the great ironic contrasts to his changeability. The irony is itself symptomatic of one further aspect of the modern condition—in Mark Goble's words, "the relationship between modernity and history, one that looks to technology as a means to preserve and ultimately transmit a material past."[22] Equally, as Goble makes clear by citing Michel Chion on the "acousmatic," modernity attempts to "preserve and transmit" a decidedly *immaterial* past "'systematized in the use of radio, telephones, and phonograph records,' all of which allow us to hear, in the 'here and now,' something that isn't really there."[23] This "acousmatic" experience is an important aspect of "the detachment of modernity itself," as Comentale argues—"detachment not as a kind of death or even a new birth, but as the very means of continuity, the possibility of stability amid change."[24] Photography, cinema, and the print media, of course, are further means of establishing "continuity" and "stability amid change."

That Guthrie appealed to "continuity" and "stability" is beyond doubt. Some of his writings reveal his intense desire to ensure that his work would be preserved in concrete form, standing amid the whirlwinds of change—the desire that his "scribbling might stay," regardless of whether he went "down or up or anywhere."[25] Concrete preservation was part of the "identity" that he was determined to maintain—hence the evident desperation with which he once appealed to some unnamed hosts in the wake of a performance with Cisco Houston: "You will do us a big favor by please sending us a few copies of the picture you took of us in action against Dewey at the Chicago Stadium Sunday Sept. 24, 1944. We have no real good action shot of us playing together. Pleeeeeze. We will be more than glad to pay all the expenses involved."[26]

Guthrie was highly sensitive to the possibilities of oblivion, were such provisions not made—not only on his own behalf but on those of his friends as well, particularly Lead Belly. Having argued strenuously more than once that Lead Belly's voice should have been broadcast more frequently on the radio and preserved on record, he confided to his notebook:

> Some of the worlds best poetry
> Comes out of the mouth
> of Huddie Leadbelly
>   If it was only recorded
>   Or wrote down somewhere
>   I'm pretty sure
>   It would stand up
>   Alongside any
>   Of the books
>   In the library.[27]

And if, for whatever reason, the "scribbling" might *not* stay—if there were, in history, a blank space where the output of Woody Guthrie might have been—what would happen then? We can appreciate it almost viscerally when we consider what we no longer have: Guthrie's original oil paintings meant for the cover of the first edition of *Bound for Glory*. They are as tantalizingly absent as the "Hoodises," and like those sculptures so pregnant with interpretive possibilities, we have only approximate substitutes—Guthrie's description—to give us an inkling of what has been lost:

> I got to New York okay and spent the night painting on 3 jacket covers.
>
> The scene is three people, a man, a woman, and a child, evidently migrants (and in this life ain't we all migrants?)—
>
> The man is carrying a bed-roll on his back and is walking away from you. The woman is at his elbow always at his side—and possibly not satisfied at all to be on the road—yet she is happiest when she is backing him up because he is the man she loves and she loves the work he does. The child is a boy with his back also turned toward you. He is a few steps in the distance. The three are in a reddish and

brownish foreground and it looks like the heat of the desert—and they're walking toward a big white power dam jammed down between a couple of mountains—and back of the dam is a big lake of water which makes the background all blue and cool looking—and the sky is blue also. There is a power building at the dam sight and some electric cables strung along to a steel derrick which sweep[s] from the power house to the derrick and out of the picture.

I've done 3 pictures in oil colors on canvas—some little shades here and there are different and I'm signing my name in big letters to two of them. Dutton's expert will letter them. He'll do the "Bound for Glory" up in the pretty blue sky.[28]

Guthrie claimed to have been told by Joy Doerflinger, E. P. Dutton's editor, that "the fact that the writer of the book also illustrated it and made the jacket, that fact alone, would sell another 2000 or 3000 books."[29] But whether it was Doerflinger or another executive, somebody at Dutton decided in the end that Guthrie's painting should not adorn the cover of *Bound for Glory*. With that decision, gone too were all Guthrie's visual references about the Dust Bowl migrants being bound for the benevolent modernity that he had attached to electricity and the Bonneville dam projects. Gone are the "big white power dam," the "electric cables," the "steel derrick," and the "power house." Even the "pretty blue sky" is gone. Guthrie's migrants now have no destination except "Glory," wherever—or whatever—that is (fig. 14).

None of this is to say that even concrete preservation would be a guarantee that Guthrie's "scribbling might stay"—or that it would have any progressive impact at all. Once issued, his art would lie where it fell or go where it was taken, perhaps to be used in manners well beyond his intent. The destination was not always salutary, as is disclosed in one undated, uncharacteristically angry letter discovered in the Woody Guthrie Archives:

> To whoever wants $250 for Woody's folio "My New Found Land"
> Please see me. I will be glad to pay you one hard sock in the jaw.
> You got some fucking nerve. Woody's songs belong to the people.
> The money raised is trying to find a cure for his disease. But I guess
> money-grubbing bastards like you would not understand—
> Pete Seeger[30]

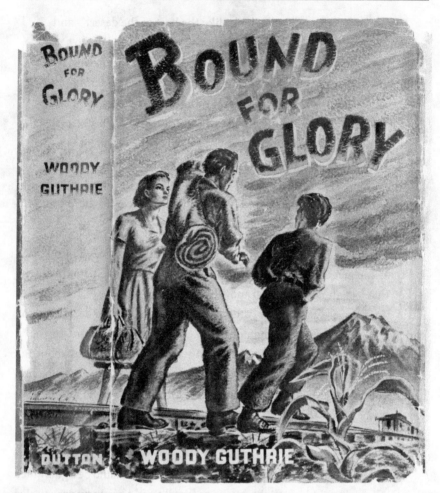

Fig. 14. Dust jacket artwork, first edition of *Bound for Glory*, 1943. Photo courtesy of Kate Blalack, Woody Guthrie Archives.

Still, one might always act, perhaps quixotically, *as if*—as if all the words and images might have a positive impact; as if all the violent forces of modernity would *not* bury one's efforts in the tempest of change; as if one's "scribbling might stay"—even if it might conflict with some "scribbling" laid down elsewhere. Guthrie, "constant changer" though he was, maintained at least one other constant, besides his changeability. It is inscribed into the final two lines of his unpublished poem, "Roaches Run":

Wife tired out
Baby is crying
I'll try anything
If it's worth trying.[31]

When Jean-Paul Sartre was asked in 1964 to reflect upon his first novel, *Nausea*, published twenty-six years earlier, he said that what he had lacked when writing it was "a sense of reality": "I have changed since. I have slowly learned to experience reality. I have seen children dying of hunger. Over against a dying child *Nausea* cannot act as a counterweight."[32] As Toril Moi asked skeptically, "Who will feel illuminated by the thought that *Nausea* will not save a dying child? The answer is clear: only someone who once fervently hoped that it would."[33] By the time he made that statement, Sartre—suffering from ill health and practically blind—had seen ample evidence of the "broken promise" of modernity and the apparent ineffectualness of art in the face of it. The capacity to change—"I have changed since"—had brought Sartre to the point of negation. There was, perhaps, no longer any point in his "scribbling" (although he continued to write—what else could he do?).

Woody Guthrie did not live long enough to give up on his art, even nominally; however much he changed, he never changed so much as *that*. When his hand and his voice were stilled, it was only because Huntington's disease had decreed it so. His eleventh-hour retreat into the arms of Jesus his "doctor," or Christian Science, was a direct response to the involuntary stilling of his hand and voice. There is no evidence that Guthrie ever thought that his art might have saved a dying child, but he did think that it might "prove to you that this is your world" or "make you take pride in yourself and in your work."[34] And if, in his own heart, he never really believed that art could do even this, he always acted *as if* he did. This was perhaps the most important constant in an otherwise dizzying, protean life and time.

Notes

Abbreviations

AFC   Archive of Folk Culture, American Folklife Center, Library of Congress, Washington, D.C.

WGA   Woody Guthrie Archives, Woody Guthrie Center, Tulsa, Oklahoma

WGP   Woody Guthrie Papers, Moses and Frances Asch Collection, Ralph Rinzler Folklife Archives and Collections, Smithsonian Center for Folklife and Cultural Heritage, Smithsonian Institution, Washington, D.C.

Introduction

1. Chris Harman, *A People's History of the World: From the Stone Age to the New Millennium* (New York: Verso, 2008), 619.

2. WGA, Notebooks, box 1, no. 19, p. 139.

3. Hartmut Rosa, *Social Acceleration: A New Theory of Modernity*, translated by Jonathan Trejo-Mathys (New York: Columbia University Press, 2013), 21, 319. Italics in original.

4. Alan Lomax quoted in Edward P. Comentale, *Sweet Air: Modernism, Regionalism and American Popular Song* (Urbana: University of Illinois Press, 2013), 37.

5. Comentale, *Sweet Air*, 123, 124.

6. Unidentified cotton farmer from Ellis, Texas, quoted in Mark Allan Jackson, *Prophet Singer: The Voice and Vision of Woody Guthrie* (Jackson: University Press of Mississippi, 2007), 66.

7. Millard Lampell quoted in Mark Allan Jackson, "Playing Legend Maker: Woody Guthrie's 'Jackhammer John,'" in *The Life, Music and Thought of Woody Guthrie: A Critical Appraisal*, ed. John S. Partington (Farnham, UK: Ashgate, 2011), 61–62.

8. Charles F. McGovern, "Woody Guthrie's American Century," in Robert Santelli and Emily Davison, eds., *Hard Travelin': The Life and Legacy of Woody Guthrie* (Hanover, N.H.: Wesleyan University Press, 1999), 114.

9. Ibid., 115–16.

10. Christopher Butler, *Modernism: A Very Short Introduction* (Oxford: Oxford University Press, 2010), 1–14.

11. Michael Denning, *The Cultural Front: The Laboring of American Culture in the Twentieth Century* (New York: Verso, 1998), 26–28.

12. Elaine O'Brien et al., eds., *Modern Art in Africa, Asia, and Latin America: An Introduction to Global Modernisms* (Oxford: Wiley-Blackwell, 2012).

13. Comentale, *Sweet Air*, 111.

14. Le Corbusier, *Towards a New Architecture* (1923; New York: Dover, 1985), 126.

15. John Steinbeck, *The Grapes of Wrath* (1939; London: Penguin, 2006), 24.

16. Denning, *The Cultural Front*, 28.

17. Clyde Langford quoted in Alan B. Govenar, *Texas Blues: The Rise of a Contemporary Sound* (College Station: Texas A&M University Press, 2008), 60.

18. Corey Harris quoted in Peter Guralnick et al., eds., *Martin Scorsese Presents the Blues* (New York: Amistad/HarperCollins, 2005), 56.

Chapter 1

1. Wayland Bishop, director of Okfuskee County History Center, email to Will Kaufman, January 14, 2015.

2. Ed Cray, *Ramblin' Man: The Life and Times of Woody Guthrie* (New York: W. W. Norton, 2004), 5.

3. Woody Guthrie, "My Life," in *American Folksong*, ed. Moses Asch (New York: Oak Publications, 1961), 2.

4. Joe Klein, *Woody Guthrie: A Life* (New York: Delta, 1980), 16.

5. Guthrie, "My Life," 1.

6. Cray, *Ramblin' Man*, 23, quoting *Okemah Ledger* of August 26, 1920.

7. Guthrie, "My Life," 2.

8. "Growing Up in Oklahoma," on *Woody Guthrie: American Radical Patriot* (Rounder, 2013), disc 1, track 2; "More Talk of Growing up in Okemah," ibid., disc 1, track 4.

9. Matt Jennings quoted in Cray, *Ramblin' Man*, 46.

10. Klein, *Woody Guthrie*, 60.

11. Century of Progress programs quoted in Steve J. Wurtzler, *Electric Sounds: Technological Change and the Rise of Corporate Mass Media* (New York: Columbia University Press, 2007), 118.

12. Donald Worster, *Dust Bowl: The Southern Plains in the 1930s* (Oxford, UK: Oxford University Press, 1982) 6–7, 13.

13. Lee Hays quoted in Ronald D. Cohen, *Woody Guthrie: Writing America's Songs* (New York: Routledge, 2012), 11.

14. Guthrie, "My Life," 4.

15. Cohen, *Woody Guthrie*, 14–15.

16. Guthrie, "My Life," 4.

17. Pare Lorentz, director, *The Fight for Life* (US Film Service, 1940). The seventy-minute film is available in its entirety on YouTube: https://www.youtube.com/watch?v=aOKjRBDTNso. Amid the overwhelming scenes of urban and industrial

dereliction, Guthrie is briefly seen at about 58:20 into the film, sitting on a tenement stoop and strumming a guitar. It is clearly not him playing on the musical soundtrack.

18. Klein, *Woody Guthrie*, 139.

19. Cray, *Ramblin' Man*, 161.

20. Alan Lomax quoted in David King Dunaway, *How Can I Keep from Singing? The Ballad of Pete Seeger* (New York: Villard Books, 2008), 69.

21. Ellen G. Landau, "Classic in Its Own Way: The Art of Woody Guthrie," in Santelli and Davidson, *Hard Travelin'*, 87.

22. Steven Brower and Nora Guthrie, eds., *Woody Guthrie Artworks* (New York: Rizzoli, 2005).

23. Cray, *Ramblin' Man*, 183.

24. Lomax quoted in Cohen, *Woody Guthrie*, 21.

25. Klein, *Woody Guthrie*, 170.

26. Sue Guthrie quoted in Cray, *Ramblin' Man*, 200.

27. Millard Lampell quoted in Klein, *Woody Guthrie*, 209–10.

28. Pete Seeger quoted in Cray, *Ramblin' Man*, 228.

29. Cray, *Ramblin' Man*, 263.

30. Jeff Place, "Woody Guthrie's Recorded Legacy," in Santelli and Davidson, *Hard Travelin'*, 62.

31. Cray, *Ramblin' Man*, 285.

32. Landau, "Classic in Its Own Way," 98–99.

33. Guthrie quoted in Klein, *Woody Guthrie*, 359–60.

34. Klein, *Woody Guthrie*, 379.

35. Cray, *Ramblin' Man*, 378.

36. Guthrie to Marjorie Guthrie, December 12, 1956, quoted in Klein, *Woody Guthrie*, 438.

37. Guthrie to the Guthrie children, December 14, 1956, quoted in ibid., 438.

Chapter 2

1. Guthrie to "Dear Friends" at unnamed magazine, July 18, 1944, WGA, Manuscripts 9, series 1, box 4, folder 6.

2. Guthrie to Marjorie Mazia, November 17, 1942, WGA, Correspondence 1, box 1, folder 44.

3. Brian Jones, "Finding the Avant-Garde in the Old-Time: John Cohen in the American Folk Revival," *American Music* 28, no. 4 (Winter 2010): 408.

4. Ibid.

5. Thomas Crow, *The Long March of Pop: Art, Music and Design, 1930–1995* (New Haven: Yale University Press, 2014), 7, 12.

6. Comentale, *Sweet Air*, 122.

7. Regina Bendix, "Authenticity," in *Folklore: An Encyclopedia of Beliefs, Customs, Tales, Music, and Art*, vol. 1, ed. Charlie T. McCormick and Kim Kennedy White (Santa Barbara: ABC-Clio, 2011), 187.

8. Virginia Woolf, "Phases of Fiction," in *Collected Essays*, vol. 2 (London: Hogarth Press, 1966), 83.

9. WGA, Notebooks, box 1, no. 11, pp. 8–10 (December 17, 1942).

10. WGA, Notebooks, box 1, no. 10, p. 11.

11. WGA, Notebooks, box 1, no. 62, p. 35.

12. Comentale, *Sweet Air*, 135, 136.

13. WGA, Notebooks, box 1, no. 10, p. 11 (November 13–15, 1942).

14. Mark Goble, *Beautiful Circuits: Modernism and the Mediated Life* (New York: Columbia University Press, 2010), 192.

15. WGA, Notebooks, box 1, no. 62, p. 34 (November 10, 1947).

16. WGA, Notebooks, box 1, no. 39, p. 6.

17. Comentale, *Sweet Air*, 136.

18. Guthrie, "People Are Words," November 29, 1943, WGA, Notebooks, box 1, no. 19, p. 77.

19. Daniel Tammet, *Born on a Blue Day: Inside the Extraordinary Mind of an Autistic Savant* (New York: Free Press, 2006), 2.

20. Klein, *Woody Guthrie*, 462–63.

21. Guthrie, "I Hate," August 3, 1947, WGA, Notebooks 1, no. 54, p. 66.

22. Guthrie, "Pictures," October 1944, WGA, Notebooks 1, no. 31, p. 78.

23. Guthrie, "Old Words," September 20, 1948, WGA, Notebooks 2, no. 2, p. 27.

24. Guthrie to Moses Asch, August 1, 1946, WGA, Correspondence 1, box 1, folder 6.

25. Guthrie, "No Rich," ca. August 1947, WGA, Notebooks 1, no. 57, 139.

26. Guthrie, note below lyrics to "Cumberland Mountain Farms," WGA, Songs 1.

27. Guthrie, "You're the Big Poet," August 13, 1947, WGA, Notebooks 1, no. 57, p. 88.

28. Guthrie, "Words and Workers," ca. mid-1943, WGA, Notebooks 1, no. 19, p. 43.

29. Comentale, *Sweet Air*, 125–26.

30. Woody Guthrie, *House of Earth* (New York: HarperCollins/Infinitum Nihil, 2013), 24, 172.

31. Peter Nicholls, *Modernisms: A Literary Guide* (Berkeley: University of California Press, 1995), 202.

32. Guthrie, "Big Smudge," August 3, 1947, WGA, Notebooks 1, no. 54, p. 53.

33. Guthrie to Marjorie Mazia, August 29, 1942, WGA, Correspondence 1, box 2, folder 8.

34. Guthrie, "Hoodis," [1946], WGA, Manuscripts 1, box 4, folder 36, p. 1.

35. Ibid., 3–4.

36. Ibid., 8.

37. Joyce quoted in Richard Ellmann, *James Joyce* (Oxford: Oxford University Press, 1982), 521.

38. Guthrie, "Hoodis," [1946], WGA, Manuscripts 1, box 4, folder 36, p. 13.

39. Theodor Adorno, "Cultural Criticism and Society" (1949), in *Prisms*, translated by Shierry Weber Nicholsen (Cambridge, Mass.: MIT Press, 1981), 34; Philip Roth, "Writing American Fiction," in *Reading Myself and Others* (New York: Farrar, Straus and Giroux, 1975), 120.

40. Guthrie quoted in Klein, *Woody Guthrie*, 327.

41. Guthrie, "Hoodis," [1946], WGA, Manuscripts 1, box 4, folder 36, p. 10.

42. Norman Brosterman, *Inventing Kindergarten* (New York: Harry N. Abrams, Inc., 1997), 7.

43. Ibid., 37.

44. Frank Lloyd Wright quoted in Brosterman, *Inventing Kindergarten*, 138.

45. Guthrie, "Child Sitting," WGA, Manuscripts 9, series 1, box 4, folder 33, pp. 5–6.

46. Ibid., 6.

47. Guthrie, "Stackabones," 1943, WGA, Notebooks 1, no. 23, p. 25; Guthrie, "Hoodoo Voodoo," on Billy Bragg and Wilco, *Mermaid Avenue: The Complete Sessions* (Nonesuch, 2012), disc 1, track 5.

48. Woody Guthrie, *Songs to Grow On for Mother and Child* (Folkways, 1956).

49. Brosterman, *Inventing Kindergarten*, 51.

50. WGA, Notebooks 1, no. 35, pp. 26–27 (October 1944).

51. Jim Longhi, *Woody, Cisco, and Me: With Woody Guthrie in the Merchant Marine* (Urbana: University of Illinois Press, 1997), 258–59.

52. Mark Franko, *The Work of Dance: Labor, Movement, and Identity in the 1930s* (Middletown, Conn.: Wesleyan University Press, 2002), 99, 102.

53. WGA, Notebooks 1, no. 19, pp. 11–15.

54. WGA, Notebooks 1, no. 11, pp. 26–27 (December 17, 1942).

55. WGA, Notebooks 1, no. 19, pp. 50–51.

56. Guthrie to Pete and Toshi Seeger, February 27, 1947, WGA, Correspondence 1, box 3, folder 23.

Chapter 3

1. The details of Guthrie's journey are from Cray, *Ramblin' Man*, 162–63.

2. Robert W. Rydell, *World of Fairs: The Century-of-Progress Expositions* (Chicago: University of Chicago Press, 1993), 78.

3. Norman Bel Geddes, *Magic Motorways* (New York: Random House, 1940), 3.

4. Edward Dimendberg, "The Will to Motorization: Cinema, Highways, and Modernity," *October* 73 (Summer 1995), 116.

5. Bel Geddes, *Magic Motorways*, 4, 18, 30–31.

6. Ibid., 8.

7. WGA, Notebooks 1, no. 6, p. vii.

8. Denning, *The Cultural Front*, 26–27.

9. Roland Barthes quoted in Wolfgang Sachs, *For Love of the Automobile: Looking Back into the History of Our Desires*, translated by Don Renau (Berkeley: University of California Press, 1992), 91.

10. Guthrie, "Old Gray Team of Hosses," WGA, Notebooks 1, no. 6, p. 185.

11. Guthrie, "Cadillac Cadillac," WGA, Songs 1, box 2.

12. Guthrie, "Cadillac Eight," WGA, Songs 1, box 2.

13. Guthrie, "Real Estate Mover," WGA, Notebooks 2, no. 2, p. 53.

14. Guthrie to Alan Lomax, June 7, 1942, WGA, Correspondence 1, box 1, folder 39.

15. WGA, Woodrow W. Guthrie FBI Files, Personal Papers, box 2, folder 48.1.

16. Guthrie, "Talking Dust Bowl Blues," *Dust Bowl Ballads* (1940, Buddha, 2000).

17. Guthrie, "Downtown Traffic Blues," WGA, Notebooks 1, no. 5, p. 51.

18. WGA, Notebooks 1, no. 4, p. 92.

19. Guthrie, "You're Bound to Get Lousy in the Lincoln Heights Jail," WGA, Notebooks 1, no. 4, p. 155.

20. Guthrie, "No Parking Place Down Here," WGA, Notebooks 2, no. 10, p. 36.

21. Guthrie, "Car Song," on *The Asch Recordings*, vol. 1 (Smithsonian Folkways, 1999), track 2.

22. Guthrie, "Windshield Wiper," WGA, Notebooks 2, no. 7, p. 15.

23. Guthrie, "Flush and Drain," WGA, Notebooks 1, no. 54, p. 30.

24. WGA, Notebooks 1, no. 22, p. 86.

25. WGA, Notebooks 1, no. 16, pp. 64–65.

26. WGA, Notebooks 1, no. 4, p. 199.

27. Guthrie, "Put It Light," WGA, Notebooks 1, no. 9, p. 39.

28. WGA, Notebooks 1, no. 52, p. 60.

29. Roland Marchand, "The Designers Go to the Fair II: Norman Bel Geddes, the General Motors 'Futurama,' and the Visit to the Factory Transformed," *Design Issues* 8, no. 2 (Spring 1992): 29.

30. Dimendberg, "The Will to Motorization," 126.

31. Alan Lomax, Woody Guthrie, and Pete Seeger, eds., *Hard Hitting Songs for Hard-Hit People* (New York: Oak Publications, 1967), 62.

32. Denning, *The Cultural Front*, 29.

33. Guthrie, "Stepstone," on *The Asch Recordings*, vol. 2, track 12.

34. WGA, Notebooks 1, no. 4, p. 30. "They called us cowards for running and hiding along the road. We called them cowards for running and hiding at home." Guthrie to Marjorie Mazia, September 10, 1945, WGA, Correspondence 1, box 2, folder 5.

35. "Hobo's Lullaby" (Goebel Reeves), on Guthrie, *The Asch Recordings*, vol. 1.

36. WGA, Notebooks 1, no. 4, p. 57.

37. WGA, Notebooks 1, no. 11, p. 40.

38. Guthrie, "Little Mama," November 29, 1943, WGA, Notebooks 1, no. 19, p. 73.

39. WGA, Notebooks 1, no. 42, pp. 8–11 (August 28, 1945).

40. Guthrie, "On Ballad Singers," March 20, 1946, WGA, Manuscripts 9, box 4, folder 26.

41. Wayne Hampton, *Guerrilla Minstrels* (Knoxville: University of Tennessee Press, 1986), 213.

42. Guthrie to Marjorie Mazia, September 10, 1945, WGA, Correspondence 1, box 2, folder 5.

43. Guthrie, notes to "Ain't a Gonna Do," WGP, Song Texts, box 1, folder 1.

44. Guthrie to Marjorie Mazia, January 20, 1944, WGA, Correspondence 1, box 1, folder 49.

45. Guthrie to Marjorie Mazia, September 10, 1945, WGA, Correspondence 1, box 2, folder 8.

46. Guthrie, "This Road," WGA, Songs 1, box 9.

47. WGA, Notebooks 1, no. 22, pp. 34–35.

48. Guthrie, "Stackabones," WGA, Notebooks 1, no. 23, p. 55.

49. Guthrie, "Stackabones," 59; "orgastic future": F. Scott Fitzgerald, *The Great Gatsby* (1925, New York: Scribner, 2004), 180.

50. Guthrie, "I Ain't Got No Home," KFVD air check recording (1937), track 4. unlabeled CD, Ralph Rinzler Archives, Center for Folklife and Cultural Heritage, Smithsonian Institution, Washington, D.C.

51. "Will Rogers Highway," on *Woody Guthrie: American Radical Patriot*, disc 4, track 11.

52. Guthrie, *Seeds of Man* (New York: Pocket Books, 1977), 122.

53. Guthrie, "Gates of Heaven," WGA, Notebooks 2, no. 7, p. 17.

54. Guthrie, "Setting by the Highway," WGA, Notebooks 2, no. 3, p. 58.

55. Guthrie, "New Road Blues," WGA, Notebooks 1, no. 6, p. 108.

56. WGA, Notebooks 1, no. 4, p. 185.

57. Guthrie, "The Government Road," WGA, Notebooks 1, no. 4, p. 184.

58. WGA, Notebooks 1, no. 6, p. vii.

Chapter 4

1. Woody Guthrie, *Bound for Glory* (New York: Dutton, 1943), 300–301.

2. Klein, *Woody Guthrie*, 41.

3. John Gillespie Magee Jr., "High Flight," in *Flight: A Celebration of 100 Years in Art and Literature*, ed. Anne Collins Goodyear et al. (New York: Welcome Books, 2003), 63.

4. Guthrie, *Bound for Glory*, 299.

5. Roy Acuff, "Streamlined Cannonball," on *Wabash Cannonball* (Hickory Records, 1965).

6. Norm Cohen, *Long Steel Rail: The Railroad in American Folksong* (Urbana: University of Illinois Press, 2000): 596–602.

7. Guthrie, "Little Black Train," on *The Asch Recordings*, vol. 2.

8. Guthrie, "The White Ghost Train," WGA, Notebooks 1, no. 3, p. 103.

9. Guthrie, "Better World," on *The Asch Recordings*, vol. 3.

10. WGA, Notebooks 1, no. 35, p. 33.

11. Jim Cox, *Rails across Dixie: A History of Passenger Trains in the American South* (Jefferson, NC: McFarland, 2011), 164.

12. Guthrie, "Railroad Guys," WGA, Songs 1, box 7.

13. Guthrie, "I Aint Satisfied," WGA, Notebooks 1, no. 4, p. 196.

14. WGA, Notebooks 1, no. 4, p. 197.

15. Guthrie, "On My Railroad," WGA, Songs 1, box 7.

16. Guthrie, "Gyro Locomotive," WGA, Notebooks 1, no. 31, p. 56.

17. Guthrie to Marjorie Mazia, December 9, 1942, WGA, Correspondence 1, box 1, folder 44.

18. Guthrie, "Union Train," WGA, Notebooks 1, no. 3, p. 113.

19. Guthrie, "War Songs Are Work Songs," ca. 1942, WGA, Manuscripts 9, box 3, folder 22.

20. Mary Guthrie Boyle quoted in Nora Guthrie et al., *My Name Is New York: Ramblin' around Woody Guthrie's Town* (Brooklyn: powerHouse Books, 2012), 27.

21. WGA, Notebooks 1, no. 4, p. 249.

22. Guthrie, "The New York Trains," WGA, Notebooks 1, no. 4, p. 249. A recorded version by the Del McCroury Band is on Nora Guthrie et al., *My Name Is New York: Ramblin' around Woody Guthrie's Town* (Woody Guthrie Publications, 2014), disc 3, track 2.

23. Woody Guthrie, *Woody Sez* (New York: Grosset and Dunlap, 1975), 107.

24. Guthrie, "Talkin' Subway Blues," in Nora Guthrie et al., *My Name Is New York,* 25.

25. Cray, *Ramblin' Man,* 367.

26. The uncataloged tapes of Guthrie's final recording session are housed in the Moses and Frances Asch Collection, Ralph Rinzler Archives, Smithsonian Institution, Washington, D.C.

27. Guthrie, "Perty Good Train," WGA, Notebooks 2, no. 10, p. 50.

28. Will Kaufman, *Woody Guthrie, American Radical* (Urbana: University of Illinois Press, 2011), 80 (Quin quote), 98 (Doerflinger).

29. Cohen, *Long Steel Rail,* 602.

30. Guthrie, "Airline to Heaven," WGA, Notebooks 1, no. 4, p. 127. A recorded version by Billy Bragg and Wilco is on *Mermaid Avenue: The Complete Sessions* (Nonesuch, 2012), disc 2, track 1.

31. Guthrie, "High Priced Cars," WGA, Notebooks 1, no. 5, p. 53.

32. Lauren Rabinovitz, *Electric Dreamland: Amusement Parks, Movies, and American Modernity* (New York: Columbia University Press, 2012), 11.

33. Wolfgang Schivelbusch, *The Railway Journey: The Industrialization of Time and Space in the Nineteenth Century* (Oakland: University of California Press, 2014), 33.

34. Guthrie had long before signaled his awareness of the expansive part played by labor in keeping the airplanes flying. During the war he wrote "My Daddy Flies That Ship in the Sky," in which a pilot's bragging little girl is told by her playmates, "My daddy builds the planes" and "My daddy works at the place where they land." On Guthrie, *The Asch Recordings,* vol. 3 (Smithsonian Folkways, 1999).

35. WGA, Notebooks 1, no. 47, pp. 2–3.

36. Pete Seeger to Guthrie, undated, on typed copy of Guthrie, "Airplane," WGA, Songs 1, box 1.

37. Guthrie, "Airplane," WGA, Songs 1, box 1.

38. Guthrie, "Lady in the Plane," WGA, Notebooks 2, no. 9, p. 122.

39. WGA, Notebooks 1, no. 47, p. 23.

40. Guthrie, "Looking Down on You," WGA, Notebooks 1, no. 47, p. 18.

41. The migrants remained unnamed until 2013 when, thanks to the investigative efforts of Tim Z. Hernandez, a memorial at Los Gatos was erected to their memory. See Hernandez, *All They Will Call You* (Tucson: University of Arizona Press, 2017). See also Juan Mora-Torres, "Woody Guthrie's 'Deportee': Migrants, Death, and Namelessness," *PilsenPortal,* June 24, 2013, http://chicagovoz.org/2013/06/24/woody-guthries-deportee-migrants-death-and-namelessness; Vani Kannan, "Memorializing 'Deportees': Conversations with Tim Hernandez and Lance Canales," *Woody Guthrie Annual* 1 (2015): 83–100, http://pops.uclan.ac.uk/index.php/WGA/article/view/298/122.

42. Guthrie, "Deportee." Lyrics online at Woody Guthrie Publications, http://woodyguthrie.org/Lyrics/Plane_Wreck_At_Los_Gatos.htm.

43. Guthrie to John A. Lomax, 2004/04, Woody Guthrie and Carl Sandburg Correspondence, box 33.02, Alan Lomax Collection, American Folklife Center, Library of Congress, Washington, D.C.

44. Guthrie to Pete Seeger and family, April 12, 1949, WGA, Correspondence 1, box 3, folder 24.

45. Guthrie to his unnamed Oklahoma family, April 21, 1949, WGA, Correspondence 1, box 3, folder 38.

46. John Greenway, *American Folksongs of Protest* (New York: A. S. Barnes, 1953), 288. Guthrie aficionados will recognize the lyric's image reworked into the song, "California Stars," recorded by Billy Bragg and Wilco, *Mermaid Avenue: The Complete Sessions* (Nonesuch, 2012), disc 1, track 2.

47. Guthrie, "My Oklahoma," WGA, Correspondence 1, box 3, folder 27.

48. Cohen, *Long Steel Rail*, 602.

49. Guthrie, "Woke Up This Morning with a Foggy Brain," WGA, Songs 1, box 10.

50. Guthrie, "Talking Hitler's Head Off Blues," WGA, Notebooks 1, no. 3, p. 100.

51. Guthrie, "Jet Plane," WGA, Songs 2, notebook 64, p. 243.

52. Guthrie, "My Flying Saucer," recorded by Billy Bragg and Wilco, *Mermaid Avenue: The Complete Sessions* (Nonesuch, 2012), disc 2, track 2.

53. Billy Bragg quoted in Peter Applebomel, "New Glimpses of Woody Guthrie's Imagination," *New York Times*, April 27, 1998.

54. Angela Hague, "UFOs," in *Conspiracy Theories in American History: An Encyclopedia*, vol. 2., ed. Peter Knight (Santa Barbara: ABC-Clio, 2003), 699–704.

55. Guthrie quoted in Kaufman, *Woody Guthrie, American Radical*, 143–44.

56. Guthrie, *Skybally*, WGA, Manuscripts 6, box 8, folder 16.

57. "Ezekiel Saw the Wheel," Woody Guthrie, in *My Dusty Road*, disc 4 (Rounder, 2009), track 9.

58. Guthrie, "Ezekiel Saw the Wheel," *YouTube*, https://www.youtube.com/watch?v=VxhDwqwMgaY.

Chapter 5

1. Rosa, *Social Acceleration*, 156.

2. Tom Gunning, "Re-Newing Old Technologies: Astonishment, Second Nature, and the Uncanny in Technology from the Previous Turn-of-the-Century," in *Rethinking Media Change: The Aesthetics of Transition*, ed. David Thorburn and Henry Jenkins (Cambridge, Mass.: MIT Press, 2003), 40–41.

3. Zygmunt Bauman, *Modernity and Ambivalence* (Cambridge, Mass.: Polity Press, 1991), 151.

4. Guthrie, "Talking Columbia," in *The Columbia River Collection* (Rounder, 1988), track 4.

5. Guthrie, "I Can't Be Happy This a Way," WGA, Notebooks 1, no. 4, 214.

6. Guthrie to Millard Lampell, 1941, WGA, Correspondence 1, box 1, folder 34.

7. Guthrie to Alan Lomax, September 19, 1940, WGA, Correspondence 1, box 1, folder 39.

8. Hampton, *Guerrilla Minstrels*, 132.

9. See Will Kaufman, "Lonesome Radical Soul," in *Woody Guthrie, American Radical*, 110–44.

10. Guthrie, *House of Earth*, 165–66.

11. WGA, Notebooks 1, no. 54, p. 34.

12. Guthrie, "Wires That Won't Burn," ibid.

13. Guthrie, "Ranian's Finbow and Me," January 25, 1948, WGA, Manuscripts 9, box 7, folder 3. Robert Cantwell refers to the "sticker produced for war workers, typically seen on lathes and drill presses, that Woody Guthrie posted on his guitar: 'This machine kills fascists.'" Cantwell, *When We Were Good: The Folk Revival* (Cambridge, Mass.: Harvard University Press, 1996), 102.

14. WGA, Notebooks 1, no. 19, 4.

15. Guthrie to Marjorie Mazia [December 1942], WGA, Correspondence 1, box 1, folder 44.

16. Guthrie, "Jack Hammer Blues," WGA, Notebooks 1, no. 4, p. 200.

17. Guthrie, "Dust Can't Kill Me," WGA, Notebooks 1, no. 5, p. 15.

18. Guthrie, "Poor, Hard-Working Man Blues," Songs of Woody Guthrie manuscript, 1940/004, Woody Guthrie Manuscript Collection, box 1, folder 13, p. 92, Archive of Folk Culture, American Folklife Center, Library of Congress, Washington, D.C.

19. Guthrie, *House of Earth*, 160.

20. WGA, Notebooks 1, no. 46, p. 22.

21. WGA, Notebooks 1, no. 4, p. 36.

22. Worster, *Dust Bowl*, 97.

23. Stuart Udall to Guthrie, April 6, 1966, WGP, Correspondence: By and about Woody Guthrie, box 4, folder 4/5.

24. Silber quoted in Cray, *Ramblin' Man*, 389.

25. Daniel B. Botkin, "My Recollections of Woody Guthrie," Danielbbotkin.com, July 20, 2012, http://www.danielbbotkin.com/?s=Guthrie.

26. Thomas DeGregori, *Bountiful Harvest: Technology, Food Safety, and the Environment* (Washington, D.C.: Cato Institute, 2002), 193.

27. Guthrie, "If I Was Everything on Earth," in "Alonzo Zilch's Own Collection of Original Songs and Ballads," Woody Guthrie Manuscript Collection, box 1, folder 9, Archive of Folk Culture, American Folklife Center, Library of Congress, Washington, D.C.

28. Guthrie, *Bound for Glory*, 114.

29. Guthrie, *Bound for Glory*, 250.

30. Guthrie, *Seeds of Man*, 124.

31. Guthrie, "Lumber Is King," in *Woody Guthrie, Roll on Columbia: The Columbia River Songs*, ed. Bill Murlin (Portland, Ore.: Bonneville Power Administration, 1988), 67.

32. Guthrie to Millard Lampell, September 9, 1941, WGA, Correspondence 1, box 1, folder 34.

33. "Columbia River," in *Cleaner Rivers for Oregon*, Oregon Environmental Council, 2007, http://oeconline.org/wp-content/uploads/2014/10/cleaner-rivers-report.pdf, 7–8. I am grateful to Daniel B. Botkin for directing me to this source.

34. Guthrie, "Lumber Is King," in Murlin, *Woody Guthrie, Roll on Columbia*, 67.

35. See Lynette Boone, "Development of the Columbia River and Impacts on Native American Cultures and the Environment," in *Roll on Columbia: Woody Guthrie and the Bonneville Power Administration* (website supplement to documentary film by same title), University of Oregon, https://library.uoregon.edu/ec/wguthrie/development.html.

36. Guthrie, *Bound for Glory*, 203–204.

37. Guthrie, "Garbage Waves," WGA, Notebooks 1, no. 57, 108.

38. Woody Guthrie, "Silicosis Is Killin' Me," in Lomax, Guthrie, and Seeger, *Hard Hitting Songs for Hard-Hit People*, 134.

39. Guthrie, "Dead from the Dust," WGA, Songs 1, box 3.

40. Guthrie, "Smoggy Old Smog," WGA, Notebooks 2, no. 9, p. 44.

41. Guthrie, "On Top of Old Smoggy," WGA, Notebooks 2, no. 9, p. 48.

42. Guthrie, "Smoggy Mountain Top," WGA, Notebooks 2, no. 9, p. 46.

43. WGA, Notebooks 1, no. 35, p. 55.

Chapter 6

1. Goble, *Beautiful Circuits*, 3, 122.

2. Sam Halliday, *Sonic Modernity: Representing Sound in Literature, Culture, and the Arts* (Edinburgh: Edinburgh University Press, 2013), 9.

3. Guthrie to Will and Herta Geer, February 6, 1945, WGA, Correspondence 1, box 1, folder 18.

4. Guthrie to Marjorie Mazia, November 17, 1952, WGA, Correspondence 1, box 1, folder 44.

5. WGA, Notebooks 1, no. 22, p. 149.

6. Guthrie, "Marjorie," WGA, Notebooks 2, no. 10, p. 19.

7. Guthrie, "DRexell 23883," October 21, 1950, WGA, Notebooks 2, no. 6, p. 44.

8. Goble, *Beautiful Circuits*, 192.

9. Comentale, *Sweet Air*, 13.

10. Mike Adams, *Lee de Forest: King of Radio, Television, and Film* (New York: Copernicus, 2012), xii, 106.

11. Comentale, *Sweet Air*, 111, 113.

12. Denning, *The Cultural Front*, 42.

13. See June S. MacArthur, "Farm Radios: Communication before Rural Electrification," *Farm Collector*, March 2001, http://www.farmcollector.com/.

14. Cray, *Ramblin' Man*, 29.

15. "Tulsa Radio Memories," Tulsatvmemories.com, http://tulsatvmemories.com/tulrkvoo.html.

16. Klein, *Woody Guthrie*, 55.

17. Cray, *Ramblin' Man*, 49–50.

18. Ibid., 53.

19. Guthrie, *House of Earth*, 108–109. Further page references are cited parenthetically in the text.

20. Comentale, *Sweet Air*, 108–109, 114. Comentale quotes Bob Coltman, "Across the Chasm: How the Depression Changed Country Music," *Old Time Music* 23 (Winter 1976–77): 6.

21. Wurtzler, *Electric Sounds*, 198.

22. Ibid., 196–97.

23. Comentale, *Sweet Air*, 109.

24. Wurtzler, *Electric Sounds*, 63, 69.

25. Denning, *The Cultural Front*, 43.

26. Ibid., 47.

27. Klein, *Woody Guthrie*, 104.

28. Guthrie, note written below lyrics to "More Purty Gals Than One," *Woody and Lefty Lou's Favorite Collection, Old Time Hill Country Songs* (Gardena, Calif.: Spanish American Institute Press, 1937), unpaginated, WGP, box 2, folder 4.

29. Peter La Chapelle, *Proud to Be an Okie: Cultural Politics, Country Music, and Migration to Southern California* (Berkeley: University of California Press, 2007), 58.

30. Guthrie, "Songs, People, Papers," September 1, 1946, WGA, Manuscripts 9, box 4, folder 31.

31. Klein, *Woody Guthrie*, 105.

32. Guthrie, "Songs, People, Papers."

33. Alan Lomax quoted in Denning, *The Cultural Front*, 91.

34. Cray, *Ramblin' Man*, 182–83.

35. Guthrie to Alan Lomax, September 17, 1940, WGA, Correspondence 1, box 1, folder 39.

36. Guthrie, "Pipe Smoking Time," quoted in Klein, *Woody Guthrie*, 179.

37. WGA, Notebooks 1, no. 4, p. 245.

38. Guthrie, note below lyrics to "Christmas Talking Blues," WGA, Songs 1, box 2.

39. Guthrie to Alan Lomax, February 20, 1941, WGA, Correspondence 1, box 1, folder 39.

40. New York *World-Telegram*, quoted in Klein, *Woody Guthrie*, 229.

41. Denning, *The Cultural Front*, 82. See also Allan M. Winkler, *The Politics of Propaganda: The Office of War Information, 1942–1945* (New Haven: Yale University Press, 1978), 65–66.

42. Guthrie, "Union Radio," November 30, 1943, WGA, Notebooks 1, no. 19, p. 107.

43. Guthrie to Marjorie Mazia, November 17, 1942, WGA, Correspondence 1, box 1, folder 44.

44. Guthrie, "Notes on 'East Texas Red,'" WGP, Song Texts, box 1, folder 3.

45. Guthrie, "War Songs and Work Songs," WGA, Manuscripts 1, series 9, box 3, folder 22.

46. Guthrie to Marjorie Mazia, June 8, 1944, WGA, Correspondence 1, box 1, folder 50.

47. Guthrie to Marjorie Mazia, January 20, 1944, WGA, Correspondence 1, box 1, folder 49.

48. "BBC: Children's Hour, July 7, 1944," *Woody at 100: The Woody Guthrie Centennial Collection* (Smithsonian Folkways, 2012), disc 3, track 6.

49. Guthrie to Marjorie Mazia [July 1944], WGA, Correspondence 1, box 1, folder 50. See also Alan Lomax et al., *The Martins and the Coys* (Rounder, 2000).

50. Guthrie, "WNEW," in *Born to Win*, ed. Robert Shelton (New York: Collier, 1967), 224–25.

51. WGA, Notebooks 1, no. 26, pp. 96–97. Although WNEW had an association with the *Daily News*, maintaining a broadcast desk in the paper's office, it was not owned by Patterson McCormick, but rather by Milton Biow and the Arde Bulova watch company. See Nightingale Gordon, *WNEW—Where the Melody Lingers On, 1934–1984* (New York: WNEW, 1984).

52. Guthrie quoted in Klein, *Woody Guthrie*, 300.

53. Guthrie to Marjorie Mazia, July 18, 1945, WGA, Correspondence 1, box 2, folder 4.

54. Guthrie, "Railroad Cricket," quoted in Cray, *Ramblin' Man*, 202.

55. Ibid., 202–203; Klein, *Woody Guthrie*, 184; Shelton in Guthrie, *Born to Win*, 145; Guthrie, "The Singing Cricket and Huddie Ledbetter," in *Born to Win*, 149.

Chapter 7

1. WGA, Notebooks 1, no. 13, p. 26.

2. Douglas Gomery, *The Coming of Sound: A History* (New York: Routledge, 2005), 152–53.

3. Wurtzler, *Electric Sounds*, 64.

4. Comentale, *Sweet Air*, 24; Denning, *The Cultural Front*, 47.

5. Guthrie, "To a Union Show Troup," ca. 1941, WGA, Manuscripts 1, series 9, box 1, folder 12.

6. Guthrie, "Me . . . and Ingrid," in *Pastures of Plenty*, ed. Dave Marsh and Harold Leventhal (New York: HarperPerennial, 1990), 189. Originally published in *Sunday Worker*, January 12, 1947.

7. Comentale, *Sweet Air*, 68.

8. Cray, *Ramblin' Man*, 43.

9. William Howland Kenney, *Recorded Music in American Life: The Phonograph and Popular Memory, 1890–1945* (New York: Oxford University Press, 1999), 153.

10. La Chapelle, *Proud to Be an Okie*, 56–57.

11. Guthrie, *Woody Sez*, 126.

12. Guthrie to Pete Seeger, March 19, 1941, WGA, Correspondence 1, box 3, folder 23.

13. Irwin Silber, publisher's foreword to Lomax, Guthrie, and Seeger, eds., *Hard Hitting Songs for Hard-Hit People*, 11.

14. Alan Lomax, compiler's postscript to Lomax, Guthrie, and Seeger, eds., *Hard Hitting Songs for Hard-Hit People*, 366.

15. Woody Guthrie, introduction to Lomax, Guthrie, and Seeger, eds., *Hard Hitting Songs for Hard-Hit People*, 25.

16. Denning, *The Cultural Front*, 41.

17. "Woody Guthrie's Personal Record Collection," finding aid. Woody Guthrie Center, http://woodyguthriecenter.org/archives/collection/1856-2.

18. Guthrie to Mary Jo Edgmon and family, Dec. 1, 1950, WGA, Correspondence 1, box 1, folder 14.

19. Guthrie to Marjorie Mazia, August 5, 1945, WGA, Correspondence 1, box 2, folder 5.

20. Guthrie to Marjorie Mazia, December 12, 1944, WGA, Correspondence 1, box 1, folder 49.

21. Guthrie, "Hard Hitting Songs by Hard Hit People," ca. 1941, WGA, Manuscripts 1, series 9, box 1, folder 11.

22. Guthrie, "Folk Songs" July 25, 1944, WGA, Manuscripts 1, series 9, box 4, folder 7.

23. In addition to Comentale's *Sweet Air,* see Richard A. Peterson, *Creating Country Music: Fabricating Authenticity* (Chicago: University of Chicago Press, 1999); Elijah Wald, *Escaping the Delta: Robert Johnson and the Invention of the Blues* (New York: HarperCollins, 2004); Pamela Fox, *Natural Acts: Gender, Race, and Rusticity in Country Music* (Ann Arbor: University of Michigan Press, 2009).

24. Comentale, *Sweet Air,* 34.

25. Fox, *Natural Acts,* 6.

26. Al Richmond quoted in Cray, *Ramblin' Man,* 171; Bess Hawes quoted in Cray, *Ramblin' Man,* 231; Moses Asch, interview with Guy Logsdon, July 1974, in Logsdon, introduction to liner notes to Guthrie, *The Asch Recordings,* vol. 3 (Smithsonian Folkways, 1999); Alan Lomax, "To whom it may concern," 1941 reference letter for Woody Guthrie, WGA, Correspondence 2, box 2, folder 16. In the same 1941 letter, Lomax calls Guthrie "a fine actor" as well as "a completely authentic and sensitive singer," which raises some tension between authenticity and performance.

27. Guthrie, "Singing High Balladree," January 23, 1947, WGA, Manuscripts 1, series 9, box 4, folder 46.

28. Hampton, *Guerrilla Minstrels,* 109.

29. Denning, *The Cultural Front,* 270.

30. Ibid., 355.

31. "Riding the Rails," *Woody Guthrie: American Radical Patriot,* disc 3, track 12.

32. Woody Guthrie, introduction to "I'm Going' Down That Road Feeling Bad," in Lomax, Guthrie, and Seeger, *Hard Hitting Songs for Hard-Hit People,* 215. Mark Allan Jackson claims that Guthrie's "story seems unlikely," although he doesn't elaborate. See Jackson, *Prophet Singer,* 73.

33. Cray, *Ramblin' Man,* 180.

34. Ibid., 180–81n.

35. Guthrie, "Hard Hitting Songs by Hard Hit People," ca. 1941, WGA, Manuscripts 1, series 9, box 1, folder 11.

36. WGA, Notebooks 1, no. 4, p. 25.

37. "California as One of the 48 States," *Woody Guthrie: American Radical Patriot,* disc 4, track 10.

38. "Will Rogers Highway," *Woody Guthrie: American Radical Patriot,* disc 4, track 11.

39. P. David Marshall, *Celebrity and Power: Fame in Contemporary Culture* (Minneapolis: University of Minnesota Press, 1997), 4, 82.

40. Guthrie, "Ingrid Bergman," on Billy Bragg and Wilco, *Mermaid Avenue: The Complete Sessions* (Nonesuch, 2012), disc 1, track 8. Bragg notes that, in at least one sense, the interest between Guthrie and Bergman was mutual. He posts on his official Facebook page: "For those of you thinking that Woody and Ingrid didn't have much in common, somewhere in the Woody Guthrie Archive is a newspaper clipping of a photograph of a young Ingrid Bergman reading Woody's novel 'Bound for Glory.' As Woody's daughter Nora said when she showed me the clipping, 'Who knew?'" Facebook, billybraggofficial, https://www.facebook.com/billybraggofficial/posts/103241393132926, February 3, 2012.

41. Colorado Senator Edwin C. Johnson quoted in Donald Spoto, *Notorious: The Life of Ingrid Bergman* (Boston: Da Capo Press, 2001), 295–96.

42. WGA, Notebooks 2, no. 6, p. 63 (May 4, 1949).

43. Guthrie, "Me . . . and Ingrid," *Pastures of Plenty*, 187.

44. Ibid., *Pastures of Plenty*, 187–89.

45. Cray, *Ramblin' Man*, 156.

46. Guthrie, "Songs, People, Papers," September 1, 1946, WGA, Manuscripts 9, box 4, folder 31.

47. Denning, *The Cultural Front*, 18.

48. Guthrie to Marjorie Mazia, October 14, 1945, WGA, Correspondence 1, box 1, folder 36.

49. Guthrie to Aliza Greenblatt, March 20, 1944, WGA, Correspondence 1, box 1, folder 24.

50. "Finding Aid for the Irving Lerner Papers, 1935–1978," Online Archive of California, http://www.oac.cdlib.org/findaid/ark:/13030/tf0n39n6p6/entire_text.

51. Woody Guthrie, "Greasy String" (letter to Irving Lerner, July 17, 1946), in *Born to Win*, ed. Robert Shelton (New York: Collier Books, 1967), 120.

52. Ibid., 122, 123.

53. Ibid., 126–27.

54. Ibid., 127–28.

55. Kaufman, *Woody Guthrie, American Radical*, 183.

56. Blain Brown, *Cinematography: Theory and Practice* (Burlington, Mass.: Focal Press, 2012), 210.

57. Nick Dawson, *Being Hal Ashby: Life of a Hollywood Rebel* (Lexington: University Press of Kentucky, 2009), 169–70.

58. WGA, Notebooks 1, no. 7, 42 (September 25, 1940).

59. Guthrie to unnamed Oklahoma family members, April 21, 1949, WGA, Correspondence 1, box 3, folder 38.

60. Guthrie to "Dear Bobby" ("Bubby" Greenblatt), April 12, 1949, WGA, Correspondence 1, box 1, folder 24.

Chapter 8

1. Guthrie to Marjorie Mazia, August 9, 1945, WGA, Correspondence 1, box 2, folder 5.

2. Guthrie, *Woody Sez*, 71.

3. Guthrie, "My Peace," on Arlo Guthrie and Wenzel, *Every 100 Years* (Indigo Musik, 2010).

4. "Two years ago [1996] a shopkeeper in his hometown erected a sign saying 'Okemah: Home of Woody Guthrie,' which was quickly vandalised with the footnote 'Commist (sic) draft dodger and red.' They took it down." Andrew Collins, "From Dagenham to the Dust Bowl," *New Statesman*, March 6, 1998, 30.

5. Guthrie to Marjorie Mazia, August 9, 1945, WGA, Correspondence 1, box 2, folder 5.

6. See Kaufman, *Woody Guthrie, American Radical*, 82–109.

7. Guthrie, "Singing High Balladree," January 23, 1947, WGA, Manuscripts 9, box 3, folder 46.

8. WGA, Notebooks 1, no. 28, p. 75.

9. Guthrie to Marjorie Mazia, November 17, 1942, WGA, Correspondence 1, box 1, folder 44.

10. Guthrie to Marjorie Mazia, [1942], WGA, Correspondence 1, box 1, folder 44.

11. Guthrie, "You're Gone, You Fascists, You're Gone," WGA, Notebooks 1, no. 3, p. 116.

12. Guthrie, "Postage Stamp," July 19, 1944, WGA, Manuscripts 9, box 4, folder 6.

13. WGA, Notebooks 1, no. 28, p. 45.

14. Guthrie to Mary Jo Guthrie, from Glasgow [1944], WGA, Correspondence 1, box 1, folder 14.

15. WGA, Notebooks 1, no. 29, p. 14.

16. WGA, Notebooks 1, no. 10, p. 6.

17.   We were seamen three
         Cisco, Jimmy and me;
         Shipped out to beat the fascists
         Across the land and sea.

Guthrie, "Seamen Three," in *Pastures of Plenty,* ed. Dave Marsh and Harold Leventhal (New York: HarperPerennial, 1990), 134–35.

18. Guthrie, "Palermo," WGA, Notebooks 1, no. 38, p. 7.

19. Ibid., p. 12.

20. Ibid.,14–17. Regarding "Sicilian . . . Hoovervilles": "There are flies crawling over babies faces. There are little pot bellies by the hundreds swelled up with the gas that is caused by malnutrition. There youll see the torn holes in the flour sack dresses that the kids wear. Red, fevered skin is showing through these clothes like the blistered hide of the several hundred thousand Okies that crawled and walked and marched across a couple of thousand miles of red hot desert to get from Oklahoma's trash pile to California's green pretty places." Guthrie to Marjorie Mazia, April 12, 1942. WGA, Correspondence 1, box 1, folder 43.

21. Guthrie, "Palermo," WGA, Notebooks 1, no. 37a, p. 25.

22. Ibid., pp. 26–27.

23. Guthrie, "Freedom's Fire," WGA, Correspondence 1, box 2, folder 8.

24. Guthrie, "Dance around My Atom Fire," WGP, Song Texts, box 1, folder 3.

25. Guthrie, "People's Songs and Its People," March 19, 1946, WGA, Manuscripts 9, box 4, folder 25.

26. Guthrie, "My Eyes Do See All over This World," WGA, Notebooks 1, no. 47, p. 22.

27. Richard Clendenin, quoted in Andrew Goliszek, *In the Name of Science: A History of Secret Programs, Medical Research, and Human Experimentation* (Boston: St. Martin's Press, 2003), 48.

28. Kenneth Gatland, *Manned Spacecraft* (New York: Macmillan, 1976), 100–101.

29. WGA, Notebooks 1, no. 47, p. 27.

30. Asaf A. Siddiqi, *Sputnik and the Soviet Space Challenge* (Gainesville: University Press of Florida, 2003), 24–41.

31. Guthrie, "That Moon Told Me," WGA, Notebooks 1, no. 54, p. 106.

32. Guthrie, "I Don't Like Your 'Lantic Pact," WGA, Notebooks 2, no. 2, p. 60.

33. Guthrie to Harry S. Truman, July 31, 1949. Reprinted in Guthrie, *Born to Win*, ed. Robert Shelton (New York: Collier Books, 1967), 91–92.

34. Guthrie, "The Hour Cometh," WGA, Notebooks 2, no. 7, p. 23.

35. Wada Haruki, *The Korean War: An International History* (Lanham, Md.: Rowman and Littlefield, 2014), 29; Stanley Sandler, *The Korean War: An Interpretative History* (London: UCL Press, 1999), 40, 226.

36. Guthrie, "When I Get Home," WGA, Notebooks 2, no. 3, p. 60.

37. On the day after the Japanese surrender, Guthrie reported to Marjorie a discussion in his teletype class: "We talked about the war, about the atom, and the teacher surprised me by saying, 'Men, we've got to really give credit to that Red Army. And of course to all of the Allies, but when those Reds poured into Manchuko yesterday and the Allies blocked every port and hit with every plane, well, the Jap Landlords just counted their ashes and their dead bodies and saw it was hopeless to keep on any longer.'" Guthrie to Marjorie Mazia, August 10, 1945, WGA, Correspondence 1, box 2, folder 6.

38. Guthrie, "Peoples Army," WGA, Notebooks 2, no. 2, p. 41.

39. Guthrie, "World's on Afire," WGA, Notebooks 2, no. 10, p. 53.

40. Guthrie to Stetson Kennedy, August 15, 1950, WGA, Correspondence 1, box 1, folder 32.

41. Guthrie, "Brooklyn and This Bomb," WGA, Notebooks 2, no. 11, p. 3.

42. WGA, Notebooks 2, no. 12, p. 64.

43. Guthrie, "Talkin Atom Bomb," WGA, Notebooks 2, no. 9, p. 130.

44. Guthrie, "Germy Bomb," WGA, Songs 2, notebook 1, p. 64.

45. Du Bois, statement on behalf of Peace Information Center, August 24, 1950, Harold Leventhal Proletarian Archive, box 3, 2006–0003–3, folder 21, McFarlin Library, Department of Special Collections and University Archives, University of Tulsa, Oklahoma.

46. Guthrie, "Korea and Me," WGA, Songs 2, notebook 64, p. 216. See also "Out Korea," WGA, Songs 2, notebook 64, p. 165.

47. Guthrie, "Thirty 8th Parallel," WGA, Songs 2, notebook 64, p. 194.

48. Guthrie, "Korean Quicksands," WGA, Songs 2, notebook 64, p. 206.

49. Guthrie, "Korean Waltz," WGA, Songs 2, notebook 64, p. 212; "Korean Quickstep," Songs 2, notebook 64, p. 196; "Korean Boogy," Songs 2, notebook 64, p. 211.

50. Guthrie, "Korea Send Me Home Blues," WGA, Songs 2, notebook 64, p. 204; "Korea Boggyhole Blues," Songs 2, notebook 64, p. 205; "Korean Blues," Songs 2, notebook 64, p. 203.

51. Guthrie, "Korean Girly," WGA, Songs 2, notebook 64, p. 209.

52. Guthrie, "Goldine Grain," WGA, Notebooks 2, no. 9, p. 86.

53. Guthrie, "Ponta Delegata," WGA, Notebooks 2, no. 11, p. 9.

54. Guthrie, "Name Wanted," WGA, Notebooks 2, no. 11, p. 13; Cray, *Ramblin' Man*, 350.

55. Guthrie, "Post War Junk Pile," WGA, Notebooks 2, no. 11, p. 11. See also Guthrie, "Mad Raver," WGA, Notebooks 2, no. 7, p. 27, with its conclusion:

> If we build a nut house
> Wide enough to hold us all;
> It'll reach up higher than the blue sky
> With a fence around the little brown world.

56. Guthrie's songs on behalf of the 1952 Progressive Party candidates include "Rube & Peace & Me," "Heyyy Rube," "Hallinan Hold My Hand," "Ruben & Rachelle" (written with Herta Geer), "Polly Put the Kettle On," and "Talkin' World Peace." All in WGA, Notebooks 2, no. 9, pp. 76–100.

57. Guthrie, "I'm Not Ikey," WGA, Songs 2, notebook 1, p. 64; "Ikey He Lye," Notebooks 2, no. 11, p. 33. In the latter song, the Democrat Stevenson fares little better:

> Some big shake up down th' cellar, I run downta see;
> Steve Steevey tossin' bottles 'ginst them walls at me;
> Steve's kind has got t' go, go,
> His kind got t' saddle up'n go!

Guthrie's "Hy Lolly" completes the postmortem: "If I'd voted Rube in 'steada old Ikeyboy . . . / I'd have peace and lots more joy, joy." WGA, Notebooks 2, no. 11, p. 31.

58. Guthrie, "Dear Mister Eisenhower," WGA, Notebooks 2, no. 3, p. 117.

59. Guthrie, "Hot Seat," WGA, Notebooks 2, no. 7, p. 71.

60. Irving Kaufman quoted in Jessica Wang, *American Science in an Age of Anxiety: Scientists, Anticommunism, and the Cold War* (Chapel Hill: University of North Carolina Press, 1999), 292.

61. Guthrie, "Narrow Margins," WGA, Notebooks 2, no. 3, p. 92.

62. Guthrie, "Last Mile," WGA, Notebooks 2, no. 7, p. 70.

63. Guthrie, "Windy Cloud," WGA, Notebooks 2, no. 6, p. 22. Guthrie was hardly alone in painting Stalin as a peacemaker. Paul Robeson's elegy, "To You, Beloved Comrade" (1953), literally cries, "Glory to Stalin," praising his "deep humanity" and "wise understanding" in the "fight for peace." See Philip S. Foner, ed., *Paul Robeson Speaks* (New York: Citadel, 1978), 347–49.

64. Judy Kutulas, *The Long War: The Intellectual People's Front and Anti-Stalinism, 1930–1940* (Durham, N.C.: Duke University Press, 1995), 64–67.

65. Bruce Cumings, *The Korean War: A History* (New York: Modern Library, 2011), 34.

66. WGA, Notebooks 2, no. 12, p. 79.

Chapter 9

1. Guthrie to Marjorie Mazia, January 25, 1943, WGA, Correspondence 1, box 1, folder 45. By 1949, when he was writing a series of songs on venereal disease for a Columbia University public information project, Guthrie concluded, more conventionally: "Penicillin's th' only gun in th' world that'll drop that old / Veedee stone dead in its track." Guthrie, "Veedee Talkin Seaman," WGA, Notebooks 2, no. 9, p. 12.

2. Guthrie, "Jesus My Doctor," WGA, Songs 1, box 2.

3. Guthrie to Marjorie Guthrie, [August 1956], WGA, Correspondence 1, box 3, folder 12.

4. Guthrie to Arlo Guthrie, August 18, 1956, WGA, Correspondence 1, box 3, folder 9. Guthrie's idiosyncratic syntax and word construction—his "linguistic anarchy," as Joe Klein calls it—were characteristic symptoms of the middle stages of Huntington's disease. Klein, *Woody Guthrie*, 379.

5. Paul Peppis, *Sciences of Modernism: Ethnography, Sexology, and Psychology* (Cambridge, UK: Cambridge University Press, 2014), 7.

6. Guthrie, "Atom Dance," WGA, Correspondence 1, box 2, folder 8.

7. Guthrie, "My Eyes Do See All over This World," WGA, Notebooks 1, no. 20, p. 23.

8. Guthrie, "Heaven," WGP, Song Texts, box 1, folder 4.

9. WGA, Notebooks 1, no. 43, p. 13.

10. Richard Reuss's archival list, "Political Books Owned by Woody Guthrie," includes V. I. Lenin's *Theory of the Agrarian Question* (1938), Karl Marx's *Capital, the Communist Manifesto, and Other Writings* (1932), the *Selected Correspondence* of Marx and Engels (1942), Josef Stalin's *Leninism* (1940) and *Leninism: Selected Writings* (1942), and Friedrich Engels's *Dialectics of Nature* (1940). Guthrie's annotation to the latter title reads: "Bought and paid for by WG 1947 to try to see what goes on around this place." Richard Reuss Papers, box 3, folder 1, Office of Archives and Records Management, Herman B. Wells Library, Indiana University, Bloomington.

11. George Novack, "Dialectical Materialism," *Fourth International* 1, no. 4 (August 1940): 108–11, https://www.marxists.org/archive/novack/works/1940/aug/x01.htm.

12. Guthrie to Marjorie Mazia, ca. late 1942 or early 1943, WGA, Correspondence 1, box 1, folder 44.

13. Novack, "Dialectical Materialism."

14. WGA, Notebooks 1, no. 28, p. 4.

15. WGA, Notebooks 1, no. 19, p. 56. In a notebook entry of 1944, Guthrie jotted: "I've just been reading Darwin's book on the Origin of Species and the Descent of Man. Well, even if I had of been born a monkey, I know I would have been a union one." WGA, Notebooks 2, no. 10, p. 71.

16. WGA, Notebooks 1, no. 26, pp. 26–27.

17. WGA, Notebooks 1, no. 50, p. 18.

18. Guthrie to Marjorie Mazia, November 17, 1942, WGA, Correspondence 1, box 1, folder 44.

19. Guthrie to Marjorie Mazia, January 16, 1943, WGA, Correspondence 1, box 1, folder 45.

20. Guthrie, "Our Kitchen," WGA, Notebooks 1, no. 19, pp. 84–85.

21. Guthrie, "All Artists," WGA, Notebooks 1, no. 19, pp. 48–49.

22. WGA, Notebooks 1, no. 43, p. 45.

23. Ibid., p. 15.

24. Stephen Jay Gould, "Nurturing Nature," in *An Urchin in the Storm: Essays about Books and Ideas* (London: Penguin, 1990), 153–54; Howard Zinn interviewed on *Howard Zinn: You Can't Be Neutral on a Moving Train*, dir. Deb Ellis and Denis Mueller (First Run Features, 2010).

25. WGA, Notebooks 1, no. 43, p. 10.

26. Ibid., p. 39.

27. Guthrie, "High Balladry," WGA, Notebooks 1, no. 31, p. 77.

28. WGA, Notebooks 1, no. 43, p. 41.

29. Ibid., p. 6.

30. Ibid., p. 7.

31. Ibid., pp. 8–9.

32. Ibid., p. 14.

33. Ibid., p. 17.

34. Guthrie to Marjorie Mazia, November 5, 1945, WGA, Correspondence 1, box 2, folder 10.

35. Guthrie to Marjorie Mazia, October 14, 1945, WGA, Correspondence 1, box 2, folder 10.

36. Guthrie to Marjorie Mazia, May 8, 1947, WGA, Correspondence 1, box 2, folder 12.

37. Guthrie to Marjorie Mazia, March 7, 1943, WGA, Correspondence 4, postcard 1943k.

38. WGA, Notebooks 1, no. 16, p. 21.

39. WGA, Notebooks 1, no. 11, pp. 19–20.

40. Ibid., p. 15.

41. Ibid., pp. 31–32.

42. WGA, Notebooks 1, no. 6, p. 33.

43. Guthrie, "Lessons in Human Engineering," WGA, Notebooks 1, no. 15, pp. 3–4.

44. Guthrie, "Trouble Busting," chap. 12 in *Bound for Glory*.

45. WGA, Notebooks 1, no. 50, p. 24.

46. WGA, Notebooks 1, no. 15, pp. 42–43.

47. WGA, Notebooks 1, no. 11, p. 49.

48. Guthrie, "Psyko Man," WGA, Notebooks 2, no. 10, p. 77.

49. Guthrie, "My Id & My Ego," WGA, Songs 1, box 6.

50. Cray, *Ramblin' Man*, 352.

51. Guthrie, "Schizofreenick Extravert," WGA, Notebooks 2, no. 3, p. 75.

52. Guthrie, "One Thing the Atom Can't Do," WGA, Notebooks 2, no. 2, p. 25.

53. Guthrie, "Old Atom Hunter," WGA, Notebooks 2, no. 7, p. 115.

54. Guthrie to "Bubby Waitzman," June 14, 1949, WGA Notebooks 1, no. 69, pp. 114–15.

55. WGA, Notebooks 2, no. 8, pp. 21–35.

56. Guthrie, note to "Einstein Theme Song," August 1950, WGA, Manuscripts 9, box

7, folder 31. See also "Einstein Brings Back Light Rays" in Guthrie, *Born to Win*, 193–94. "The post-war rush of science and technology had left him at a loss. And yet, he was fascinated by the abstractions of modern science (if not the realities). Albert Einstein was a particular hero and, according to several accounts, Woody went down to Princeton University and visited the man one day." Klein, *Woody Guthrie*, 364.

57. WGA, Notebooks 2, no. 8, p. 72.

58. WGA, Notebooks 1, no. 28, p. ii.

Chapter 10

1. Marshall Berman, *All That Is Solid Melts into Air: The Experience of Modernity* (New York: Penguin, 1988), 15.

2. I.W.W. Preamble, in Patrick Renshaw, *The Wobblies: The Story of Syndicalism in the United States* (London: Eyre and Spottiswoode, 1967), 2.

3. Guthrie to Marjorie Mazia, November 17, 1942, WGA, Correspondence, series 1, box 1, folder 44.

4. Guthrie, "Good Old Union Feeling," WGP, Song Texts, box 1, folder 3.

5. Hampton, *Guerrilla Minstrels*, 130.

6. Guthrie, to unnamed recipient, "Work," WGA, Correspondence 1, box 1, folder 50.

7. Guthrie to Marjorie Mazia, August 9, 1945, WGA, Correspondence 1, box 2, folder 5.

8. Denning, *The Cultural Front*, 98.

9. Guthrie to Marjorie Mazia, August 28, 1945. WGA, Notebooks 1, no. 42, pp. 40–41.

10. Guthrie, "Work Songs for Working People," ca. 1941, WGA, Manuscripts 1, series 9, box 1, folder 11.

11. WGA, Notebooks 1, no. 16, p. 11.

12. Guthrie, notes to "Girl in the Red, White, and Blue," WGP, Song Texts, box 1, folder 3.

13. Guthrie to Marjorie Mazia, December 27, 1942, WGA, Notebooks 1, no. 12, pp. 10–11.

14. Guthrie's copy of Vernon L. Parrington, *Main Currents in American Thought*, vol. 1 (New York: Harcourt, Brace, 1930), 65, in Center for Folklore and Cultural Heritage, Smithsonian Institution.

15. Guthrie, "When the Pickets Start to Marching," June 3, 1949, WGA, Notebooks 2, no. 2, p. 52.

16. Guthrie, "Hard Hitting Songs by Hard Hit People," WGA, Manuscripts 1, series 9, box 1, folder 11.

17. Guthrie, "Victory of the Whelan Strikers," WGA, Notebooks 2, no. 2, p. 45.

18. Guthrie to Marjorie Mazia, April 5, 1943, WGA, Correspondence 1, box 1, folder 47.

19. WGA, Notebooks 1, no. 37a, p. 20.

20. Guthrie, untitled poem, WGA, Notebooks 1, no. 22, p. 96.

21. Guthrie, *House of Earth*, 151–52.

22. WGA, Notebooks 1, no. 37a, pp. 19–20.

23. David Hollinger, "How Wide the Circle of the 'We?' American Intellectuals and the Problem of the Ethnos since World War II," *American Historical Review* 98, no. 2 (April 1993): 318.

24. Guthrie to Marjorie Mazia and Cathy Ann Guthrie, June 11, 1944, WGA, Correspondence 1, box 1, folder 50.

25. Guthrie to Marjorie Mazia and Cathy Ann Guthrie, July 4, 1944, WGA, Correspondence 1, box 1, folder 50.

26. Guthrie to the Almanac Singers, [March 1941], WGA, Correspondence 1, box 1, folder 3.

27. Guthrie, "Ten Songs," unpublished manuscript, WGP, Typescripts, Woody Guthrie Songs, box 2, folder 3.

28. Guthrie, *Pastures of Plenty*, 207.

29. Guthrie, "Living + Dying + Singing," 1942, WGA, Notebooks 1, no. 9, p. 37.

30. Robbie Lieberman, *My Song Is My Weapon: People's Songs, American Communism, and the Politics of Culture, 1930–50* (Chicago: University of Illinois Press, 1995), 34.

31. Denning, *The Cultural Front*, 329.

32. Guthrie, "Arvin Migratory Labor Camp," WGA, Manuscripts 2, box 1, folder 4.

33. Dunaway, *How Can I Keep from Singing?*, 134–35.

34. Cray, *Ramblin' Man*, 322.

35. Pete Seeger, "People's Songs and Singers," *New Masses*, July 16, 1946, 9.

36. Guthrie, *Pastures of Plenty*, 205.

37. WGA, Notebooks 1, no. 26, pp. 24–25.

Chapter 11

1. Denning, *The Cultural Front*, 28.

2. Milton Cantor, *The Divided Left: American Radicalism, 1900–1975* (New York: Hill and Wang, 1978), 13–14.

3. Denning, *The Cultural Front*, 30, 137.

4. WGA, Notebooks 1, no. 10, p. 6; "She Came Along to Me," Billy Bragg and Wilco, *Mermaid Avenue: The Complete Sessions*, disc 1, track 6.

5. Bill Nowlin, *Woody Guthrie: American Radical Patriot* (Cambridge, Mass.: Rounder, 2013), 27–28. As Guthrie wrote in a short notebook entry in 1947: "No human here among us has got any right to walk up to any other human and to tell you what to do, and when and how to do it. I can't tell you to be a dancer nor to be a wife aboot the hoose. All of this is your own deciding in a democracy." WGA, Notebooks 1, no. 52, p. 75.

6. Guthrie, "Whitman's Swimmy Waters," August 10, 1947, WGA, Notebooks 1, no. 57, p. 77.

7. Bryan K. Garman, *A Race of Singers: Whitman's Working Class Hero from Guthrie to Springsteen* (Chapel Hill: University of North Carolina Press, 2000), 115.

8. Brower and Guthrie, eds., *Woody Guthrie Artworks*, 194–95; Jonatha Brooke, *The Works* (Bad Dog Records, 2008).

9. Guthrie to Ed Robbin, no date, reprinted in Robbin, *Woody Guthrie and Me* (Berkeley: Lancaster-Miller Publishers, 1979), 151. Robbin judges this letter to have been "written in 1941 at Almanac House" (148).

10. Cray, *Ramblin' Man*, 380.

11. Guthrie, "Folk Songs," July 1944, WGA, Manuscripts 9, box 4, folder 7.

12. Denning, *The Cultural Front*, 29.

13. "Some people with Huntington's disease may act in a disinhibited way that is embarrassing to others. Disinhibited behaviour may take a variety of forms. People may act impulsively or rashly without thought. . . . They may make socially inappropriate remarks, for example making personal comments about a person who is within earshot. They may behave in a sexually disinhibited way, such as making sexual advances to a partner in front of the children. Such behaviour results from a breakdown in patients' social awareness and ability to think through and appreciate the social consequences of actions." *Huntington's Disease: Behavioral Problems* (Liverpool, UK: Huntington's Disease Association, May 2015), http://hda.org.uk/hda/factsheets.

14. See Kaufman, *Woody Guthrie, American Radical*, 47–50.

15. Guthrie, "Union Maid," on *The Asch Recordings*, vol. 3. Hampton, *Guerrilla Minstrels*, 128–29, notes that feminist irritation with this patronizing verse resulted, by 1973, in a new verse written by Nancy Katz:

> A woman's struggle is hard
> Even with a union card,
> She's got to stand on her own two feet,
> And not be a servant of the male elite.
> It's time to take a stand,
> Keep working hand in hand,
> There's a job that's got to be done
> And a fight that's got to be won.

See also Emily S. P. Baxter, "'You Gals Who Want to Be Free': A Feminist Perspective on the Evolution of Woody Guthrie's 'Union Maid,'" *Woody Guthrie Annual* 1 (2015): 63–71, http://pops.uclan.ac.uk/index.php/WGA/article/view/285/111; Jodie Childers, "Pete Seeger and the Origins of 'Union Maid,'" *Woody Guthrie Annual* 1 (2015): 72–75, http://pops.uclan.ac.uk/index.php/WGA/article/view/299/123.

16. WGA, Notebooks 1, no. 10, p. 6.

17. Guthrie, "Psalm," ibid.

18. Guthrie, "The Girl in the Red, White, and Blue," WGP, Song Texts, box 1, folder 3.

19. Guthrie, "The Ranger's Command," on *The Asch Recordings*, vol. 4.

20. Guthrie, "Miss Pavilichenko," on *The Asch Recordings*, vol. 3.

21. Guthrie, "Harriet Tubman's Ballad," on *Long Ways to Travel: The Unreleased Folkways Masters, 1944–1949* (Smithsonian Folkways, 1994).

22. Guthrie, "Tuccumcari Striker," WGA, Notebooks 2, no. 3, p. 98.

23. WGA, Notebooks 1, no. 11, p. 20 (December 17, 1942).

24. Guthrie to Marjorie Mazia, March 7, 1943, WGA, Correspondence 4, postcard 1943n.

25. Denning, *The Cultural Front*, 139.

26. Guthrie, "Revolutionary Mind," WGP, Song Texts, box 1, folder 7.

27. Garman, *A Race of Singers*, 108.

28. Ibid., 116. "When [Floyd] Dell asked in the *New Masses*, 'What is the correct revolutionary proletarian attitude toward sex?' in 1927, he started a discussion of the attitudes that the revolutionary movement might take toward marriage." James B. Gilbert, *Writers and Partisans: A History of Literary Radicalism in America* (New York: Wiley and Sons, 1968), 56.

29. Garman, *A Race of Singers*, 108.

30. Guthrie, "My Teeneager Girl," WGA, Notebooks 2, no. 3, p. 1.

31. WGA, Notebooks 1, no. 50, p. 48.

32. Guthrie, "Baby Knocker," WGA, Notebooks 2, no. 3, p. 116.

33. Cray, *Ramblin' Man*, 302.

34. Garman, *A Race of Singers*, 110.

35. Denning, *The Cultural Front*, 137.

36. Guthrie, *House of Earth*, 168.

37. Guthrie's 1944 daybook, WGA, Notebooks 1, no. 28, p. 47.

38. Guthrie quoted in Klein, *Woody Guthrie*, 264.

39. WGA, Notebooks 2, no. 12, p. 60.

40. WGA, Notebooks 1, no. 54, 43 (August 7, 1947).

41. WGA, Notebooks 1, no. 54, p. 49 (August 2, 1947).

42. WGA, Notebooks 1, no. 52, p. 10 (August 1947).

43. Guthrie, "Whores and Wives," August 6, 1947, WGA, Notebooks 1, no. 54, p. 65.

44. WGA, Notebooks 1, no. 50, p. 42.

45. WGA, Notebooks 1, no. 40, p. 43.

46. WGA, Notebooks 1, no. 50, p. 20.

47. WGA, Notebooks 1, no. 11, pp. 61–62.

48. Nowlin, *Woody Guthrie*, 28.

49. Guthrie, "Dance Out and Grab," August 7, 1947, WGA, Notebooks 1, no. 54, p. 63.

50. Guthrie, "Slow Marriages," October 19, 1947, WGA, Notebooks 1, no. 52, p. 74.

51. Guthrie, "Wife # Three," WGA, Notebooks 2, no. 9, p. 84.

52. "Anneke took a secretarial job with Bellevue Hospital that spring and, reluctantly, left Lorina in Woody's care each day. She'd return home to find the baby wet, undiapered, and bawling wildly in a soaking crib; and Woody passed out on the bed." Klein, *Woody Guthrie*, 421.

53. Guthrie to Marjorie Guthrie, October 10, 1956, WGA, Correspondence 1, box 3, folder 10.

Chapter 12

1. See Jackson, "Skin Trouble," chap. 4 in *Prophet Singer*; Kaufman, "Long Road to Peekskill," chap. 6 in *Woody Guthrie, American Radical*.

2. Goble, *Beautiful Circuits*, 298.

3. Guthrie, undated note jotted below lyrics to "Lonesome Road Blues" / "Goin' Down the Road Feelin' Bad," WGA, Notebooks 1, no. 4, p. 63.

4. Ronald Radano, *Lying Up a Nation: Race and Black Music* (Chicago: University of Chicago Press, 2003), 33.

5. Guthrie to Marjorie Guthrie, May 8, 1947, WGA, Correspondence 1, box 2, folder 12.

6. Denning, *The Cultural Front*, 35.

7. Ibid., 260.

8. Guthrie, *Woody Guthrie: American Radical Patriot*, disc 4, track 10. Guthrie would later protest against the stigmatization of Japanese Americans, not only in *Bound for Glory* but also in such newspapers as the *Japanese American Pacific Citizen*, in which he urged "Japanese American G.I.'s and workers to write their own folk and protest songs." Guthrie to Moses Asch and Marian Ditsler, December 6, 1945, WGA Correspondence 1, box 1, folder 6.

9. La Chapelle, *Proud to Be an Okie*, 66. "While newspaper characterizations of migrants as hordes or swarms invoked the specter of 'Yellow Peril' alarmism, one Bakersfield movie theater equally discriminated against blacks and white Dust Bowlers by segregating both from the general white moviegoing population, posting a sign that read: 'Negroes and Okies Upstairs.'" Ibid., 28–29.

10. Ibid., 66, 78.

11. Robbin, *Woody Guthrie and Me*, 8, 40–41.

12. Undated annotation to manuscript lyrics of "Do Re Mi," WGP, Typescripts: Woody Guthrie Songs, box 2, folder 3.

13. Guthrie quoted in Douglas Brinkley and Johnny Depp, "Introduction," *House of Earth*, xxvii.

14. Irwin Silber quoted in Cray, *Ramblin' Man*, 216.

15. Cray, *Ramblin' Man*, 242.

16. Susanne A. Shavelson, "Aliza Greenblatt, 1885–1975," *Jewish Women's Archive Encyclopedia*, http://jwa.org/encyclopedia/article/greenblat-aliza.

17. Aaron Lansky, *Outwitting History: The Amazing Adventures of a Man Who Rescued a Million Yiddish Books* (Chapel Hill: Algonquin Books, 2004), 98.

18. Guthrie quoted in Klein, *Woody Guthrie*, 308.

19. Guthrie to Marjorie Mazia, November 17, 1942, WGA, Correspondence 1, box 1, folder 44.

20. Guthrie, "Ilsa Koch," WGA, Songs 1, box 2, folder 12. The song has been recorded on Klezmatics, *Wonder Wheel* (Jewish Music Group, 2006), track 16, with Guthrie's own voice intoning, "Somebody turned Ilsa Koch free . . . They let old Ilsa Koch go."

21. Anton La Guardia, *Holy Land, Unholy War: Israelis and Palestinians* (London: Penguin, 2007), 76.

22. Zygmunt Bauman, *Modernity and the Holocaust* (Cambridge, Mass.: Polity Press, 2000), 74.

23. "Palestine Refugees," United Nations Relief and Works Agency, http://www.unrwa.org/palestine-refugees.

24. Guthrie, "Talking News Blues," in Guthrie, *New Found Land*, typed manuscript, Alan Lomax Collection, AFC 2004/04, Woody Guthrie Manuscripts, box 33.02, folder 20.

25. Guthrie, annotation to "Go and Leave Me," WGP, Song Texts, box 1, folder 3.

26. For a cogent account of this most bitter chapter of British imperial history, see David Cesarani, *Major Farran's Hat: The Untold Story of the Struggle to Establish the Jewish State* (Cambridge, Mass.: Da Capo Press, 2009).

27. Guthrie, "Old Churchill," August 4, 1947, WGA, Notebooks 1, no. 54, p. 130.

28. Guthrie, "Wet Peach Seed," August 23, 1947, WGA, Notebooks 1, no. 52, p. 31.

29. Guthrie to Moses Asch, November 7, 1947, WGA, Correspondence 1, box 1, folder 8.

30. Among the category of "Rare Books Annotated by Woody Guthrie" in the Woody Guthrie Archives, those from 1948 include such titles as *Suggestions for Hanukkah Programs, How to Celebrate Hanukah at Home, Chanukah Feast of Lights, Chanukkah Songster,* and *Maccabee—1948.*

31. See Guthrie, "The Many and the Few" and "Hanukkah Dance" on *The Asch Recordings,* vol. 3 (Smithsonian Folkways, 1998).

32. Klezmatics, *Happy Joyous Hanukkah* (Jewish Music Group, 2006) and *Wonder Wheel* (Jewish Music Group, 2009). "Headdy Down" is on the latter. See also Ray Allen, "Holy Ground: The Klezmatics Channel Woody Guthrie," *Woody Guthrie Annual* 1 (2015): 41–62, http://pops.uclan.ac.uk/index.php/WGA/article/view/297/121.

33. Guthrie to Moses Asch [May or June 1949]. WGA, Manuscripts 9, box 7, folder 23.2.

34. Eric J. Sundquist, *Strangers in the Land: Blacks, Jews, Post-Holocaust America* (Cambridge, Mass.: Harvard University Press, 2005).

35. Guthrie, "Peekskill Golfing Grounds," WGA, Songs 1, box 2, folder 21.

36. "Boots" Casetta quoted in Ronald D. Cohen and Dave Samuelson, accompanying text to *Songs for Political Action: Folk Music, Topical Songs, and the American Left, 1926–1953* (Hambergen, Germany: Bear Family Records, 1996), 166. "The Peekskill Story," in its entirety, is on disc 8, track 22.

37. Will Kaufman, "Woody Guthrie, 'Old Man Trump,' and a Real Estate Empire's Racist Foundations," *The Conversation,* January 21, 2016: https://theconversation.com/woody-guthrie-old-man-trump-and-a-real-estate-empires-racist-foundations-53026.

38. Charles Densen, *Coney Island: Lost and Found* (Berkeley: Ten Speed Press, 2002), 76.

39. Gwenda Blair, *The Trumps: Three Generations That Built an Empire* (New York: Simon and Schuster, 2000), 145.

40. Wayne Barrett and Jon Campbell, "How a Young Donald Trump Forced His Way from Avenue Z to Manhattan," *Village Voice,* July 20, 2015, http://www.villagevoice.com/news/how-a-young-donald-trump-forced-his-way-from-avenue-z-to-manhattan-7380462.

41. Guthrie, "Black Feet," August 16, 1947, WGA, Notebooks 1, no. 57, p. 91.

42. Guthrie, "Beach Haven Way," October 18, 1950, WGA, Notebooks 2, no. 10, p. 47.

43. Guthrie, "Racial Hate at Beach Haven," February 26, 1952, WGA, Notebooks 2, no. 9, p. 107.

44. Ibid.

45. Guthrie, "Trump Made a Tramp Out of Me," photocopied lyric sheet courtesy of Judy Bell, TRO-Essex Music, Ltd., New York. See also Will Kaufman, "In Another

Newly Discovered Song, Woody Guthrie Continues His Assault on 'Old Man Trump,'" *The Conversation,* September 6, 2016, https://theconversation.com/in-another-newly-discovered-song-woody-guthrie-continues-his-assault-on-old-man-trump-64221.

46. Guthrie to Stetson Kennedy, November 5, 1951, WGA, Correspondence 1, box 1, folder 1.

47. Guthrie, "Beach Haven Race Hate," 1954, WGA, Notebooks 2, no. 2, p. 73.

48. Guthrie, "Beach Haven Ain't My Home," May 3, 1952, WGA, Songs 2, notebook 1, p. 64. In 2016, Ryan Harvey, along with Tom Morello and Ani DiFranco, incorporated some of Guthrie's Beach Haven writings into the song "Old Man Trump" (Firebrand Records).

49. WGA, Notebooks 2, no. 9, p. 47.

50. WGA, Notebooks 2, no. 11, p. 55 (December 25, 1952).

51. Guthrie to Stetson Kennedy, August 15, 1950, WGA, Correspondence 1, box 1, folder 32.

52. Guthrie, "My Big Mixed Race," WGA, Notebooks 2, no. 2, p. 67. Ellipses in original.

53. WGA, Notebooks 1, no. 33, p. 35 (July 21, 1944).

54. Guthrie to Marianne "Jolly" Smolens, March 31, 1951, private collection of Barry and Judy Ollman.

55. Stetson Kennedy quoted in Jorge Arévalo Mateus, "Beluthahatchee Blues: An Interview with Stetson Kennedy," in Chris Green et al., eds. *Radicalism in the South since Reconstruction* (New York: Palgrave Macmillan, 2006), 221.

56. Ibid., 221, 222.

57. Guthrie in Klein, *Woody Guthrie,* 360–61.

58. Guthrie, "I Hit You," August 16, 1947, WGA, Notebooks 1, no. 57, p. 90.

59. WGA, Notebooks 1, no. 10, p. 6 (June 10–11, 1942).

60. Urmilla Seshagiri, *Race and the Modernist Imagination* (Ithaca: Cornell University Press, 2010), 17.

61. See Paul Gilroy, *The Black Atlantic: Modernity and Double-Consciousness* (Cambridge, Mass.: Harvard University Press, 1993).

62. Ezra Pound, "In a Station of the Metro" (1919), in *New Selected Poems and Translations,* ed. Richard Sieburth (New York: New Directions, 2010), 39.

63. Ezra Pound, "N.Y." (1917), in *New Selected Poems and Translations,* 27.

Chapter 13

1. John Cohen quoted in Phillip Buehler, ed., *Woody Guthrie's Wardy Forty: The Interviews* (Mount Kisco: Woody Guthrie Publications, 2013), 16–17.

2. T. S. Eliot, "The Waste Land" (1922), in Eliot, *The Complete Poems and Plays: 1909–1950* (Orlando: Harcourt Brace, 1980), 48 (lines 372–77).

3. Guthrie, "My Name Is New York," in Nora Guthrie et al., *My Name Is New York,* 11; Guthrie, "Los Angeles New Year's Flood," *Woody Guthrie: American Radical Patriot,* disc 4, track 13; Guthrie, "Shook Old Frisco Down," WGA Notebooks 1, no. 4, p. 134.

4. "Under car wheels": Guthrie, "My Name Is New York," *My Name Is New York,* 11.

5. Comentale, *Sweet Air,* 157.

6. "Hooded hordes": Eliot, "The Waste Land," 48 (line 368); Guthrie, "Voice," in *Pastures of Plenty*, xxvi.

7. Rabinovitz, *Electric Dreamland*, 16.

8. WGA, Notebooks 1, no. 4, p. 68.

9. Guthrie, "Bright & Shining City," WGA, Notebooks 1, no. 4, p. 58.

10. Thomas Jefferson, "Query 19," in *Notes on the State of Virginia*, 1787, American Studies, University of Virginia, http://xroads.virginia.edu/~hyper/JEFFERSON/ch19.html.

11. Guthrie's KFVD air check is captured on an unlabeled CD in the Smithsonian Institution, Center for Folklife and Cultural Heritage; Guthrie, "I'm A-Goin' Back to the Farm," Songs of Woody Guthrie, ms., p. 203, Library of Congress, AFC 1940/004, Woody Guthrie Manuscript Collection, box 1, folder 13; Guthrie, "Left in This World Alone," WGA, Notebooks 1, no. 4, p. 102.

12. Guthrie, "Listening to the Wind that Blows," WGA, Notebooks 1, no. 4, p. 139. Beneath the lyrics Guthrie writes: "Me and Lefty Lou sung the dickens out of this one."

13. Guthrie, note below lyrics to "Foggy Mountain Top," WGA, Notebooks 1, no. 4, p. 74.

14. KFVD fan letter quoted in Klein, *Woody Guthrie*, 93.

15. La Chapelle, *Proud to Be an Okie*, 7.

16. Denning, *The Cultural Front*, 11–12.

17. Guthrie, *Woody Sez*, 107.

18. Nora Guthrie et al., *My Name Is New York*, 23.

19. Saul Bellow quoted in Klein, *Woody Guthrie*, 162.

20. Jorge Arévalo Mateus, introduction to Nora Guthrie et al., *My Name Is New York*, 8.

21. Guthrie to Marjorie Mazia, ca. September–December 1942, WGA, Correspondence 1, box 1, folder 44.

22. Guthrie, "This Is the House Where the Almanacs Used to Stay," in Nora Guthrie, et al., *My Name Is New York*, 41.

23. Seeger quoted in Dunaway, *How Can I Keep from Singing?*, xxii.

24. Guthrie, "The Almanacs and Me," ms. p. 2, WGA, Manuscripts 2, box 1, folder 2.

25. Arévalo Mateus, introduction to Nora Guthrie et al., *My Name Is New York*, 9.

26. WGA, Notebooks 1, no. 12, pp. 48–49 (September 20, 1946).

27. WGA, Notebooks 1, no. 16, pp. 61–62.

28. WGA, Notebooks 1, no. 22, 206–208 (March 6, 1943).

29. Marjorie Guthrie quoted in Buehler, ed., *Woody Guthrie's Wardy Forty: The Interviews*, 89.

30. Guthrie to Marjorie Mazia, July 6, 1942, WGA, Correspondence 4, postcard 1942k.

31. Congregationalist minister Rollin Lynde Hartt on Coney Island, quoted in Rabinovitz, *Electric Dreamland*, 1.

32. Guthrie to Marjorie Mazia, August 28, 1945, WGA, Notebooks 1, no. 42, p. 16.

33. Guthrie to Marjorie Mazia, [1943], WGA, Correspondence 1, box 1, folder 48.

34. Guthrie, "Go Coney Island Roll on the Sand," WGA, Notebooks 1, no. 53, pp. 7–8. A recorded version by the Demolition String Band with Stephan Said is on Nora Guthrie et al., *My Name Is New York Audio Book*, disc 3, track 13.

35. Guthrie in Cathy's notebook, November 30, 1943, WGA, Notebooks 1, no. 18, pp. 125–26.

36. Guthrie to Marjorie Mazia, August 28, 1945, Notebooks 1, no. 42, p. 19.

37. Ibid.

38. Guthrie, "Whistle Birdy," October 24, 1950, WGA, Notebooks 2, no. 3, p. 25.

39. WGA, Notebooks 1, no. 54, p. 47 (August 2, 1947).

40. Guthrie, "My New York City," April 5, 1947, WGA, Songs 1, box 6. A recorded version by Mike and Ruthie is on Nora Guthrie et al., *My Name Is New York Audio Book*, disc 3, track 4.

41. WGA, Notebooks 1, no. 62, p. 140 (November 10, 1947).

42. Guthrie to "Peoples Songs & Peoples Artists, Both, and to Peter Seeger, & Wally Hillie, & all other interested parties," April 16, 1948, WGA, Correspondence 1, box 3, folder 18.

43. Guthrie to the Almanac Singers, March 1941, WGA, Correspondence 1, box 1, folder 3.

44. Guthrie, "My Ideas about the Use of Peoples Songs in the Progressive Party Movement to Elect Henry Wallace and Glen Taylor," ms. pp. 6–7, January 9 and 11, 1949, WGA, Manuscripts 1, box 7, folder 17.

45. Norma Starobin quoted in David King Dunaway and Molly Beer, eds., *Singing Out: An Oral History of America's Folk Music Revivals* (New York: Oxford University Press, 2010), 89.

46. Guthrie to Mary Jo Edgmon and family, April 12, 1949, WGA, Correspondence 1, box 1, folder 14.

47. Guthrie, "V. D. City," on *Woody Guthrie: American Radical Patriot*, disc 6, track 17.

48. Guthrie, "Brooklyn Town," on *Woody Guthrie: American Radical Patriot*, disc 6, track 21.

49. Guthrie, "Around New York," August 10, 1950, WGA, Songs 1, box 1.

50. Guthrie to Marjorie Guthrie [after August 1956], WGA, Correspondence 1, box 3, folder 12.

51. Patricia Cohen, "Bound for Local Glory at Last," *New York Times*, December 27, 2011.

Conclusion

1. Ronald Radosh, "The Communist Party's Role in the Folk Revival: From Woody Guthrie to Bob Dylan," *American Communist History* 14, no. 1 (2014): 14.

2. Kaufman, *Woody Guthrie, American Radical*, 165.

3. Kurt Vonnegut, *If This Isn't Nice, What Is?* (New York: RosettaBooks, 2013), 110.

4. Ricardo J. Quinones, *Mapping Literary Modernism* (Princeton: Princeton University Press, 1985), 105.

5. La Chapelle, *Proud to Be an Okie*, 47.

6. Comentale, *Sweet Air*, 25.

7. Guthrie to Tom Scott, November 12, 1946, WGA, Correspondence 1, box 3, folder 22.

8. Guthrie to "Dear Friends" at an unnamed magazine, July 18, 1944, WGA, Manuscripts 1, box 4, folder 6.

9. WGA, Notebooks 1, no. 31, p. 72.

10. WGA, Notebooks 1, no. 62, p. 22 (November 8, 1947).

11. WGA, Notebooks 1, no. 62, p. 23 (November 1947).

12. Wurtzler, *Electric Sounds*, 2.

13. Rosa, *Social Acceleration*, 41.

14. Richard A. Reuss with Joanne C. Reuss, *American Folk Music and Left-Wing Politics, 1927–1957* (Lanham, Md.: Scarecrow Press, 2000), 35.

15. *Woody Guthrie: American Radical Patriot*, disc 4, track 10.

16. Jones, "Finding the Avant-Garde in the Old-Time," 419.

17. WGA, Notebooks 1, no. 18, p. 136 (December 4, 1943).

18. Berman, *All That Is Solid Melts into Air*, 6.

19. WGA, Notebooks 1, no. 16, pp. 8–9.

20. WGA, Notebooks 1, no. 52, p. 30 (August 1947).

21. WGA, Media: Record Albums, box 3, A#2008–100, annotated January 16, 1945.

22. Goble, *Beautiful Circuits*, 227.

23. Ibid., 160, quoting Michel Chion, *The Voice in Cinema*, translated by Claudia Gorbman (New York: Columbia University Press, 1999).

24. Comentale, *Sweet Air*, 113.

25. Guthrie, "Another Man Done Gone." WGA, Songs 1, box 1, folder 1. Also Billy Bragg and Wilco, *Mermaid Avenue: The Complete Sessions*, disc 1, track 14.

26. Guthrie to "Dear Committee," ca. September 1944, WGA, Notebooks 1, no. 31, p. 51.

27. WGA, Notebooks 1, no. 3, p. 28.

28. WGA, Notebooks 1, no. 13, pp. 4–5.

29. Guthrie to Marjorie Mazia, November 17, 1942, WGA, Correspondence 1, box 1, folder 44.

30. Pete Seeger to unnamed recipient, WGA, Harold Leventhal Collection, box 5, folder 71 ("Writings by Pete Seeger about Woody").

31. Guthrie, "Roaches Run," WGA, Notebooks 1, no. 54, p. 77 (August 6, 1947).

32. Jean-Paul Sartre quoted in David Detmer, *Sartre Explained: From Bad Faith to Authenticity* (Peru, Ill.: Open Court, 2009), 60.

33. Toril Moi, *Sexual/Textual Politics: Feminist Literary Theory* (New York: Routledge, 2002), 182.

34. Guthrie, "WNEW," in *Born to Win*, 223.

Bibliography

Printed Sources

Adams, Mike. *Lee de Forest: King of Radio, Television, and Film*. New York: Copernicus Books, 2012.

Adorno, Theodor. "Cultural Criticism and Society." In *Prisms*, translated by Shierry Weber Nicholsen, 17–34. Cambridge, Mass.: MIT Press, 1981.

Applebomel, Peter. "New Glimpses of Woody Guthrie's Imagination." *New York Times*, April 27, 1998.

Arévalo Mateus, Jorge. "Beluthahatchee Blues: An Interview with Stetson Kennedy." In *Radicalism in the South since Reconstruction*, edited by Chris Green, Rachel Rubin, and James Smethurst, 211–26. New York: Palgrave Macmillan, 2006.

Barrett, Wayne, and Jon Campbell. "How a Young Donald Trump Forced His Way from Avenue Z to Manhattan." *Village Voice*, July 20, 2015.

Bauman, Zygmunt. *Modernity and Ambivalence*. Cambridge, Mass.: Polity Press, 1991.

———. *Modernity and the Holocaust*. Cambridge, Mass.: Polity Press, 2000.

Bel Geddes, Norman. *Magic Motorways*. New York: Random House, 1940.

Bendix, Regina. "Authenticity." In *Folklore: An Encyclopedia of Beliefs, Customs, Tales, Music, and Art*, vol. 1., edited by Charlie T. McCormick and Kim Kennedy White, 185–87. Santa Barbara: ABC-CLIO, 2011.

Berman, Marshall. *All That Is Solid Melts into Air: The Experience of Modernity*. New York: Penguin, 1988.

Blair, Gwenda. *The Trumps: Three Generations That Built an Empire*. New York: Simon and Schuster, 2000.

Brosterman, Norman. *Inventing Kindergarten*. New York: Harry N. Abrams, 1997.

Brower, Steven, and Nora Guthrie, eds. *Woody Guthrie Artworks*. New York: Rizzoli, 2005.

Brown, Blain. *Cinematography: Theory and Practice*. Burlington, Mass.: Focal Press, 2012.

Buehler, Phillip, ed. *Woody Guthrie's Wardy Forty: The Interviews*. Mount Kisco, N.Y.: Woody Guthrie Publications, 2013.

Buehler, Phillip, with Nora Guthrie and the Woody Guthrie Archives. *Woody Guthrie's Wardy Forty: Greystone Park State Hospital Revisited*. Mt. Kisco, N.Y.: Woody Guthrie Publications, 2013.

Butler, Christopher. *Modernism: A Very Short Introduction*. Oxford: Oxford University Press, 2010.

Cantor, Milton. *The Divided Left: American Radicalism, 1900–1975*. New York: Hill and Wang, 1978.

Cantwell, Robert. *When We Were Good: The Folk Revival*. Cambridge, Mass.: Harvard University Press, 1996.

Cesarani, David. *Major Farran's Hat: The Untold Story of the Struggle to Establish the Jewish State*. Cambridge, Mass.: Da Capo Press, 2009.

Cohen, Norm. *Long Steel Rail: The Railroad in American Folksong*. Urbana: University of Illinois Press, 2000.

Cohen, Patricia. "Bound for Local Glory at Last." *New York Times*, December 27, 2011.

Cohen, Ronald D. *Woody Guthrie: Writing America's Songs*. New York: Routledge, 2012.

Cohen, Ronald D., and Dave Samuelson. *Songs for Political Action: Folk Music, Topical Songs and the American Left, 1926–1953* (textual companion to CD set). Hambergen, Germany: Bear Family Records, 1996.

Collins, Andrew. "From Dagenham to the Dust Bowl." *New Statesman*, March 6, 1998, 28–30.

Comentale, Edward P. *Sweet Air: Modernism, Regionalism and American Popular Song*. Urbana: University of Illinois Press, 2013.

Cox, Jim. *Rails across Dixie: A History of Passenger Trains in the American South*. Jefferson, N.C.: McFarland, 2011.

Cray, Ed. *Ramblin' Man: The Life and Times of Woody Guthrie*. New York: W. W. Norton, 2004.

Crow, Thomas. *The Long March of Pop: Art, Music and Design, 1930–1995*. New Haven: Yale University Press, 2014.

Cumings, Bruce. *The Korean War: A History*. New York: Modern Library, 2011.

Cunningham, Agnes "Sis," and Gordon Friesen. *Red Dust and Broadsides: A Joint Autobiography*. Edited by Ronald D. Cohen. Amherst: University of Massachusetts Press, 1999.

Dawson, Nick. *Being Hal Ashby: Life of a Hollywood Rebel*. Lexington: University Press of Kentucky, 2009.

DeGregori, Thomas. *Bountiful Harvest: Technology, Food Safety, and the Environment*. Washington, D.C.: Cato Institute, 2002.

Denning, Michael. *The Cultural Front: The Laboring of American Culture in the Twentieth Century*. New York: Verso, 1998.

Densen, Charles. *Coney Island: Lost and Found*. Berkeley: Ten Speed Press, 2002.

Detmer, David. *Sartre Explained: From Bad Faith to Authenticity*. Peru, Ill.: Open Court, 2009.

Dimendberg, Edward. "The Will to Motorization: Cinema, Highways, and Modernity." *October* 73 (Summer 1995): 90–137.

Dunaway, David King. *How Can I Keep from Singing? The Ballad of Pete Seeger.* New York: Villard Books, 2008.

Dunaway, David King, and Molly Beer, eds. *Singing Out: An Oral History of America's Folk Music Revivals.* New York: Oxford University Press, 2010.

Edgmon, Mary Jo, and Guy Logsdon. *Woody's Road: Woody Guthrie's Letters Home, Drawings, Photos, and Other Unburied Treasures.* Boulder: Paradigm Publishers, 2012.

Eliot, T. S. "The Waste Land." In *The Complete Poems and Plays: 1909–1950*, 37–55. Orlando: Harcourt Brace, 1980.

Ellman, Richard. *James Joyce.* Oxford: Oxford University Press, 1982.

Filene, Benjamin. *Romancing the Folk: Public Memory and American Roots Music.* Chapel Hill: University of North Carolina Press, 2000.

Fitzgerald, F. Scott. *The Great Gatsby.* New York: Scribners, 2004. First published 1925.

Foner, Philip S., ed. *Paul Robeson Speaks.* New York: Citadel, 1978.

Fox, Pamela. *Natural Acts: Gender, Race, and Rusticity in Country Music.* Ann Arbor: University of Michigan Press, 2009.

Franko, Mark. *The Work of Dance: Labor, Movement, and Identity in the 1930s.* Middletown, Conn.: Wesleyan University Press, 2002.

Garman, Bryan K. *A Race of Singers: Whitman's Working Class Hero from Guthrie to Springsteen.* Chapel Hill: University of North Carolina Press, 2000.

Gatland, Kenneth. *Manned Spacecraft.* New York: Macmillan, 1976.

Gilbert, James B. *Writers and Partisans: A History of Literary Radicalism in America.* New York: Wiley and Sons, 1968.

Gilroy, Paul. *The Black Atlantic: Modernity and Double-Consciousness.* Cambridge, Mass.: Harvard University Press, 1993.

Goble, Mark. *Beautiful Circuits: Modernism and the Mediated Life.* New York: Columbia University Press, 2010.

Goldsmith, Peter D., *Making People's Music: Moe Asch and Folkways Records.* Washington, D.C.: Smithsonian Institution Press, 1998.

Goliszek, Andrew. *In the Name of Science: A History of Secret Programs, Medical Research, and Human Experimentation.* Boston: St. Martin's Press, 2003.

Gomery, Douglas. *The Coming of Sound: A History.* New York: Routledge, 2005.

Gordon, Nightingale. *WNEW—Where the Melody Lingers On, 1934–1984.* New York: WNEW, 1984.

Gould, Stephen Jay. *An Urchin in the Storm: Essays about Books and Ideas.* London: Penguin, 1990.

Govenar, Alan B. *Texas Blues: The Rise of a Contemporary Sound.* College Station: Texas A&M University Press, 2008.

Graff, Ellen. *Stepping Left: Dance and Politics in New York City, 1928–1942.* Durham, N.C.: Duke University Press, 1999.

Greenway, John. *American Folksongs of Protest.* New York: A. S. Barnes, 1953.

Gunning, Tom. "Re-Newing Old Technologies: Astonishment, Second Nature, and the Uncanny in Technology from the Previous Turn of the Century." In *Rethinking Media Change: The Aesthetics of Transition*, edited by David Thorburn and Henry Jenkins, 39–60. Cambridge, Mass.: MIT Press, 2003.

Guralnick, Peter, et al., eds. *Martin Scorsese Presents the Blues.* New York: Amistad/HarperCollins, 2005.

Guthrie, Nora, and Woody Guthrie Archives. *My Name Is New York: Ramblin' Around Woody Guthrie's Town.* Brooklyn: powerHouse Books, 2012.

Guthrie, Woody. *Born to Win.* Edited by Robert Shelton. New York: Collier Books, 1967.

———. *Bound for Glory.* New York: E. P. Dutton, 1943.

———. *House of Earth: A Novel.* Edited by Douglas Brinkley and Johnny Depp. New York: HarperCollins/Infinitum Nihil, 2013.

———. "My Life." In *American Folksong,* edited by Moses Asch, 1–14. New York: Oak Publications, 1961.

———. *Pastures of Plenty.* Edited by Dave Marsh and Harold Leventhal. New York: HarperPerennial, 1990.

———. *Seeds of Man: An Experience Lived and Dreamed.* New York: Pocket Books, 1977.

———. *Woody and Lefty Lou's Favorite Collection, Old Time Hill Country Songs.* Gardenia, Calif.: Spanish American Institute Press, 1937.

———. *Woody Sez.* Edited by Marjorie Guthrie, et al. New York: Grosset and Dunlap, 1975.

Hague, Angela. "UFOs." In *Conspiracy Theories in American History: An Encyclopedia,* vol. 2, edited by Peter Knight, 699–704. Santa Barbara: ABC-CLIO, 2003.

Halliday, Sam. *Sonic Modernity: Representing Sound in Literature, Culture, and the Arts.* Edinburgh: Edinburgh University Press, 2013.

Hampton, Wayne. *Guerrilla Minstrels.* Knoxville: University of Tennessee Press, 1986.

Harman, Chris. *A People's History of the World: From the Stone Age to the New Millennium.* New York: Verso, 2008.

Haruki, Wada. *The Korean War: An International History.* Lanham, Md.: Rowman and Littlefield, 2014.

Hegeman, Susan. *Patterns for America: Modernism and the Concept of Culture.* Princeton: Princeton University Press, 1999.

Hernandez, Tim Z. *All They Will Call You.* Tucson: University of Arizona Press, 2017.

Hollinger, David. "How Wide the Circle of the 'We?' American Intellectuals and the Problem of the Ethnos since World War II." *American Historical Review* 98, no. 2 (April 1993): 317–37.

Jackson, Mark Allan. "Playing Legend Maker: Woody Guthrie's 'Jackhammer John.'" In *The Life, Music and Thought of Woody Guthrie: A Critical Appraisal,* edited by John S. Partington, 51–66. Farnham, UK: Ashgate, 2011.

———. *Prophet Singer: The Voice and Vision of Woody Guthrie.* Jackson: University Press of Mississippi, 2007.

Jones, Brian. "Finding the Avant-Garde in the Old-Time: John Cohen in the American Folk Revival." *American Music* 28, no. 4 (Winter 2010): 402–435.

Kaufman, Will. *Woody Guthrie, American Radical.* Urbana: University of Illinois Press, 2011.

Kenney, William Howland. *Recorded Music in American Life: The Phonograph and Popular Memory, 1890–1945.* New York: Oxford University Press, 1999.

Klein, Joe. *Woody Guthrie: A Life*. New York: Delta, 1980.

Kutulas, Judy. *The Long War: The Intellectual People's Front and Anti-Stalinism, 1930–1940*. Durham, N.C.: Duke University Press, 1995.

La Chapelle, Peter. *Proud to Be an Okie: Cultural Politics, Country Music, and Migration to Southern California*. Berkeley: University of California Press, 2007.

La Guardia, Anton. *Holy Land, Unholy War: Israelis and Palestinians*. London: Penguin, 2007.

Landau, Ellen G. "Classic in Its Own Way: The Art of Woody Guthrie." In Santelli and Davidson, *Hard Travelin'*, 83–110.

Lansky, Aaron. *Outwitting History: The Amazing Adventures of a Man Who Rescued a Million Yiddish Books*. Chapel Hill: Algonquin Books, 2004.

Le Corbusier. *Towards a New Architecture*. New York: Dover, 1985. First published 1923.

Lieberman, Robbie. *My Song Is My Weapon: People's Songs, American Communism, and the Politics of Culture, 1930–50*. Urbana: University of Illinois Press, 1995.

Lomax, Alan, Woody Guthrie, and Pete Seeger, eds. *Hard Hitting Songs for Hard-Hit People*. New York: Oak Publications, 1967.

Longhi, Jim. *Woody, Cisco and Me: With Woody Guthrie in the Merchant Marine*. Urbana: University of Illinois Press, 1997.

MacArthur, June S. "Farm Radios: Communication before Rural Electrification." *Farm Collector*, March 2001. http://www.farmcollector.com/.

Magee, John Gillespie, Jr. "High Flight." In *Flight: A Celebration of 100 Years in Art and Literature*, edited by Anne Collins Goodyear, et al., 63. New York: Welcome Books, 2003.

Marchand, Roland. "The Designers Go to the Fair II: Norman Bel Geddes, the General Motors 'Futurama,' and the Visit to the Factory Transformed." *Design Issues* 8, no. 2 (Spring 1992): 22–40.

Marshall, P. David. *Celebrity and Power: Fame in Contemporary Culture*. Minneapolis: University of Minnesota Press, 1997.

McGovern, Charles F. "Woody Guthrie's American Century." In Santelli and Davidson, *Hard Travelin'*, 111–27.

Moi, Toril. *Sexual/Textual Politics: Feminist Literary Theory*. New York: Routledge, 2002.

Murlin, Bill, ed. *Woody Guthrie, Roll on Columbia: The Columbia River Songs*. Portland, Ore.: Bonneville Power Administration, 1988.

Nicholls, Peter. *Modernisms: A Literary Guide*. Berkeley: University of California Press, 1995.

Nowlin, Bill. *Woody Guthrie: Radical American Patriot* (textual companion to CD set). Cambridge, Mass.: Rounder, 2013.

O'Brien, Elaine, et al., eds. *Modern Art in Africa, Asia, and Latin America: An Introduction to Global Modernisms*. Oxford: Wiley-Blackwell, 2012.

Parrington, Vernon L. *Main Currents in American Thought*. New York: Harcourt, Brace, 1930.

Partington, John S., ed. *The Life, Music and Thought of Woody Guthrie: A Critical Appraisal*. Farnham, UK: Ashgate, 2011.

Peppis, Paul. *Sciences of Modernism: Ethnography, Sexology, and Psychology.* Cambridge, UK: Cambridge University Press, 2014.

Peterson, Richard A. *Creating Country Music: Fabricating Authenticity.* Chicago: University of Chicago Press, 1999.

Place, Jeff. "Woody Guthrie's Recorded Legacy." In Santelli and Davidson, *Hard Travelin'*, 57–68.

Pound, Ezra. *New Selected Poems and Translations*, edited by Richard Sieburth. New York: New Directions, 2010.

Quinones, Ricardo J. *Mapping Literary Modernism.* Princeton: Princeton University Press, 1985.

Rabinovitz, Lauren. *Electric Dreamland: Amusement Parks, Movies, and American Modernity.* New York: Columbia University Press, 2012.

Radano, Ronald. *Lying Up a Nation: Race and Black Music.* Chicago: University of Chicago Press, 2003.

Radosh, Ronald. "The Communist Party's Role in the Folk Revival: From Woody Guthrie to Bob Dylan." *American Communist History* 14, no. 1 (2014): 3–19.

Renshaw, Patrick. *The Wobblies: The Story of Syndicalism in the United States.* London: Eyre and Spottiswoode, 1967.

Reuss, Richard, with Joanne C. Reuss. *American Folk Music and Left-Wing Politics, 1927–1957.* Lanham, Md.: Scarecrow Press, 2000.

Robbin, Ed. *Woody Guthrie and Me.* Berkeley, Calif.: Lancaster-Miller, 1979.

Rosa, Hartmut. *Social Acceleration: A New Theory of Modernity.* Translated by Jonathan Trejo-Mathys. New York: Columbia University Press, 2013.

Roth, Philip. "Writing American Fiction." In *Reading Myself and Others*, 117–36. New York: Farrar, Straus and Giroux, 1975.

Rydell, Robert W. *World of Fairs: The Century-of-Progress Expositions.* Chicago: University of Chicago Press, 1993.

Sachs, Wolfgang. *For Love of the Automobile: Looking Back into the History of Our Desires.* Translated by Don Renau. Berkeley: University of California Press, 1992.

Sa'di, Ahmad H., and Lila Abu-Lughod, eds. *Nakba: Palestine, 1948, and the Claims of Memory.* New York: Columbia University Press, 2007.

Sandler, Stanley. *The Korean War: An Interpretative History.* London: UCL Press, 1999.

Santelli, Robert. *This Land Is Your Land: Woody Guthrie and the Journey of an American Folksong.* Philadelphia: Running Press, 2012.

Santelli, Robert, and Emily Davidson, eds. *Hard Travelin': The Life and Legacy of Woody Guthrie.* Hanover, N.H.: Wesleyan University Press, 1999.

Schivelbusch, Wolfgang. *The Railway Journey: The Industrialization of Time and Space in the Nineteenth Century.* Oakland: University of California Press, 2014.

Seeger, Pete. "People's Songs and Singers." *New Masses*, July 16, 1946, 9.

Seshagiri, Urmilla. *Race and the Modernist Imagination.* Ithaca: Cornell University Press, 2010.

Shaw, John. *This Land That I Love: Irving Berlin, Woody Guthrie, and the Story of Two American Anthems.* New York: Public Affairs, 2013.

Siddiqui, Asaf A. *Sputnik and the Soviet Space Challenge*. Gainesville: University Press of Florida, 2003.

Spoto, Donald. *Notorious: The Life of Ingrid Bergman*. Boston: Da Capo Press, 2001.

Steinbeck, John. *The Grapes of Wrath*. London: Penguin, 2006. First published 1939.

Sundquist, Eric J. *Strangers in the Land: Blacks, Jews, Post-Holocaust America*. Cambridge, Mass.: Harvard University Press, 2005.

Tammet, Daniel. *Born on a Blue Day: Inside the Extraordinary Mind of an Autistic Savant*. New York: Free Press, 2006.

Vonnegut, Kurt. *If This Isn't Nice, What Is?* New York: RosettaBooks, 2013.

Wald, Elijah. *Escaping the Delta: Robert Johnson and the Invention of the Blues*. New York: HarperCollins, 2004.

Wang, Jessica. *American Science in an Age of Anxiety: Scientists, Anticommunism, and the Cold War*. Chapel Hill: University of North Carolina Press, 1999.

Winkler, Allan M. *The Politics of Propaganda: The Office of War Information, 1942–1945*. New Haven: Yale University Press, 1978.

Woolf, Virginia. "Phases of Fiction." In *Collected Essays*, vol. 2, 56–102. London: Hogarth Press, 1966.

Worster, Donald. *Dust Bowl: The Southern Plains in the 1930s*. Oxford, UK: Oxford University Press, 1982.

Wurtzler, Steve J. *Electric Sounds: Technological Change and the Rise of Corporate Mass Media*. New York: Columbia University Press, 2007.

Yurchenco, Henrietta. *A Mighty Hard Road: The Woody Guthrie Story*. New York: McGraw-Hill, 1970.

Audio Sources

Acuff, Roy. *Wabash Cannonball*. Hickory Records, 1965.

Bragg, Billy, and Wilco. *Mermaid Avenue: The Complete Sessions*. Nonesuch, 2012.

Brooke, Jonatha. *The Works*. Bad Dog Records, 2008.

Farrar, Jay, et al. *New Multitudes*. Rounder, 2012.

Guthrie, Arlo, and Wenzel. *Every 100 Years*. Indigo Musik, 2010.

Guthrie, Nora, et al. *My Name Is New York: Ramblin' around Woody Guthrie's Town* (audio book). Woody Guthrie Publications, 2014.

Guthrie, Woody. *The Asch Recordings*. 4 vols. Smithsonian Folkways, 1999.

———. *Ballads of Sacco and Vanzetti*. Folkways Records, 1965.

———. *The Columbia River Collection*. Rounder, 1988.

———. *Dust Bowl Ballads*. Buddha, 2000. First released 1940.

———. *Library of Congress Recordings*. Rounder Records, 1988.

———. *The Live Wire Woody Guthrie*. Woody Guthrie Foundation, 2007.

———. *Long Ways to Travel: The Unreleased Folkways Masters, 1944–1949*. Smithsonian Folkways, 1994.

———. *My Dusty Road*. Rounder, 2009.

———. *Songs to Grow On for Mother and Child*. Folkways Records, 1956.

———. *Woody at 100: The Woody Guthrie Centennial Collection.* Smithsonian Folkways, 2012.

———. *Woody Guthrie: American Radical Patriot.* Rounder, 2013.

Harvey, Ryan, with Tom Morello and Ani DiFranco. "Old Man Trump." Firebrand Records, 2016.

Klezmatics. *Wonder Wheel.* Jewish Music Group, 2006.

———. *Woody Guthrie's Happy Joyous Hanukkah.* Jewish Music Group, 2006.

Lomax, Alan, et al. *The Martins and the Coys.* Rounder, 2000.

Songs for Political Action: Folk Music, Topical Songs, and the American Left, 1926–1953. Bear Family Records, 1996.

Video Sources

Ashby, Hal, director. *Bound for Glory.* United Artists, 1976.

Ellis, Deb, and Denis Mueller, directors. *Howard Zinn: You Can't Be Neutral on a Moving Train.* First Run Features, 2010.

Lorentz, Pare, director. *The Fight for Life.* US Film Service, 1940.

Majdic, Michael, and Denise Edwards, directors. *Roll on Columbia: Woody Guthrie and the Bonneville Power Administration.* University of Oregon, 2000.

Online Sources

Allen, Ray. "Holy Ground: The Klezmatics Channel Woody Guthrie." *Woody Guthrie Annual* 1 (2015): 41–62. http://pops.uclan.ac.uk/index.php/WGA/article/view/297/121.

Baxter, Emily S. P. "'You Gals Who Want to Be Free': A Feminist Perspective on the Evolution of Woody Guthrie's 'Union Maid.'" *Woody Guthrie Annual* 1 (2015): 63–71. http://pops.uclan.ac.uk/index.php/WGA/article/view/285/111.

Boone, Lynette. "Development of the Columbia River and Impacts on Native American Cultures and the Environment." In *Roll on Columbia: Woody Guthrie and the Bonneville Power Administration* (website supplement to documentary film of same title). University of Oregon Library. https://library.uoregon.edu/ec/wguthrie/development.html.

Botkin, Daniel B. "My Recollections of Woody Guthrie." Danielbbotkin.com, July 20, 2012. http://www.danielbbotkin.com/?s=Guthrie.

Childers, Jodie. "Pete Seeger and the Origins of 'Union Maid.'" *Woody Guthrie Annual* 1 (2015): 72–75. http://pops.uclan.ac.uk/index.php/WGA/article/view/299/123.

"Columbia River." In *Cleaner Rivers for Oregon: Why Our Rivers Need Our Help.* Oregon Environmental Council, 2007. http://oeconline.org/wp-content/uploads/2014/10/cleaner-rivers-report.pdf.

Conner, Thomas. "'Our Unseen Friend': Early Radio and the Tuning In of Woody Guthrie's Performing Persona." *Woody Guthrie Annual* 1 (2015): 18–40. http://pops.uclan.ac.uk/index.php/WGA.

"Finding Aid for the Irving Lerner Papers, 1935–1978." Online Archive of California. http://www.oac.cdlib.org/findaid/ark:/13030/tf0n39n6p6/entire_text.

Huntington's Disease: Behavioral Problems. Liverpool, UK: Huntington's Disease Association, 2015. http://hda.org.uk/hda/factsheets.

Jefferson, Thomas. *Notes on the State of Virginia.* 1787. American Studies, University of Virginia. http://xroads.virginia.edu/~hyper/JEFFERSON/toc.html.

Kannan, Vani. "Memorializing 'Deportees': Conversations with Tim Hernandez and Lance Canales." *Woody Guthrie Annual* 1 (2015): 83–100. http://pops.uclan.ac.uk/index.php/WGA/article/view/298/122.

Kaufman, Will. "In Another Newly Discovered Song, Woody Guthrie Continues His Assault on 'Old Man Trump.'" *The Conversation,* September 6, 2016: https://theconversation.com/in-another-newly-discovered-song-woody-guthrie-continues-his-assault-on-old-man-trump-64221.

———. "Woody Guthrie, 'Old Man Trump,' and a Real Estate Empire's Racist Foundations." *The Conversation,* January 21, 2016: https://theconversation.com/woody-guthrie-old-man-trump-and-a-real-estate-empires-racist-foundations-53026.

Mora-Torres, Juan. "Woody Guthrie's 'Deportee': Migrants, Death, and Namelessness." *PilsenPortal,* June 24, 2013 http://chicagovoz.org/2013/06/24/woody-guthries-deportee-migrants-death-and-namelessness.

"Palestine Refugees." United Nations Relief and Works Agency. http://www.unrwa.org/palestine-refugees.

Shavelson, Susanne A. "Aliza Greenblatt, 1885–1975." *Jewish Women's Encyclopedia*: http://jwa.org/encyclopedia/article/greenblat-aliza.

"Tulsa Radio Memories." Tulsatvmemories.com. http://tulsatvmemories.com/tulrkvoo.html.

Warde, William F. "Elements of Dialectical Materialism." By George Novack writing as William F. Warde. Marxists Internet Archive. https://www.marxists.org/archive/novack/works/1940/aug/x01.htm. First published in *Fourth International* 1, no. 4 (August 1940): 108–11.

"Woody Guthrie's Personal Record Collection." Finding aid. Woody Guthrie Center. http://woodyguthriecenter.org/archives/collection/1856-2.

Permissions

In addition to all Woody Guthrie correspondence, visual artwork, and untitled writings copyrighted by Woody Guthrie Publications, Inc., I gratefully acknowledge permission to quote from the following prose and lyric writings (all words by Woody Guthrie, © copyright Woody Guthrie Publications, Inc., all rights reserved, used by permission):

"Ain't a Gonna Do," "Airplane," "All Artists," "The Almanacs and Me," "Around New York," "Arvin Migratory Labor Camp," "Baby Knocker," "Beach Haven Ain't My Home," "Beach Haven Race Hate," "Beach Haven Way," "Better Stay in the Livery Barn," "Big Smudge," "Black Feet," "Bright & Shining City," "Brooklyn & This Bomb," "Cadillac Cadillac," "Child Sitting," "Christmas Talking Blues," "Cumberland Mountain Farms," "Dance Out and Grab," "Dear Mister Eisenhower," "Downtown Traffic Blues," "Drexell 23883," "Einstein Theme Song," "Flush and Drain," "Folk Songs," "Freedom's Fire," "Garbage Waves," "Germy Bomb," "The Girl in the Red, White, and Blue," "Go and Leave Me," "Goldine Grain," "Good Old Union Feeling," "Gyro Locomotive," "Hallinan Hold My Hand," "Hard Hitting Songs by Hard Hit People," "Heaven," "Heyyy Rube," "High Balladry," "High Priced Cars," "Hoodis," "Hot Seat," "Hy Lolly," "I Don't Like Your 'Lantic Pact," "I Hate," "I Hit You," "If I Was Everything on Earth," "Ikey He Lye," "I'm A-Goin' Back to the Farm," "I'm Not Ikey," "Jesus My Doctor," "Jet Plane," "Korea and Me," "Korea Boggy Hole Blues," "Korean Blues," "Korean Boogy," "Korean Quickstep," "Korean Waltz," "Korea Send Me Home Blues," "Lady in the Plane," "Last Mile," "Lessons in Human Engineering," "Little Mama," "Living + Dying + Singing," "Lonesome Road Blues/Goin' Down the Road Feelin' Bad," "Looking Down on You," "Mad Raver," "Marjorie," "More Purty Gals Than One," "My Big Mixed Race," "My Eyes Do See All over This World," "My Ideas about the Use of Peoples Songs in the Progressive Party Movement to Elect Henry Wallace and Glen Taylor," "My Oklahoma," "My Teeneager Girl," "Name Wanted," "Narrow Margins,"

Index

References to illustrations appear in italic type.